Colorado

Byways

Yampa River, Dinosaur National Monument *(Tour 3)*

Colorado
Byways

Backcountry Drives
For The
Whole Family

By TONY HUEGEL

WILDERNESS PRESS
BERKELEY, CA

FIRST EDITION 1999
SECOND EDITION July 2003

Published by **Wilderness Press**
          1200 5th Street
          Berkeley, CA 94710-1306
          (800) 443-7227; FAX (510) 558-1696
          mail@wildernesspress.com

Contact us for a free catalog
Visit our website at **www.wildernesspress.com**

Front cover photo: Placer Gulch (Tour 60)
Back cover photo: Rocky Mountain columbine
Frontispiece photo: Yampa River (Tour 3)

Disclaimer

Colorado Byways has been prepared to help you enjoy backcountry driving. It assumes you will be driving a high-clearance four-wheel drive vehicle that is properly equipped for backcountry travel on unpaved, sometimes unmaintained and primitive backcountry roads. It is not intended to be an exhaustive, all-encompassing authority on backcountry driving, nor is it intended to be your only source of information about the subject.

There are risks and dangers that are inevitable when driving in the backcountry. The condition of all unpaved backcountry roads can deteriorate quickly and substantially at any time. Thus, you may encounter road conditions considerably worse than what is described here. If you drive the routes listed in this book, or any other backcountry roads, you assume all risks, dangers and liabilities that may result from your actions. The author and publisher of this book disclaim any and all liability for any injury, loss or damage that you, your passengers or your vehicle may incur.

Exercise the caution and good judgment that visiting the backcountry demands. Bring the proper supplies. Be prepared for accidents, injuries, breakdowns or other problems, because help will almost always be far away and a long time coming.

Acknowledgments

I could not have produced this guidebook without the help of many people who gave generously of their time, skill, knowledge, patience and resources.

Among them are the staff of the U.S. Forest Service, Bureau of Land Management, and National Park Service in Colorado who provided essential background, facts, and insights about the lands they manage on the public's behalf.

I must thank the researchers and authors who chronicled the story of Colorado long before I came along, and whose work provided the background, insights, and information necessary to my own understanding and appreciation of this fascinating state. I encourage you to take advantage of their outstanding work, which is listed under "References" in the back of the book.

Jerry Painter's maps, graphics, design skills, and patience have been central to building the *Byways* series from its inception, and he deserves an enormous amount of credit.

I doubt that I've driven a mile researching my guidebooks and magazine articles without thanking Toyota Motor Sales and Michael Dobrin. They've allowed me to give Toyota's superb sport-utility vehicles the ultimate road tests over thousands of punishing backcountry miles, in some of the most rugged and remote wildlands in the American West. Toyota SUVs have taken me and my family through blizzards, mud, sand, blinding dust storms, triple-digit desert heat, deepwater fordings, and boulder strewn canyons comfortably, safely, securely, and with unfailing reliability. I have never had a breakdown.

Gratitude is due as well to the Post Company of Idaho Falls, Idaho, for supporting the vision that enabled me to write *Colorado Byways* and my other *Byways* guides; and to the staff of Wilderness Press for the substantial work involved in improving, sustaining and expanding the series.

My father, Frank Huegel, provided companionship over many stormy Rocky Mountain miles. Without him, they would have been lonely miles indeed. Ultimately, though, no one's support has been more important than that of my wife, Lynn MacAusland, and our children, Hannah and Land. They've endured many adventures and misadventures during the building of *Byways*, which wouldn't have been possible without them.

Contents

Preface

Hiking. Backpacking. Mountain biking. When I was younger and more footloose, I enjoyed them all. But life always seems to make more, not fewer, demands on our time and energy. Thus, over the years work, family, lawn care, and, I must admit, the passing of my physical prime took me away from those once-cherished modes of backcountry travel. As middle age loomed on the horizon, I worried that my days of wandering the wild were over.

Then I discovered that the West's most beautiful and remote regions, including wilderness areas where mechanized travel is usually prohibited, are often crossed by unpaved, often little-known backcountry roads. I learned that with a factory-stock sport-utility vehicle, my family and I could have a wildland experience in the comfort and convenience of our family "car" anytime, whether for a few hours or a few days.

Bringing whatever amenities we wanted, we could explore rugged mountain ranges, remote plateaus and isolated canyons by day and then, if we didn't want to camp, relax at a motel at night. A child in diapers? We could carry a case of them. No time to hike? I could drive. That bothersome foot? It would never hold me back again.

I'd broken free of the limitations of time, distance, and physical ability. I'd learned that America's most beautiful wildlands were no longer just for the fit and free, or those who drive motorcycles, ATVs, and modified 4x4s. Since many of the West's most rural backroads are relied on by farmers, ranchers, foresters, and such, I found most to be easily driveable, while others were rough enough to provide exhilarating moments of adventure and challenge. I didn't need a winch, a lift kit, or oversized tires and wheels. Our factory-stock daily driver, our family car, would do just fine.

Over the years, backcountry touring became a bigger and bigger part of my family's outdoor life. With our children, we got to know the beauty and history of the West in ways that would not have been possible for us otherwise. The West, we learned, is paradise for adventure driving. And Colorado may well be its capital.

Colorado Byways: Backcountry Drives For The Whole Family, part of my series of adventure driving guidebooks, will take you along many of the Centennial State's most beautiful and historic backways, which rank among the very best in the West. Some of the tours are included in the Colorado Department of Transportation's Scenic and Historic Byways program. Others are part of the U.S. Bureau of Land Management's network of National Back Country Byways. All offer exceptional opportunities to get off the beaten path and explore a state that never fails to amaze visitors. Name it, and you will find it here. Just take the off-ramp to adventure and see.

Crystal Mill *(Tour 29)*

INTRODUCTION

Bachelor Historic Loop *(Tour 69)*

The Colorado Experience
Where the past is just a short drive away

The sudden appearance of the lone wild horse startled me as I drove along the rim of Sand Wash Basin, a badland not far from where someone long ago drew imaginary boundaries and declared the territory to the south Colorado, the expanse to the north Wyoming and the region to the west Utah.

A moment earlier, I'd gazed across this no-man's land and saw only how the angled light of the morning sun could transform a bleak high-desert landscape of low hills, sagebrush, and grass into a tapestry of shadows and textures. My mind was only half here, though. The other half was still roaming the alpine tundra, glacial valleys and wildflower meadows of the mountains to the south, where I had been just the day before. Then I spotted that living vestige of the Old West, statuesque and alkali-white, eyeing me warily from perhaps 100 hundred yards away.

The Spanish brought horses to the New World in the 1500s. Some escaped into the wild, and in the centuries that followed, horses of Indians, prospectors, and ranchers broke away, too, or were set free. Today, Sand Wash Basin, the largest of four areas set aside in Colorado for these living links with the frontier West, is home to about 200 wild horses. This, my first sighting of one, was a stirring moment. But it was an ephemeral one as well, for in the time that it took to mount a telephoto lens on my camera, he was gone. Still, it was yet another reminder of how tangible and accessible Colorado's Wild West history remains for those who are willing to go where asphalt does not.

Traveling Colorado's most rural roads over sky-scraping mountain passes, along high-desert canyons and among grassy hills is a unique opportunity to experience remnants of the bygone West, as well as one of North America's most beautiful places. These roads help modern-day explorers relive Colorado's frontier years, from, say, the gold rush of 1858–59 to the early years of the 20th century. But in some places they take you far into prehistory as well.

In the semiarid northwestern corner, you can traverse energy-rich sediments laid down by a primordial sea. On the slopes of the Uncompahgre Plateau, you can watch paleontologists excavate the fossilized bones of gigantic dinosaurs. Drive the famous Alpine Loop National Back Country Byway through the San Juan Mountains, in the sparsely populated region of fire and ice occupied by Ouray, Lake City, and Silverton, and you will encounter 13,000- to 14,000-foot peaks that ring two volcanic calderas as old as 28 million years, gulches dozed by the glaciers that capped these mountains some 20,000 years ago, and ghost towns haunted by countless dashed dreams. In Canyon Pintado, an area that a pair of intrepid Spanish padres explored and named in 1776, backcountry roads let adventurous travelers ponder rock walls adorned over the centuries with mysterious images created by native people.

In the part of Colorado where maps show names like Meeker, Craig, and Maybell, you can look out across the valley of Milk Creek where, in 1879, Northern Ute Indians battled federal troops to save their way of life. At the site of Camp Hale, where the famed 10th Mountain Division of World War II trained, another valley still seems to echo with the sounds of men training to defend their way of life almost half the world away. In the south, Colorado's Spanish and Mexican heritage lives on in place names like Cortez, Durango, Sangre de Cristo, and San Juan. The name Colorado itself is Spanish, meaning reddish colored, perhaps reflecting the hue of the rock and soil in some places, or the color of the sediment-laden Colorado River. In the La Plata Mountains, named for the silver ore that fueled a furious pace of mineral exploration, road-building and settlement in the second half of the 1800s, you can follow one 19th-century road past a remnant of the early atomic age, a remote uranium mine. Or you can approach the Continental Divide on an old narrow-gauge railroad grade still blackened by the soot from steam-powered locomotives. And after imagining the hardship of the miners who bored into the mountain slopes around Aspen, drive up to the Sundeck Restaurant on the kind of famous ski slopes that have brought renewed, even unprecedented, prosperity and wealth to a number of former mining towns.

Indian people have occupied Colorado for thousands of years. Evidence of nomadic Paleo-Indians dating as far back as 14,000 years has been uncovered at Hovenweep National Monument. Nomadic hunters are thought to have stalked mastodons, mammoths, ground sloths, and antelope on the eastern plains and western plateau 6,000 years before that. By the time Europeans arrived, Arapaho, Cheyenne, Comanche, and Kiowa Indians inhabited the plains, while the Utes dominated the mountains. The first non-Indians to explore Colorado probably were members of the expedition led in 1541 by Francisco Vasques de Coronado, who may have entered Colorado from New Mexico in search of the fabled Seven Golden Cities of Cibola.

During the 1700s, Spain and France vied for control of the vast plains region. In 1762, France ceded to Spain all of Louisiana west of the Mississippi River. Fourteen years later, just as 13 Atlantic colonies launched a rebellion against British rule, two Spanish priests—Francisco Atanasio Dominguez and Silvestre Velez de Escalante—embarked on an expedition that would take them on a huge loop from Santa Fe north through western Colorado, across the Colorado River to the White River, then west into Utah, across the Green River, south to Arizona, then back to New Mexico and Santa Fe. Their goal was to find a practical overland route between Santa Fe and the missions in California along which new missions could be established, and to convert Indians to Catholicism along the way. Although they failed to achieve those goals, the two Franciscan friars and the eight men who accompanied them did explore more unknown territory than Lewis and Clark would almost three decades later. They also provided the first written record of the wilderness they crossed, gave many of its topographic features the Spanish names they still bear, and set a new standard for friendly relations with Indian people. But Spain never took advantage of its northern lands, failing both to settle them and, as it looked elsewhere for riches, to discover their enormous deposits of silver and gold.

In 1800, France's expansion-minded emperor Napoleon Bonaparte reacquired Louisiana from Spain, including eastern Colorado, only to sell out three years later to the fledgling United States, which doubled its size for $15 million. In 1806, U.S. Army Lieutenant Zebulon Montgomery Pike, for whom 14,110-foot Pike's Peak was named, led the first American expedition to explore Colorado. Another, led by Major Stephen H. Long, followed in 1820. Long labeled the Great Plains the Great American Desert, which failed to heighten interest in the region, thus leaving further exploration to the mountain men and the fur traders. By 1840 their era was over, too, but by then expansion fever was spreading in the United States. Lieutenant John C. Fremont and his guide, Kit Carson, explored the region in the 1840s. Then war broke out between Mexico and the United States in 1846. It ended in 1848 with Mexico ceding to the United States all of its southwestern territories from Texas to the Pacific Ocean, and from the Rio Grande River to the 42nd parallel. All of Colorado was now American territory.

In 1858, gold was discovered in streams where downtown Denver now stands. By the summer of 1859, under the motto "Pike's Peak or Bust!", the rush to Colorado was on. First the fortune seekers came for gold, then for silver. The plains and mountain grasslands attracted farmers and ranchers. Colorado was granted territorial status in 1861, which did nothing to ease tensions between the newcomers and the natives of the region.

On November 29, 1864, U.S. soldiers attacked a sleeping village of Cheyenne Indians on Sand Creek, in eastern Colorado. They slaughtered more than 100, perhaps as many as 200 Indians, most of them women and children. That same year, the first of many silver mines that would come to wield enormous influence on Colorado's fortunes opened near Georgetown, which became Colorado's first "silver queen." Statehood came on August 1, 1876, the centennial year of the Declaration of Independence, thereby christening Colorado the Centennial State. But three years later another page in its history was written in red in Rio Blanco County, where Indian agent Nathan Meeker attempted to force the Northern Ute Indians to give up their nomadic hunting lifestyle and stay put on farms. Meeker sent for troops to enforce his edict, resulting in a bloody battle and the death of Meeker and others near the site of the town that today bears the agent's name.

Mining was Colorado's economic and political foundation during the second half of the 19th century, and just about everyone had a stake in it. Thus, there is now an abundance of ghost towns, 19th-century structures, and diggings. Many people view them as tangible reminders of the vision, courage, and stamina of the men and women who settled even Colorado's most inhospitable locales. Others see the omnipresent ruins, shafts and tailings piles as hideous, dangerous and costly blights on a once-pristine mountain environment.

The 1870s saw Colorado's silver rush, which crowned Leadville the state's new silver queen. By 1874, the value of the silver being mined in the Southern Rocky Mountains of Colorado eclipsed that of gold. The silver boom spurred a road-building boom to meet the need for transportation routes for hauling people and supplies into the rough-and-tumble mining camps and boom towns, and ore to the smelters. The most famous roadbuilder was Otto Mears, a Russian immigrant. Eventually, narrow-gauge railroad lines, better suited to snaking along precipitous mountain slopes than standard-gauge railroads, replaced many of the wagon and stagecoach roads. Increasing numbers of tourists—the mother lode of so many old mining communities today—were drawn to Colorado's wonders via the expanding network of railroads that made the mountains and valleys so accessible. Today, many of the old toll roads and railroad grades are the same routes you can follow through some of Colorado's most rugged, spectacular and history-rich country.

In 1873, Congress passed the Coinage Act, which authorized the U.S. Treasury to stop minting silver dollars, thus decreasing demand for the metal. By 1881, silver dominated the economy of Colorado, which had become the nation's leading producer. Silver-mining interests in Colorado and elsewhere in the West began to press Congress to allow unlimited silver coinage, arguing that so-called "free silver" would bring greater prosperity to the West. In 1890, Congress passed the Sherman Silver Purchase Act, which President Benjamin Harrison signed into law. The act approximately doubled the amount of silver the government could buy at market prices, and the price of silver did rise for a time. But production continued to outpace demand, and soon the price began a steady decline. In 1893, India stopped coining silver, and the bottom fell out of the market. Mines and smelters closed throughout Colorado. Simultaneously, farmers were struck by drought, overproduction, and depressed prices. Banks closed. Towns were abandoned. Colorado's economy crashed as economic panic gripped the nation, which fell into a depression that would last for four hard years. Many blamed the depression on the Silver Purchase Act, which Congress repealed in 1893. With silver now unprofitable, more mines closed, and silver's economic reign came to an end. Gold provided some cushion for hard times, most notably at Cripple Creek, which after 1891 became one of the world's most productive gold-mining regions.

Something else changed during the 1890s. With the removal of Ute Indians to reservations and settlement of the Western Slope by non-Indians, Colorado's rough-and-tumble frontier period was brought to an end. The events of the 20th century would present the Centennial State with even more challenges, triumphs, and travails. Gold and silver would be eclipsed by fossil fuels, especially natural gas, and the Cold War would bring a uranium boom and bust. Ultimately, Colorado would become a diverse state that is effectively pursuing the golden fleeces of outdoor recreation and tourism the way it once did precious metals.

Colorado today ranks as the nation's eighth-largest state in area, encompassing 104,247 square miles. With almost 4 million people, it is the second most populous mountain state, after Arizona. Eighty percent of its population is concentrated in the cities and towns of the Front Range, along the increasingly urbanized, nearly 200-mile-long corridor that stretches from Fort Collins in the north to Pueblo in the south. Rectangular in shape, its arbitrarily drawn boundaries ignore such natural landmarks as the Continental Divide, which winds through the mountains.

Culturally, geographically, and geologically, parts of the state seem to have been annexed from its neighbors. Across the Western Slope, the tumultuous region that reposes west of the Divide, Colorado tumbles toward Utah to take in the eastern sector of the vast uplift known as the Colorado Plateau, named for the legendary river that drains the region. Here, Colorado shares with Utah some of the Colorado Plateau's most fantastic features. There are red-hued sandstone monoliths in Colorado National Monument, arches in Black Ridge Canyons, plunging river gorges in Dinosaur National Monument and Black Canyon of the Gunnison National Park, and lesser plateaus like the Uncompahgre. In the far southwest, Colorado is one of four states that meet at Four Corners. There, it shares the homeland of the ancestral Puebloan people known as the Anasazi, whose structures at Mesa Verde National Park and Hovenweep and Yucca House national monuments still hold secret the reasons for the Anasazi's mysterious disappearance from the Colorado Plateau by about 1300 A.D., after they'd occupied the region for more than a thousand years.

In the northwest, the Middle Rocky Mountain province (the Uinta Mountains) extends from Utah into Colorado. There, too, the Wyoming (or Green River) Basin reaches down into Colorado from the Cowboy State, sharing its sparse population, expansive shrublands and great deposits of fossil fuels. In the south, Colorado is imbued with the culture and look of New Mexico, while east of the Front Range, the Great Plains, which comprise 40 percent of the state, make Colorado look like neighboring Kansas, Nebraska, and Oklahoma.

Colorado's average elevation is 6,800 feet above sea level, making it the highest state, a fact that affects almost every aspect of life. The lowest point, where the Arkansas River flows into Kansas, is 3,350 feet above sea level. From the Front Range, the land soars westward toward the ramparts of the Continental Divide and the 14,433-foot summit of Mt. Elbert, the highest point in the American Rockies, just 61 feet shy of the highest peak in the Lower 48, California's Mt. Whitney. In fact, 54 Colorado peaks (the count changes as new measurements are taken) qualify as "fourteeners," summits that reach or exceed 14,000 feet. Another 740 reach 13,000 feet, and 1,090 reach 10,000 feet. These are the Southern Rocky Mountains, which are comprised of various north-south trending ranges separated by high-altitude valleys and mountain basins, or "parks." Here are the "purple mountain majesties" that inspired Katharine Lee Bates to pen "America the Beautiful" in 1893. This is the Colorado of our imagination, America's Switzerland, a region whose grandeur is Colorado's alone.

This is where you will find Rocky Mountain National Park, and historic Leadville, at 10,430 feet the highest incorporated town in the country and Colorado's geographic center. In these mountains are born the headwaters or major tributaries of the Rio Grande, Colorado, Mississippi and Missouri river systems. They give Colorado the Arkansas, South Platte, Dolores, San Juan, Gunnison, and Yampa rivers. Asphalt often will take you to more than 10,000 feet in these parts. Venture off the pavement, and you can drive another 4,000 feet closer to the clouds.

Within Colorado's borders are semidesert shrublands, mountainous sand dunes, piñon-juniper woodlands, vast grasslands, and riparian ecosystems. There are forests of aspen, cedar, spruce, pine, and fir, as well as semiarid lands where yuccas and cacti grow. Colorado has countless lakes and streams and waves of snow-salted peaks. Then, too, there are its famous meadows of brilliantly colored wildflowers, including the exquisite state flower, the Rocky Mountain (or Colorado) Columbine, which blooms in the mountains from June through August.

No matter which face of Colorado appeals to you, surprise, wonder, beauty, diversity, ever-present reminders of mankind's relentless determination to push back the frontiers of human existence are all here, all comprising the Colorado experience. You will see that much effort and energy has been spent trying to tame the place, but like the mustang that kept a wary eye on me as I drove past, it somehow manages to maintain its wild side. And that is the side you are about to see.

Town of Dinosaur

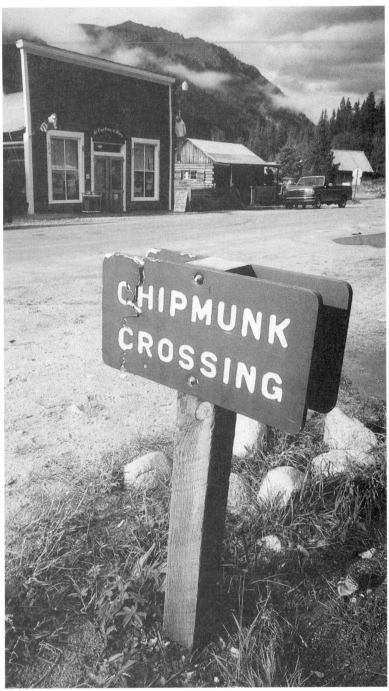

St. Elmo *(Tour 39)*

Adventuring Off The Asphalt
Backcountry Touring 101

Exploring western Colorado's alluring network of unpaved backroads, in a vehicle that is suited to rough off-highway conditions, is among the most convenient and rewarding ways to experience the state's unique mix of history and scenery. Indeed, a case can be made that sticking to the paved roads means missing the best of both. But one must take precautions, acquire certain skills, and adhere to a code of conduct to assure a safe and enjoyable experience while protecting the state's historic and cultural sites, as well as its fragile environment.

Since relatively few people who drive vehicles that are capable of off-highway travel ever take advantage of what their vehicles can do, I'm going to assume that your experience is limited, and that some basic how-to tips will be useful.

KNOW YOUR VEHICLE. Some automakers, eager to tap into the motoring public's yen for at least the visage of adventure, have begun to apply the label "sport-utility" to just about anything with wheels. Don't be fooled. Know what you're driving, and drive within the vehicle's limits as well as your own.

Familiarize yourself with your vehicle's four-wheel-drive system. Is it a full-time, part-time or automatic system? In a full-time, or permanent, 4WD system, all four wheels are continuously engaged as driving wheels; there is no 2WD mode. (A multi-mode system, however, will include a 2WD mode.) Full-time 4WD uses either a center differential or viscous coupling to allow the front and rear axles to turn independently for typical daily driving. Some systems allow the driver to "lock" the center differential so that, in poor conditions, both axles will turn together for greater traction. A part-time system uses only the rear wheels as driving wheels until the driver engages 4WD. A part-time system must be disengaged from 4WD on pavement to avoid excessive drivetrain stress. An automatic system is designed to sense on its own when 4WD should be engaged. All-wheel-drive (AWD) systems, such as those used in some passenger cars and vans, provide power to all four wheels much as full-time 4WD systems do. But AWD vehicles are usually designed for all-weather use, not all-terrain use.

Does your vehicle have a transfer case? Perhaps more than any other single feature, a transfer case identifies a vehicle suited to all-terrain travel. It sends power to the front axles as well as to the rear axles and, acting as an auxiliary transmission, provides a wider range of gear ratios for a wider range of driving conditions. Use high-range 2WD for everyday driving in normal conditions, both on pavement and off. Use high-range 4WD when added traction is helpful or necessary on loose or slick surfaces, but when conditions are not difficult. Use low-range 4WD in difficult low-speed conditions when maximum traction and power are needed, and to keep engine revs high while moving slowly through rough or steep terrain.

Does your vehicle have all-season highway tires or all-terrain tires? Tires take a terrible beating in off-highway conditions, for which the latter are designed.

Find out where the engine's air intake is, and how high it is. This is important to avoid the devastating consequences of sucking water into the engine through the air intake while fording waterways.

Does your vehicle have steel plates protecting undercarriage components like the oil pan, transfer case, and transmission? Skid plates, as they're called, are essential to avoiding the expensive and very inconvenient damage that obstacles, particularly roadbed rocks, can inflict.

KNOW WHERE YOU'RE GOING. The maps in this book are general locator maps only. For route-finding you will need a statewide map in addition to a detailed map illustrating the area you will be visiting and the route you'll be driving.

Each tour description in *Colorado Byways* recommends at least one map for route-finding. These maps often will include other useful information about the area's natural and human history, regulations, campgrounds, picnic areas, and historic sites. They often differentiate between public and private lands as well. The Forest Service's national forest visitor maps may be the best all-purpose maps, but some are out of date. They may not reflect administrative changes that have transferred responsibility for an area from one national forest or ranger district to another. Or they may depict road numbers that no longer apply, campgrounds that have become picnic areas, and roads that are now closed or whose quality has changed. Occasionally, the number on a roadside signpost will not match what's shown on the map. In some cases, different national forest maps will depict the quality of the same road differently. So buy the latest map available. Maps of various kinds can be purchased at Forest Service and U.S. Bureau of Land Management offices, bookstores, information centers and outdoor recreation equipment retailers, as well as the publisher of my *Byways* series, Wilderness Press.

Go over your maps before you begin the drive. Become familiar with sights and landmarks to watch for along the way. As you travel, keep track of your progress to avoid missing important turnoffs, places of interest and side trips.

Don't expect to find road signs. Agencies that manage backcountry roads and the wildlands they cross do post signs of various types, often simple vertical posts, but they don't last long. Vandals, especially the gun-toting kind, often make short work of them. If you reach a junction where there are several routes to choose from and none has a sign, it's usually best to follow what appears to be the most heavily used route. Global Positioning System navigation units are increasingly popular, and I'm sure some backcountry travelers find them handy at times, especially when they're trying to pinpoint an obscure point of interest. But I've not yet found a GPS unit to be necessary.

When venturing into unfamiliar territory, it's sometimes best to rely on road numbers rather than common road names, because rural and backcountry roads sometimes are known by more than one name. However, you will quickly find that roads can have more than one numerical designation as well. Counties, for example, may assign a number that is different from the one assigned by the Forest Service.

KNOW WHAT YOU'RE GETTING INTO. Colorado's backcountry byways vary widely in quality and in how much maintenance they receive. Some receive none; others get a lot. Still others receive just enough to keep them driveable without diminishing too much the sense of adventure that people like us are looking for. Many are safe and easily driven county-maintained roads. Others aren't much more than two-track trails scratched onto mountainsides more than a century ago. Many include the full range of conditions.

Some mountain roads are exceptionally narrow shelves, wide enough perhaps for the horse-drawn wagons they were "built" for but not for a full-size SUV or pickup. When in doubt, compare your vehicle's wheel spread with the width of the roadbed, and turn back if the route ahead doesn't seem safe.

Some roads, like those over Ophir, Georgia, and Weston passes, require high clearance and 4WD on one side but are passable with 2WD vehicles on the other. Even the famously frightening road over Black Bear Pass is quite easy for much of the way above Telluride.

WEATHER AND WHEN TO GO. The backcountry driving season in Colorado varies by location, the preceding winter's snowpack, elevation, climatic zone, and whether a road is subject to county maintenance. The famous Alpine Loop, in the San Juan Mountains, is often open by mid-May. But roads over high passes like Buffalo, Black Bear, Tincup, Argentine, and Mosquito may not open until July or even August, when Colorado's mountain meadows are splashed with the colors of columbine, Indian paintbrush, bluebell, and other wildflowers. Even late in summer, a small snowdrift lingering in the cool shade of a north-facing slope can still block the way. By mid-September, when Coloradans begin to enjoy autumn's fiery aspens, snow is likely in the high country, and the loftier passes begin to close. Then you can visit lower areas like spectacular Echo Park, an excellent autumn destination at the confluence of the Green and Yampa rivers in north-western Colorado's Dinosaur National Monument, or the bucolic country around Pagosa Junction, just north of the New Mexico line. Generally speaking, in a state with everything from high desert to forests and alpine tundra, you're sure to find somewhere to go from May into October.

I suggest avoiding popular hunting areas during the general hunting season, which begins the second week of October and continues into the first week of November. Most high campgrounds are closed from October to May. If one is open, it's likely that the water system has been shut down for the winter. For that reason, however, it's also likely to be free.

Agencies like the U.S. Forest Service and U.S. Bureau of Land Management are getting better at responding to recreation-oriented issues and inquiries. But their ability to stay on top of ever-changing conditions along thousands of miles of backcountry roads is limited, and their most knowledgeable people are often out in the field. So I often find it's best to inquire at local 4x4 rental shops, tour businesses, visitor information centers, and other places geared toward the state's thriving four-wheel-drive tourism trade. Sometimes I just have to go see for myself, and now and then you will, too.

Be sure to allow enough time for your chosen tour to avoid driving after nightfall. The waning of a day in the Colorado Rockies, with its alpenglow and emerging wildlife, can be something to behold. But if you get a late start or stay out after dark, you risk colliding with some hard-to-spot roadway obstacle, missing an important turn, or at least missing the sights. So unless a drive is short, as many are, get an early start. Don't drive at night.

Colorado's high deserts, mountains, and valleys have different weather patterns and climates, and rules-of-thumb that apply to one region may not apply to the others. Generally, though, the weather is nothing if not capricious and fast-changing, so be prepared for anything, anytime. This is especially true in the mountains, where sunny summer weather can give way quickly to dramatic thunder and lightning storms, even snow. But storms often pass before long, so if you're caught in one, you may only have to pull over and sit it out for an hour or so.

Precipitation can instantly make Colorado's unpaved roads dangerously slick and undriveable, even with four-wheel drive. Danger aside, driving on muddy roads is almost always a bad idea, since it creates tracks that tend to erode into ever-deepening ruts. If you get caught in a rainstorm, pull over and let it pass, then give the roadbed an hour or so to dry out.

GOING ALONE. There is security in having more than one vehicle, and more than one source of ideas and labor if things go awry. It's also fun to be with other people. But when you're on vacation, or venturing off for a few hours, a day or a weekend, you and yours will probably go alone, in a single vehicle. And that's OK, so long as your vehicle is reliable and you're prepared to handle emergencies alone. Fact is, you often will not have the road to yourself, anyway. In the more popular destinations, places like Yankee Boy Basin, Imogene Pass and Black Bear Pass, you will find yourself just one of a crowd.

RULES OF THE ROAD. There are some rules, written and unwritten, even in places where no one will be watching. The intent behind them is simple: to keep you safe, and to preserve these places from abusive and destructive activities that scar the land, damage the environment, ruin archaeological and historic sites, disturb wildlife, and interfere with people who live and work in these parts. Misconduct and mistakes can result in personal injury, damage to your vehicle, areas being closed, and perhaps even legal penalties.

Here are some things to keep in mind:
- Your vehicle must be street legal to take these drives. Obey traffic laws and regulatory signs, wear your seat belt, don't try to sneak around locked gates, and keep yourself and the kids buckled up.

- Drive only on established roads, and never make a new route or follow in the tracks of someone who did.
- Uphill traffic has the right of way, whenever practical, because it's usually easier and safer to back up to a pullout, using gravity as a brake, than to back down a slope while fighting the pull of gravity. Expect to encounter people who do not understand this.
- Be especially careful on blind curves, which are commonplace on the old railroad grades that are roads today.
- Mechanized travel of any kind, including motorcycles and mountain bikes, is not allowed in designated wilderness areas and other preserves unless a legal corridor exists, like the one through the La Garita Wilderness to the Wheeler Geologic Area.
- Do not disturb archaeological or historic artifacts and sites, many of which are on private property. Do not touch Native American rock art, which can be thousands of years old. Doing so will degrade, even destroy it. Do not use archaeological or historic sites for picnics or camping unless they are developed for those purposes, because the more time people spend at them, the more wear and tear and damage they sustain.
- If you camp, leave no trace. Camp only in established campsites, at least 200 feet from streams, ponds, and lakes to avoid damage and pollution.
- Leave gates as you find them. Don't disturb wildlife or livestock.
- Take out only what you bring in. Clean up after yourself and those who came before you. Haul out your trash.
- Old mine sites and abandoned structures are dangerous, especially for children. View them from a distance. Stay away from shafts, tunnels, and holes.
- Avoid parking on grass, because hot exhaust systems can ignite fires. That's what sparked the Big Elk Fire in Larimer County in July 2002.
- Avoid steep hillsides, stream banks, and boggy areas. Never drive across the high country's delicate alpine tundra.
- If you get stuck or lost, stay with your vehicle unless you're certain that help is nearby. A vehicle is easier to find than an individual who's wandering about. It also will provide shelter.

GO PREPARED. Things can and will go wrong out there, so always go prepared to walk back, spend the night, dig yourself out of a rut or provide emergency medical assistance.

Here's a basic checklist of some things to bring.
- A full fuel tank. It shouldn't be necessary to carry extra fuel in a container.
- A shovel. Mine has been a life-saver. Sooner or later yours will be, too.
- Toilet paper.
- A well-stocked first-aid kit.
- Very good all-terrain tires; a good (and properly inflated) spare tire and jack; a small board to support the jack on dirt or sand; a couple of cans of pressurized tire sealant; a small electric air compressor (the kind that plug into the cigarette lighter, available at department stores); and a tire pressure gauge. A warning here: Old mines sites are notorious for having rusting nails strewn about.
- Clothing suitable for inclement weather.
- Some basic tools, including jumper cables, duct tape, electrical tape, baling wire, spare fuses, multipurpose knife, tow strap, and a plastic sheet to lay on the ground. An assortment of screws, washers, nuts, and such may come in handy if you're driving an older or modified (meaning trouble-prone) vehicle.
- Maps, compass, extra eyeglasses and keys, binoculars, trash bags, flashlight or head lamp with extra batteries, matches, watch, hats, sunscreen, bug repellent.
- Food and drinks.

Except for the food, I keep much of this stuff in a large plastic storage container, like Rubbermaid's ActionPacker. It's important to tie it all down so that it doesn't get tossed about on rough terrain.

Sometimes I bring my mountain bike as a backup vehicle in case I get into a bind. I also use it to reach places that might damage my vehicle. Think about getting a CB radio, even though transmitting range is limited. These days, a cellular telephone can be handy as well, although they often don't work in remote areas.

STAY WELL. Many of the tours in *Colorado Byways* climb well over 10,000 feet above sea level, and are among the highest roads in the country. The ease with which modern vehicles travel at these elevations, however, can lull one into forgetting how thin the air is up there, and how altitude affects the human body.

High altitude is generally defined as higher than 5,280 feet above sea level. Colorado's average elevation is about 6,800 feet, although many roads go much higher. At 8,000 feet, oxygen is 40-45 percent less dense than at sea level, and humidity is 50–80 percent less. So if you live in a low-elevation place and have arrived in Colorado's high country without much time to become acclimated, hiking up one of the state's many "14ers" right away is not a good idea.

Suddenly arriving at a high-altitude environment from sea level can produce nausea, insomnia, diarrhea, restlessness, shortness of breath, and air "hunger." Other effects can include heart palpitations, rapid heart beat, headache, nasal congestion, coughing, intestinal gas, and fatigue. Initial symptoms should disappear as your body gets used to the elevation, which occurs over a few days or weeks. But if things get bad, one can experience severe coughing and edema, the abnormal accumulation of fluid in various parts of the body.

To avoid the effects of high altitude, the American Heart Association recommends that newcomers take the following steps:
• Keep physical exertion to a minimum, especially for the first couple of days. Early overexertion can result in severe and persistent symptoms.
• Eat lightly.
• Avoid alcoholic beverages for the first 48–72 hours. Alcohol aggravates high-altitude sickness.
• If you have a history of heart, circulatory, or lung disease, check with your doctor before visiting high-elevation places. Respiratory ailments in particular should be completely resolved first.
• If you experience symptoms of altitude sickness, decrease your physical activity, and seek medical attention.
• Use sunscreen to protect your skin from the harmful effects of the intense ultraviolet rays at high elevations.

Do not drink from streams and lakes. Runoff laden with heavy metals and other unhealthful substances is part of Colorado's mining legacy. Then, too, there is the chance of ingesting giardia, an intestinal parasite that can cause a number of unpleasant physical effects, including diarrhea, cramping, fever, and foul-smelling burps.

OFF-HIGHWAY DRIVING. Most of the time, just driving more slowly and cautiously than you do on paved roads is all it takes for trouble-free backroad travel. But when the going gets rough, as it often will, try these suggestions:

Think ahead. If you have a part-time 4WD system, engage it before you actually need it.

When in doubt, scout. If the road ahead seems risky, walk it and see.

Adjust tire pressure to suit the terrain. Most of the time, standard tire pressure will suffice. But deep mud and soft, dry sand can require temporarily airing down each tire (letting air out) to 15–18 psi or even lower to expand the tire's "footprint" for greater flotation. Dampening soft, dry sand can make it more firm. On rocky terrain, airing down will soften the ride and lessen the punishment the roadbed inflicts on your vehicle. In particularly rocky and steep terrain, partially deflated tires will conform better to roadbed rocks, giving them better grip. Be sure to reinflate the tires before driving at speed or on pavement, using a small electric air compressor.

Shallow mud and fresh snow can be underlain by a more solid base, so normal tire inflation or even over-inflation can help tires penetrate to terra firma.

Avoid mud. If you are caught in a downpour, pull onto firm ground and let the storm pass. Then wait an hour or so to let the road dry out.

If you begin to lose traction in mud, turn the steering wheel rapidly one way and then the other to help the tires bite. Try not to spin your tires, which tears up the road and can get you stuck, or stuck worse than you already are. If you get stuck in mud, dig out the sides of the tires to relieve suction. Then pack rocks, sticks, and other debris around the tires for traction.

Maintain steady forward momentum in sand, mud, and snow. Go as slow as you can, but as fast as you must. Higher gears can be more effective than lower gears.

Tire chains, while heavy, are easy to pack and can save the day.

Stick to the high points. When the going gets particularly rough, shift into low range, go slow and steady, and keep the tires on the road's high spots, thus keeping the undercarriage high and away from obstacles that can damage the differentials, or so-called "pumpkins." Let the tires roll over the rocks. Do not let large rocks pass directly beneath the vehicle, or you may damage the undercarriage.

All thumbs? You won't be for long if you forget to keep them on top of the steering wheel. Otherwise, the wheel's spokes can badly injure your thumbs if a front wheel is suddenly jerked in an unexpected direction by a roadbed obstacle. If the steering wheel is being rocked back and forth, keep your hands loose, at 10 and 2 o'clock.

Another tip for rough ground is to lean forward, keeping your back away from the seat back. That way you won't be tossed about so much.

Straddle ruts, letting them pass beneath the vehicle. It's best not to try to cross ruts, but if you must, do so at an angle, easing one tire at a time into and across it. Same for depressions, dips and ditches. If you get stuck, raise the vehicle with the jack and fill in the space beneath and around the affected wheels with dirt and debris until you've built up a base they can roll on (it can help to make it high enough so that the wheel's on a down-slope).

To get over a ledge, either use the rock ramp that is likely to be there already, or use a few nearby rocks to build one. If you've had to build a rudimentary ramp to get over an obstacle, don't leave an excavation site behind. Some people actually like going over obstacles the hard way, and may well appreciate it if you return the site to the condition in which you found it.

Expect deadfall. Once in a while you might encounter a fallen tree or limb in the road. It might be possible to drive across it, crossing at an angle and putting one wheel at a time over it. If you carry a folding saw, as I do, you might be able to cut it. Or you can use your tow strap to pull it out of the way.

Have someone act as a "spotter" to help you maneuver through difficult places, and use low range and a low transmission gear for better control.

If your vehicle gets high-centered, that is, the undercarriage is hung up on an obstacle like a rock—jack it up and see if the obstacle can be removed. Or build small ramps, using dirt and rocks, beneath the tires so you can drive off the obstacle.

Take that hill! Before climbing a particularly steep hill, first learn what's at the top and on the other side. Depending on how steep it is and how much power your vehicle has, shift into first or second gear/low range. Accelerate as you climb, keep moving, then slow down as you near the top. Some hills will have been badly chewed up by spinning tires. In that case, using low range, try to keep your wheels on the high spots.

If the engine stalls on the way up, stop and immediately set the parking brake hard and tight. Here, an automatic transmission should help you get going again relatively easily. If you have a manual transmission, you may be able to restart the engine by shifting into first gear/low range, turning the engine over without clutching and letting the starter motor pull the vehicle forward until the engine restarts and takes over. Otherwise, you'll have to play the clutch, hand brake and accelerator simultaneously to get going again without rolling backward.

If you can't make it up, don't try to turn around or turn sideways to the hill. Stop, and put the transmission in reverse/low range. If you have outside mirrors that are easily adjusted, tilt them so that you can see what the rear tires are doing. Then slowly back straight down. Never descend in neutral, relying on the brakes.

If you must apply the brakes, do so lightly and steadily to avoid breaking the tires' grip. Go straight down steep inclines, using low range and the lowest driving gear so the engine can help brake (automatic transmissions, which I think are best overall, don't do as well at this as manual transmissions).

Avoid side-hill traverses if you can. Occasionally, mountain roads do cross steep slopes, sometimes tilting the vehicle "off-camber," toward the downhill side. It's an unnerving experience for me, especially if the road has become wet and a bit slick. Lean heavily toward caution under such circumstances, and remove cargo from the roof to lower the vehicle's already-high center of gravity. It can help to turn the front wheels into the hill, if it's a steep slope. If you decide not to continue, do not attempt to turn around. Tilt the exterior mirrors so that you can watch the rear tires, shift into reverse/low range for greater control, and slowly back up (a spotter will help) until you reach a place where you can turn around safely.

Avoid crossing waterways if you can. Crossing streams, rivers and such is fun, but it also stirs up sediment and erodes stream banks. If you must cross, use a stick to check the depth, comparing the depth to your vehicle. Don't cross if the current is fast. Check for deep holes, and use established crossings.

Cross slowly to reduce the amount of sediment you stir up. A slow, steady crossing also will make less of a bow wake, thus minimizing erosion of the streambanks. (In deep water, however, a bow wake can create a helpful air pocket for the engine.)

Be aware of where your engine's air intake is. It may not be high enough to ford deep water. If it isn't, it'll suck water into the engine, causing severe damage.

In deep crossings, it's possible for water to be drawn into your vehicle's gear boxes unless the vents have been raised to a level that will keep them out of the water. Consider extending the front and rear differential vents up into the engine compartment, using long sections of hose. This also helps to keep them clear of dust and dirt, which can clog them.

Once across, stop and inspect the vehicle. The brakes will be wet, so use them a few times to dry them out. Your tires also will be wet, and may not grip the roadbed as well as when dry.

Do not attempt to cross a road or streambed during a flash flood, unless you want to become part of the scenery.

ACCESSORIES, MAINTENANCE, AND OPTIONS. Stock 4WD vehicles, not the pretenders but the genuine articles, are built to go places that sedans, vans and station wagons either cannot go, or shouldn't. Despite their comforts, they are rugged and reliable transport. They can go from the showroom straight into the hills without modifications.

There are many good ones, but my preference is for Toyotas. I find them tough, capable, comfortable and reliable, all of which are important to me, since I sometimes spend months traveling the remote backways of the West under all sorts of conditions, and often alone.

One of my two 4Runners has a 5-speed manual transmission and a 4-cylinder engine, which I find to be adequate. The other has a V6 and an automatic transmission, which I prefer. Manual transmissions are more responsive and tend to provide slightly better fuel mileage, and they do a better job at engine braking. But clutch-equipped vehicles usually require the driver to fully depress the pedal when starting the engine, which can be a problem while stopped on a steep hill. (My 5-speed 4Runner has a standard dash button that I can push to bypass the clutch when starting the engine.) If the engine stalls on a steep incline, you can put the transmission in first gear/low range and let the starter motor crank the engine while simultaneously pulling the vehicle forward. It's also possible to compression-start the engine (by pushing it or rolling downhill) if the starter fails or the battery dies (neither of which has ever happened to me in the wild). Still, I think automatics make driving in rough terrain much simpler, since they don't require drivers with three feet—one for the gas, another for the clutch and a third for the brake.

I've come to appreciate options that I once dismissed as unnecessary. Electric outside mirrors, for example, will pay for themselves the first time you have to back up on a narrow track above a killer drop-off. I was no fan of sunroofs, either, until I started exploring narrow, high-walled canyons.

Some new light trucks have sophisticated and effective 4-wheel electronic traction-control systems that are intended to eliminate wheel spin by instantly transferring power from spinning wheels to the wheel or wheels with traction. A few, like Toyota's 4Runner and Land Cruiser, can be purchased with factory-installed locking differentials, a.k.a. "lockers." These mechanisms vastly improve a vehicle's ability to get through nasty conditions by equalizing power to the driving wheels and temporarily eliminating a differential's tendency to transfer power to the wheel or wheels with the least traction. Both of my 4Runners have rear locking differentials.

There is a huge four-wheel-drive accessories market, but are those add-ons necessary? It depends on how much, and what type of adventure motoring you plan to do. The requirements of serious four-wheeling on difficult routes like Pearl Pass (a serious 4x4 trail that exceeds the scope and theme of this book) differ from those of general backcountry touring. The former can require extensive mechanical modifications, which can degrade on-highway performance and reliability. On most backcountry roads, stock vehicles do just fine.

Still, if you enjoy traveling the backcountry, there are real benefits to extra lights, beefier tires, a more versatile roof carrier, heavier skid plates, perhaps even an after-market locking differential. I've never owned a winch, but there have been times ...

Don't skimp on maintenance. Backcountry roads can give even the toughest vehicle a workout, so follow the recommendations in your owner's manual for dusty, wet and muddy off-highway driving.

When you get back to town, head for the car wash. It's important to clean the wheels, brakes and undercarriage to prevent rust, corrosion and other damage. You also don't want to carry home the mud, dirt and debris that has collected underneath, because the transportation of spores, insects, and other organisms to disparate geographic regions via off-highway vehicles can cause serious environmental problems.

PRESERVE THE PRIVILEGE. With so much historic, scenic and conveniently reached backcountry, Colorado ranks among the very top adventure driving venues in North America. I'd like to keep it that way. If you're interested in preserving the privilege of exploring these places, consider joining Tread Lightly!, Inc., a non-profit organization that promotes safe and environmentally responsible off-highway travel. It is based in Ogden, Utah. Call 1-800-966-9900.

As you travel the backways of Colorado, tell me what you've found, whether it's a mistake in the book, a useful tip, or a trip that you'd recommend for future editions. Write to me in care of Wilderness Press, 1200 5th Street, Berkeley, CA, 94710.

MAKING IT FUN FOR ALL. Keeping kids, especially teenagers, happy on car trips has always been tough. But there are some things you can do to make touring the backcountry fun and interesting for them.
- Don't just drive. Stop, and stop often. In western Colorado, historic sites and spectacular scenery are just about everywhere. Watch for wildlife, especially early in the morning and evening.
- Get some books on the history of the area you'll be visiting. In summer, a wildflower identification book is just about mandatory in a state that may be as famous for its brilliant displays of natural color as it is for ski hills.
- Make a photocopy of the area on the map where you'll be traveling. Let them help you navigate and identify peaks, creeks, historic sites, and other landmarks.
- Bring at least one personal cassette player with headphones, and the kids' favorite tapes. Before leaving, go to your local public library and check out some children's tapes. Books on tape, which I often listen to on long highway drives, are great diversions for children.

- Other items that have helped to keep the peace in our back seat are an inexpensive point-and-shoot camera the kids can use, and inexpensive binoculars.
- If you have a responsible, licensed teenage driver on board, let him or her drive now and then. The sooner a teen learns backcountry driving skills, the longer he or she will remain an enthusiastic participant. And someday, perhaps in an emergency, you may need a co-pilot.
- Bring snacks, preferably the non-sticky kind, and drinks. There will be plenty of bumps on your adventures, so cups with spill-proof tops are essential. Plastic garbage bags, paper towels, changes of clothing and wet wipes are handy to have along as well.
- Safety is always a concern, for hazards exist. Don't let children get close to old mine sites and deteriorating buildings. For that matter, adults should stay clear of them as well. If you want a closer look, use binoculars.

Whether you travel with children or not, don't make the drive everything. Make it part of a day that draws on the array of experiences that Colorado has to offer. Plan a picnic. See the sights. Hike to some mountain top or lake. Bring your mountain bikes. And don't forget pillows, for someone's bound to get sleepy. Finally, do something civilized when the day is done: Go out to dinner.

Echo Park, Dinosaur National Monument *(Tour 2)*

How to Use *Colorado Byways*

LOCATION: Where the drive is.

HIGHLIGHTS: What's best about the drive.

DIFFICULTY: This is subjective, since opinions and levels of experience will differ. Conditions can and do change due to weather, slides, washouts and other circumstances. I assume you are not a serious four-wheeler, but somebody traveling in a stock, high-clearance 4-wheel-drive (4WD) vehicle with all-terrain tires and a transfer case with high and low range.

That said, the ratings are: *easy*, which means it won't require four-wheel drive in good weather; *moderate*, which means high clearance, all-terrain tires, and four-wheel drive will be necessary, and the going will be slow, steep, and/or rough in places; and *difficult*, which means very rough and slow, using four-wheel drive and low-range gears, with some chance that you will scrape part of your vehicle on an obstacle. Some routes include all three categories. A road that isn't particularly difficult can still pose such hazards as drop-offs and blind curves.

TIME & DISTANCE: The approximate time it takes to complete the drive, excluding travel time getting to the starting point and any stops you might make along the way. Odometer accuracy varies among vehicles, so your measurements of distances may differ somewhat from mine.

MAPS: Each drive description is accompanied by a locator map, with the route highlighted. You will need two additional maps for route-finding: a statewide map, and a map or brochure with sufficient detail to guide you. I recommend specific maps and other helpful references for each drive. My favorite maps are those produced by *National Geographic Maps/Trails Illustrated*. National forest visitor maps are very good all-purpose maps, but they don't show elevation contours. I find Bureau of Land Management maps useful but difficult to read. I also like the Automobile Club of Southern California's *Indian Country* for southwestern Colorado, and the statewide *Recreational Map of Colorado*, published by GTR Mapping. U.S. Geologic Survey maps are excellent. *Jeep Trails of the San Juans*, by North Star Mapping, is detailed and useful. Each route also cites the relevant map in DeLorme's statewide *Colorado Atlas and Gazetteer*.

INFORMATION: An information source, usually a government agency, such as the U.S. Forest Service or Bureau of Land Management. Sometimes it will be a local chamber of commerce or information center. Addresses and telephone numbers are listed in the Appendix.

GETTING THERE: How to reach the starting point. Some tours can be driven in the opposite direction from the way I describe, so the starting point can be at either end. Check each map for the circled S (start) and F (finish).

REST STOPS: Places to picnic, camp, see a historic or cultural site, or answer the call of nature with a modicum of dignity.

THE DRIVE: In this section I provide details of the drive, such as historical background and historic sites, which turns to take, how far it is from point to point, and what you will see along the way.

ALSO TRY: A nearby route that may or may not be described in detail.

ABBREVIATIONS: ACSC: Automobile Club of Southern California. **ATV:** all-terrain vehicle. **BLM:** Bureau of Land Management. **GMUG:** Grand Mesa-Uncompahgre-Gunnison National Forests. **MYA:** million years ago. **USFS:** U.S. Forest Service. **USGS:** U.S. Geological Survey.

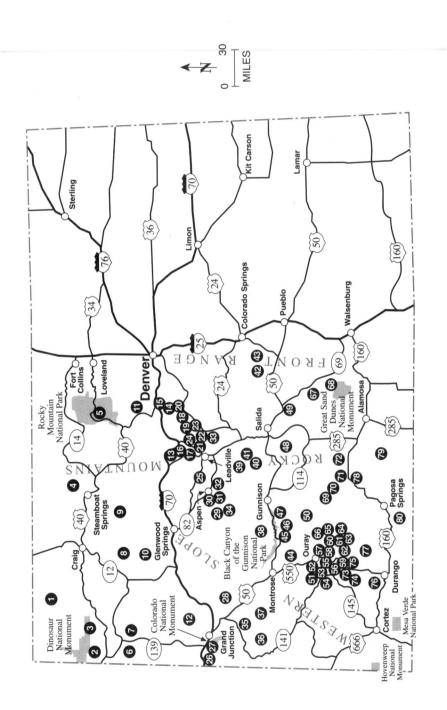

Map Symbols

TOUR ROUTE:

Start	Ⓢ
Finish	Ⓕ
Travel direction	⇄
Paved road	〰
Unpaved road	〰
Primitive road	〰

Paved road	〰
Unpaved road	〰
Primitive road	〰
Hiking Trail	- - - - - - -
Lake	⬭
Stream	∼
Mountain	⋀⋀

Forest Service road	43
Interstate highway	70
U.S. highway	50
State or county road	89
North indicator	↗
Point of interest	📷
Campground	⛰
Toilet	🚻
Site or building	■
Ranger station	⚑
Continental Divide	∼⌣
Parking	P
Picnic area	🛆
City or town	○

Guide To Tour Highlight Icons

Caution	Photo opportunities	Picnicking	Camping
Restaurant	Hiking	Mountain Biking	Wildlife viewing	Rock hounding
Fishing	Wildflowers	Arches	Rock Art	Historic sites

Author's Favorites

Echo Park and Yampa Bench roads (Tours 2 and 3): Most visitors to Dinosaur National Monument don't venture beyond the famous fossil quarry. But more adventurous types can travel these two backways to the breathtaking high-walled canyons of the Green and Yampa rivers. The views of this uplifted and deeply incised landscape rank with the best on the Colorado Plateau.

Rock Art Tour (Tour 6): Native people have occupied the semiarid canyons and valleys of Colorado for thousands of years. In the area that Spanish explorers named Canyon Pintado (Painted Canyon), they left many mysterious symbols etched and painted onto the faces of cliffs, rocks and overhangs. This tour provides outstanding opportunities to view both prehistoric and historic rock art sites in the comfort of your SUV.

Crystal/Lead King Basin (Tour 29): With its combination of historic sites, mountain scenery and exhilarating four-wheeling, I think this tour ranks among the best in the state. You'll enjoy seeing the historic marble operation at the town of Marble, the old Crystal Mill and the remote hamlet of Crystal. The mix of soaring peaks, lakes, and river gorges, as well as some white-knuckle driving, guarantee that there will never be a dull moment. The only downsides are that it is slick and dangerous when wet, and it is popular. Be prepared to share the one-lane roads.

Yankee Boy Basin (Tour 52): This convenient tour out of Ouray will take you deep into Colorado's mountain scenery and 19th-century mining history. You can make this a day-long journey if you like, taking in the side-trip to Box Canyon Falls and Park, the sights along spectacular Canyon Creek, meadows of wildflowers, historic sites and, if you're up to it, the hike to Blue Lakes in the Mt. Sneffels Wilderness. This route links up with the drive over Imogene Pass.

Imogene Pass (Tour 53): This is a busy but spectacular backroad between Telluride and Ouray. It offers just enough entry-level four-wheeling (rocky stretches, stream crossings, narrow ledges, even a tunnel) to make it a perfect SUV outing. The old mines at Camp Bird and Tomboy rank high in local lore, and the alpine meadows, glacial gulches and views of the San Juan Mountains are among the most beautiful in Colorado. People congregate on the 13,114-foot pass, especially at the sign, a favorite photo spot. If you do likewise, be considerate of others who also would like to record the moment.

Alpine Loop National Back Country Byway (Tours 57, 61, 65 and 66): This historic circuit, and other nearby roads in the vicinity of the Continental Divide, comprise the most famous network of backcountry roads in the state, and with good reason. Linking Ouray, Silverton, and Lake City — the so-called Alpine Triangle — the Alpine Loop offers a full range of driving experiences, from graded county roads to rugged 4x4 tracks. All of them pass through magnificent alpine scenery, although much of it remains scarred by thoughtless 19th-century mining practices. The ghost town of Animas Forks is one of the best in the West. If you have time for only one Rocky Mountain tour, this is the one to take.

THE DRIVES

Echo Park Road, Dinosaur National Monument *(Tour 2)*

Whispering Cave, Dinosaur National Monument *(Tour 2)*

Sand Wash Basin Loop

LOCATION: Northwest of Maybell. Moffat County.

HIGHLIGHTS: This semiarid basin offers starkly beautiful scenery, particularly along the pink-hued Vermillion Bluffs and from the 8,120-foot summit of Lookout Mountain. It encompasses the 160,000-acre Sand Wash Basin Wild Horse Management Area, the largest of Colorado's four wild horse refuges. You're sure to see many of these icons of the old West, as well as pronghorn, raptors and other wildlife. It's best in spring, when colts and fillies are born, and fall. There are many alternative roads to explore in this area, ranging from easy 2WD to difficult 4WD routes.

DIFFICULTY: Easy when dry; impassable when wet. Summers can be very hot, winters extremely cold.

TIME & DISTANCE: 4–5 hours; 64 miles.

MAPS: BLM's Canyon of Lodore. DeLorme p. 13.

INFORMATION: BLM's Little Snake Field Office.

GETTING THERE: Take state Highway 318 northwest for 15.5 miles from the junction with U.S. 40 at Maybell. After crossing the Little Snake River, turn right (north) onto county Road 75.

REST STOPS: There are none, except for the top of Lookout Mountain. There also are no services or facilities; go prepared. You can camp at Maybell Park, a fee campground on U.S. 40 in Maybell.

THE DRIVE: The Spanish brought horses to the New World in the 1500s. In the centuries that followed, many escaped from farmers, ranchers, miners and Indians, or were turned loose. Today, Colorado has four wild-horse preserves. This desert basin, home to about 200 horses, is the largest. Road 75 heads north along the Little Snake River, then climbs onto Sevenmile Ridge. To the west (left) lies Sand Wash Basin, a pale, forbidding yet intriguing badland. You may encounter pronghorn racing northward, as well as piles of horse manure in the road, called "stud piles," that studs leave to mark their territories. Continue north on Road 75. By mile 21.8, Road 75 has climbed onto a bench and brought you to a T. Go west (left), toward Lookout Mountain, following Road 67 on the rim of the basin. Take Road 67, which eventually will fade to a two-track, to a sagebrush plain. Road 67 will bend south, and by mile 32.6 you should see the spur to the right up Lookout Mountain. From there, Road 67 descends into the basin itself. Soon it will enter a long draw, angle west, and then climb out. At the Y where Road 126 goes south (right), follow Road 67 north (left) and then south as it goes around the ridge. The road will improve, and then cross Sand Wash. Pass up roads 126 and 40, go around some color-banded hills, and you will soon find yourself at the highway, only two miles west of where your adventure began.

ALSO TRY: Irish Canyon on Road 10 N north of Highway 318, about 24 miles farther northwest. It's famous for its varied geology and ancient petroglyphs.

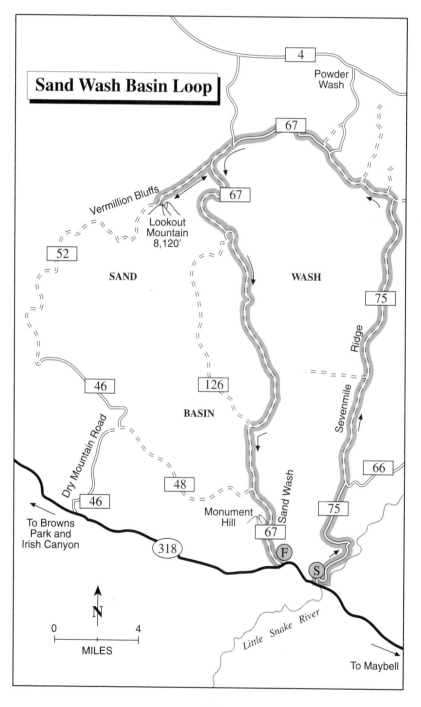

Sand Wash Basin Loop

4

Powder
Wash

67

67

Vermillion Bluffs

Lookout
Mountain
8,120'

52

SAND

WASH

75

Sevenmile Ridge

46

126

BASIN

Dry Mountain Road

48

66

46

Monument
Hill

Sand Wash

75

To Browns
Park and
Irish Canyon

318

67

F

S

N

0   4
MILES

Little Snake River

To Maybell

Echo Park Road

LOCATION: Dinosaur National Monument.

HIGHLIGHTS: The canyons of the Green and Yampa rivers are awesome. You also will see ancient Indian rock art (petroglyphs), historic Chew Ranch and Whispering Cave. Echo Park is a beautiful oasis near the confluence of the Yampa and Green. This tour connects with Yampa Bench Road (Tour 3). Best September to early October.

DIFFICULTY: Easy when dry, but impassable when wet even with 4WD. Storms can occur in summer. The roads may be closed in winter.

TIME & DISTANCE: 1.5 hours and 13 miles one-way.

MAPS: Trails Illustrated No. 220 (Dinosaur National Monument). DeLorme pp. 12, 22. Get the park's flyer for Echo Park and Yampa Bench roads. The guide to Harpers Corner Scenic Drive, *Journey Through Time*, is useful, too.

INFORMATION: Dinosaur National Monument.

GETTING THERE: From Dinosaur town, take U.S. 40 east 2 miles to park headquarters. Take Harpers Corner Scenic Drive for 25.9 miles to Echo Park Road, on the right.

REST STOPS: Echo Park has a campground. The water there is turned off for the cold-weather season. Swimming is dangerous. Fuel, lodging and supplies are available in Dinosaur, but not in the park.

THE DRIVE: Most visitors only see the dinosaur bone quarry north of Jensen. But the park's 210,000 acres in Utah and Colorado include spectacular geologic features, two great tributaries of the Colorado River, ancient rock art and historic homesteads. The Earth's crust here has been squeezed, warped, tilted and cracked, then worn down by erosion. As you descend 2,000 feet toward the Yampa Bench and then to Echo Park, you'll see in the varicolored, multitextured cliffs the pages of the Earth's history. The layers of exposed sedimentary rock—the red Moenkopi Formation, the cream-colored Weber Formation and the cliff-forming Wingate sandstone—record long-gone seas, mud flats, water courses, desert dunes and dislocations of the Earth's crust over hundreds of millions of years. After driving down Iron Springs Wash, the road enters the monument at mile 3.4. At mile 4.8 it enters Sand Canyon, walled by Weber Formation cliffs and domes. Things open up by mile 7.6, presenting a sweeping vista. Go left at the Y (Yampa Bench Road, Tour 3, is right), following Moffat County Road 156. At mile 9 is Chew Ranch, worked from 1910 into the 1970s. Soon the road passes below walls of yellow-gray rock. At mile 10.7 is a pullout. On a cliff above the stream to the left, among the cottonwoods, are the elaborate Fremont-culture Pool Creek petroglyphs, figures pecked into the rock perhaps 1,000 years ago. Ahead is Whispering Cave, a crack at the base of a cliff. Finally, you will arrive at a bend in the Green River and a tranquil flat dominated by massive Steamboat Rock. This is Echo Park. In 1825, a trapping party led by William H. Ashley became the first Europeans to enter Echo Park, which was named by explorer John Wesley Powell in 1869. In the 1950s, the U.S. Bureau of Reclamation proposed building a dam downstream, in Whirlpool Canyon. That would have inundated Echo Park and backed water up Lodore and Yampa canyons. Conservationists defeated the plan in the first major victory for the modern environmental movement. However, Glen Canyon Dam, on the Colorado River in northern Arizona, was built instead.

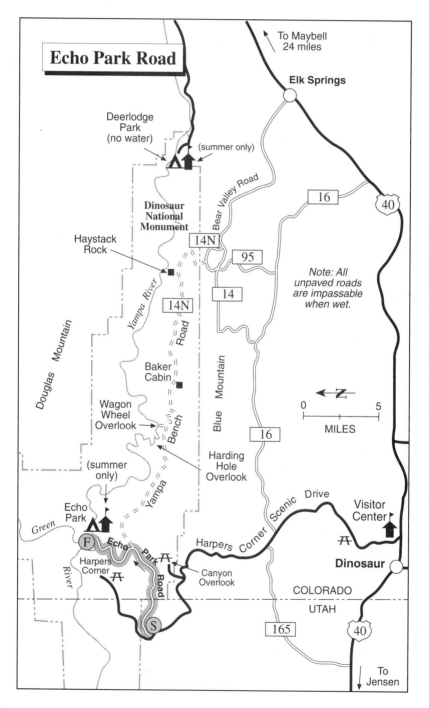

Yampa Bench Road

LOCATION: Dinosaur National Monument.

HIGHLIGHTS: This remote little road provides dramatic views of the spectacular canyon of the Yampa River, the last free-flowing river in the Colorado River system. It connects with the road to Echo Park (Tour 2). The weather's usually best September to early October.

DIFFICULTY: Easy when dry but impassable when wet, even with 4WD. Storms can occur in summer. The roads may be closed in winter.

TIME & DISTANCE: 5 hours (excluding Echo Park). It's 8 miles from Harpers Corner Scenic Drive to the junction with Echo Park Road, then about 42 miles to U.S. 40 at Elk Springs.

MAPS: Trails Illustrated No. 220 (Dinosaur National Monument). Get the park's flyer about this and other dirt roads in the area. DeLorme pp. 22–23.

INFORMATION: Dinosaur National Monument.

GETTING THERE: From the town of Dinosaur, take U.S. 40 east 2 miles to park headquarters. Take Harpers Corner Scenic Drive north for 25.9 miles to the turnoff for Echo Park, on the right. Follow Echo Park Road 8 miles through Iron Springs Wash and Sand Canyon to the junction with Yampa Bench Road (county Road 14N). **From U.S. 40 at Elk Springs,** take county Road 14 (Bear Valley Road) west. In 13.6 miles turn north (right) onto county Road 14N.

REST STOPS: Echo Park Campground is 5 miles from the Echo Park Road/Yampa Bench Road junction. (The water is turned off in the cold-weather season.) The overlooks are great, but be careful near the cliffs. Stay on trails to avoid destroying the soil's microbiotic crust.

THE DRIVE: Over millions of years, layers of rock far below the Earth's surface were lifted, buckled and warped. The Yampa (Ute for "big medicine") River, meanwhile, kept cutting downward. Today, the deep rock canyon it has eroded through cream-colored Weber Sandstone is an awesome sight akin to Utah's famous canyon country. At the west end, after descending down Iron Springs Wash amid the red layers of the Moenkopi Formation, and then between the soaring sandstone walls of Sand Canyon, the road delivers you to the Yampa Bench. This uplifted slab of the Earth's crust rises gently northward from the base of higher benches, cliffs and mountains to the south. But then, with absolute suddenness, the land ends at the brink of a 1,000-foot precipice, the Yampa River Canyon. The beauty of the cliffs and domes along the canyon is unending, perhaps even overwhelming at times, as is the silence. The view from Haystack Rock, a slickrock monolith where peregrine falcons nest from April to mid-July (when the overlook is closed), is almost dizzying. There is also human history. Baker Cabin, for example, is named for the family that struggled for 12 years, beginning in 1918, to scratch a living from the land at the mouth of Johnson Draw. At the drive's east end, the road climbs onto Blue Mountain to join Bear Valley Road, which passes scenic Disappointment Draw before reaching U.S. 40.

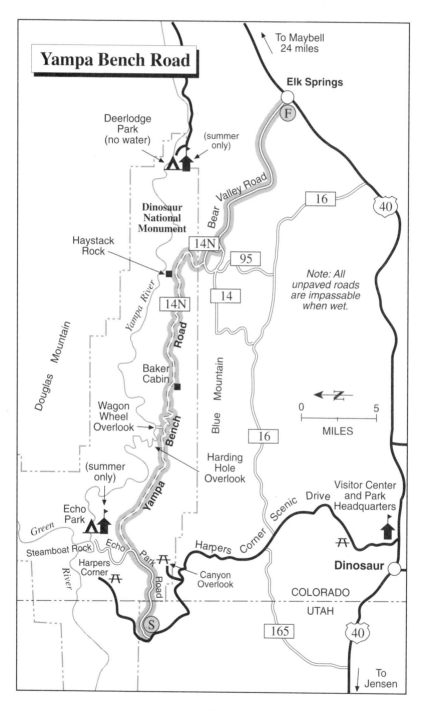

Yampa Bench Road

To Maybell
24 miles

Elk Springs

F

Deerlodge
Park
(no water)

(summer
only)

Bear Valley Road

16

40

**Dinosaur
National
Monument**

14N

95

Haystack
Rock

14

Note: All
unpaved roads
are impassable
when wet.

Yampa River

14N

Road

Douglas Mountain

Baker
Cabin

Blue Mountain

Wagon
Wheel
Overlook

Bench

0   5

MILES

16

Harding
Hole
Overlook

Scenic   Drive

Visitor Center
and Park
Headquarters

(summer
only)

Echo
Park

Yampa

Harpers   Corner

Green

Echo   Park

Steamboat Rock

Dinosaur

Harpers
Corner

Road

Canyon
Overlook

River

COLORADO

UTAH

S

165

40

To
Jensen

Buffalo Pass

LOCATION: In the Park Range on the Continental Divide, between Steamboat Springs (Routt County) and Hebron, on state Highway 14 (Jackson County). Medicine Bow-Routt National Forests.

HIGHLIGHTS: While the scenery is not as dramatic as in the San Juans, there are outstanding vistas on the west side across Steamboat Springs and the Yampa River Valley to distant mountains, valleys and plateaus; and eastward across the broad, rolling rangelands and hay fields of North Park to the lofty peaks of the Medicine Bow Mountains and Rocky Mountain National Park. On the 10,180-foot summit are subalpine meadows strewn with granite boulders. Don't pass up Steamboat Springs, which is much more than a ski town.

DIFFICULTY: Easy, although a bit rocky in places. On top, watch out for fallen snags (dead trees) in the roadway. Snow usually blocks this road until about mid-July.

TIME & DISTANCE: 1.5–2 hours; 33.7 miles.

MAPS: Routt National Forest. Trails Illustrated No. 117 (Clark, Buffalo Pass). *Recreational Map of Colorado*. DeLorme pp. 16–17, 26.

INFORMATION: Medicine Bow-Routt National Forests; Hahns Peak/Bears Ears Ranger District (west side); Parks Ranger District (east side; Walden office).

GETTING THERE: From Steamboat Springs (as is described in The Drive), take 7th Street north from the main drag, Lincoln Avenue/U.S. 40. Follow Missouri Avenue to North Park Road, which angles right and becomes county Road 36 (Strawberry Park Road). Follow Road 36 to Road 60; go right at the signs for Buffalo Pass and Highway 14. **From the east,** take Highway 14 to Hebron, and go west on county Road 24.

REST STOPS: Dry Lake and Granite campgrounds on the west side; Summit Lake campground on the pass; Grizzly Creek, Teal Lake and Hidden Lakes campgrounds on the east side.

THE DRIVE: The silhouettes of mountains and valleys roll off to the west as you climb more than 3,000 feet from Steamboat Springs toward the Continental Divide, or descend to the Yampa River Valley if you're going in the opposite direction. Soon you're in conifer forest, crossing a sub-alpine meadow strewn with pink and gray granite rocks and boulders. They recall the glacial icecaps that blanketed the flat uplands here in Pleistocene time, about 10,000 to 2 million years ago. At the summit of the Divide you will see Summit Lake. Just north of the lake and the campground is the southern boundary of the Mt. Zirkel Wilderness, which has a number of similar lakes. Single-lane Road 60 becomes rougher here as it wends through forest and boulder-salted meadows. About 18 miles from Steamboat Springs the descending road emerges from the forest, and a sweeping vista appears across North Park, the most northerly of Colorado's high and vast mountain grasslands. About 22 miles from Steamboat Springs the road passes Grizzly Guard Station and Grizzly Creek Campground. Soon you're among rolling meadows, forested hills and vast sagebrush and grass rangelands, descending on a graded two-lane dirt and gravel road. At about mile 26.5 you're on asphalt and, 7.3 miles farther, at Highway 14 at Hebron. From here you can go south to U.S. 40 and return to Steamboat Springs.

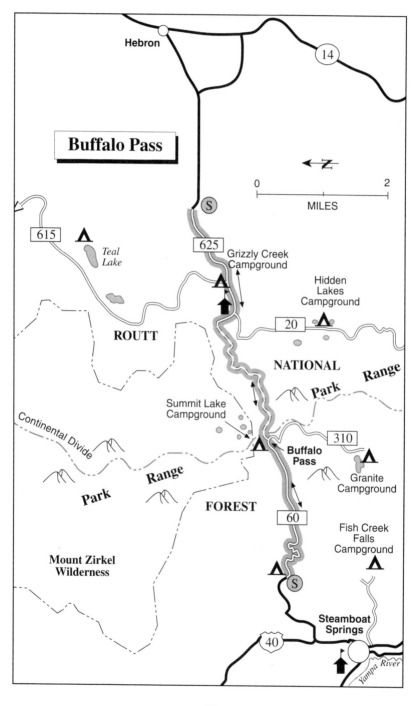

Old Fall River Road

LOCATION: Rocky Mountain National Park. It begins at Horseshoe Park and ends at Trail Ridge Road on Fall River Pass.

HIGHLIGHTS: This fabulously scenic byway, the first motor vehicle route across the park, was built between 1913 and 1920. Ascending 3,200 feet (to 11,796 feet), it provides magnificent mountain scenery as well as a tour of ecosystems, from riparian zones along the Fall River and its tributaries to meadows, woodlands, subalpine forests and alpine tundra. Watch for wildlife, too.

DIFFICULTY: Easy, on a single-lane gravel shelf road with hairpin turns and long drop-offs. It has been a one-way (uphill only) road since 1932, after construction of the more easily driven Trail Ridge Road. Vehicles over 25 feet long and towed trailers are not permitted. Be prepared for November-like weather anytime at the higher elevations, and severe afternoon thunderstorms. Can be closed temporarily by weather conditions. Open July 4 to mid-October.

TIME & DISTANCE: 1.5 hours; 9 miles.

MAPS: The park brochure. Trails Illustrated No. 200 (Rocky Mountain National Park). DeLorme p. 29.

INFORMATION: Rocky Mountain National Park. Be sure to bring a copy of the Rocky Mountain Nature Association's inexpensive but informative booklet *Old Fall River Road*, available at visitor centers and a dispenser at the start of the drive. It explains the natural and human history at specific mileage points.

GETTING THERE: From Horseshoe Park, drive past Lawn Lake Trailhead and the Alluvial Fan to Endovalley. There you will see the obvious start of Old Fall River Road.

REST STOPS: There are toilets and telephones at Lawn Lake Trailhead, and a picnic area at Endovalley. You will see many beautiful places to stop along the drive, but be sure to use the pullouts. You will find supplies, souvenirs and a snack bar at the end of the drive at historic Fall River Store, originally built in 1936 as a rest stop for travelers like yourself. The Alpine Visitor Center is here as well.

THE DRIVE: The road climbs the north wall of Fall River Canyon, and rises along the slopes of Mt. Chapin. Here you're among the lodgepole pine, Douglas fir and Englemann spruce of the upper montane zone. At mile 1.4 is the short hike to 25-foot-high Chasm Falls. Soon you will enter the spruce-fir subalpine ecosystem. By milepost 3 you will see high to the right a fantastic array of spires, pinnacles and cliffs. The rock terraces farther on were built in the 1920s to reinforce the road. At mile 7.6 is a narrow shelf section. Pass through the "krummholz," a transition zone between subalpine forest and alpine tundra where the gnarled and stunted trees reflect the harsh climate, and ahead lies the treeless, cold, blustery yet sensitive alpine zone. At mile 8.7 is a section of road dubbed the "Big Drift," where snow drifts 20 to 30 feet deep made spring road-opening especially difficult. The road ends at Fall River Pass.

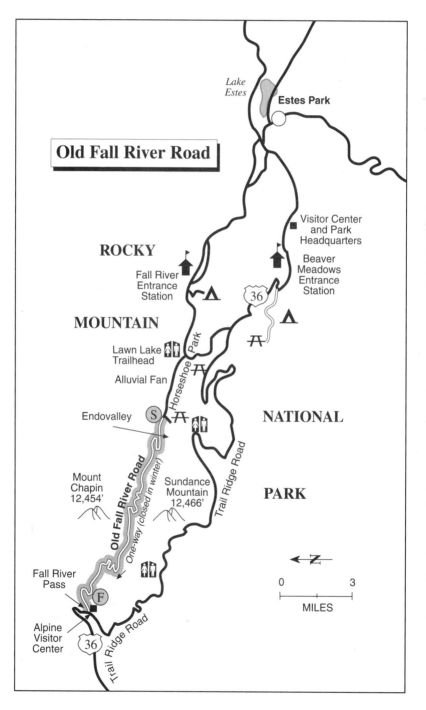

Old Fall River Road

Lake Estes

Estes Park

ROCKY

Visitor Center and Park Headquarters

Fall River Entrance Station

Beaver Meadows Entrance Station

36

MOUNTAIN

Lawn Lake Trailhead

Alluvial Fan

Horseshoe Park

Endovalley

S

NATIONAL

Mount Chapin 12,454'

Old Fall River Road

One-way (closed in winter)

Sundance Mountain 12,466'

Trail Ridge Road

PARK

Fall River Pass

F

Alpine Visitor Center

36

Trail Ridge Road

N

0   3

MILES

Town of Dinosaur

Carrot Man rock art site *(Tour 6)*

Rock Art Tour

LOCATION: South of Rangely; Rio Blanco County. Canyon Pintado Historic District.

HIGHLIGHTS: Numerous prehistoric and historic Native American petroglyphs (figures pecked into the rock) and pictographs (figures painted on the rock).

DIFFICULTY: Easy on the main roads, moderate on some roads to the sites. Roads may be impassable when wet. This route passes through a natural gas field, so watch for trucks. The many unsigned roads can be confusing. Avoid this trip during fall hunting season.

TIME & DISTANCE: 6–8 hours; roughly 75 miles, depending on how many sites you choose to visit.

MAPS: Get the *Rangely* brochure that includes a general map of the tour area with specific instructions on how to get to the rock art sites, and descriptions of what you will see. Use the BLM's Rangely and Douglas Pass maps for route-finding. Also useful are USGS' Rio Blanco County maps 1 and 5. DeLorme pp. 22, 32.

INFORMATION: Rangely Area Chamber of Commerce. BLM's White River Field Office.

GETTING THERE: North of Douglas Pass and south of Rangely, take state Highway 139 to Little Horse Draw. Turn west there, onto graded county Road 116. In 4.7 miles angle right at a Y up a pink-gravel road. To go in the opposite direction, in Rangely turn south onto South White Avenue, which becomes Dragon Road. Pavement ends in 2.6 miles. The latter is the way I take you.

REST STOPS: No facilities. It's best not to linger at archaeological sites to avoid overuse. Rangely Camper Park, a public fee campground at the north edge of town, is pleasant.

THE DRIVE: On Sept. 8, 1776, an expedition led by two Spanish friars—Francisco Atanasio Dominguez and Silvestre Velez de Escalante—who were searching for a route between Santa Fe, New Mexico, and Monterey, California, emerged from East Douglas Canyon into the canyon now traversed by Highway 139. They noted the strange figures painted on the rocks, and named the area Canyon Pintado (Painted Canyon). Follow Dragon Road south, paying close attention to the mileages in the brochure and on your odometer while watching for BLM rock art site markers. Particularly intriguing is the Carrot Man site at mile 11.6. The Fremont Culture figures on an overhang include human-like pictographs and older animal-like petroglyphs. They are at least 800 years old. About 2.6 miles farther down Dragon Road turn left (east) onto county Road 113, and note your mileage. The backway descends to Big Horse Draw, passes a windmill, crosses a wash, then parallels the wash. 3.6 miles from Dragon Road is a T; go right. 2.1 miles farther is another T, with a natural gas facility on the right. Go left on the graded road. This is Road 116. In a few miles you'll pass Road 107 on the left; keep right at the next fork. The road will switchback down into a canyon with terraced walls. Soon you will reach a Y. Keeping left, go east through a gas facility. This is Little Horse Draw.

In about 4.6 miles you'll be at Highway 139. Head north toward Rangely, and continue the tour at the sites along Canyon Pintado, both along and off the highway.

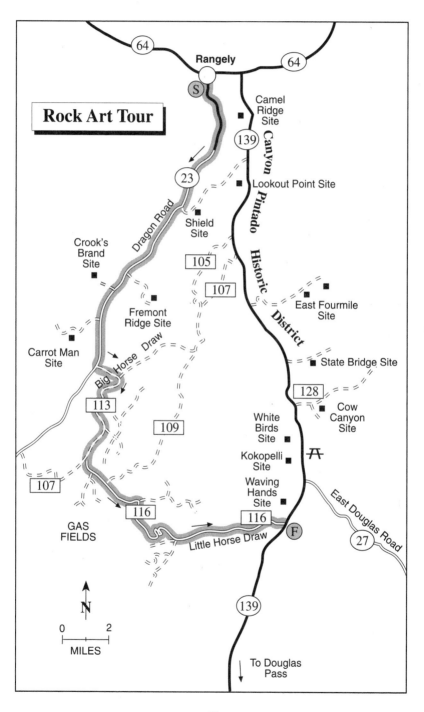

Rock Art Tour

Cathedral Bluffs

LOCATION: Rio Blanco County southeast of Rangely; south of state Highway 64 and east of state Highway 139.

HIGHLIGHTS: This is a remote sojourn through plateau country with outstanding vistas across semiarid northwestern Colorado into Utah and Wyoming. Wildlife includes wild horses, mountain lions, elk, mule deer, bears, and raptors. Vegetation ranges from sagebrush to stands of aspen and fir. Dramatic Cathedral Bluffs alone are worth the long drive. It dead-ends, but the return trip has great views, too.

DIFFICULTY: Easy but long, and the roads can be impassable when wet. It's a big commitment to go all the way, which you needn't do. Keep track of turns at each intersection.

TIME & DISTANCE: 5 hours round-trip; 101 miles.

MAPS: BLM's Rangely and Douglas Pass maps. *Recreational Map of Colorado*. DeLorme pp. 22–23, 32–33.

INFORMATION: BLM's White River Field Office.

GETTING THERE: Take Highway 64 about 9.5 miles east of Rangely. Turn south onto county Road 122.

REST STOPS: Stop anywhere. At the end, there's a pit toilet and primitive camping at Square S Summer Range State Wildlife Area, but expect to share the shade with cattle. There are no services or facilities otherwise. Get fuel, food and water in Rangely. The Rangely Camper Park, a fee campground operated by the Western Rio Blanco Metropolitan Recreation and Park District, is pleasant, with grassy sites beneath tall cottonwoods. Watch for the sign in town.

THE DRIVE: Gravel Road 122 twists and climbs for 14 miles through pale, sedimentary hills and shrublands to Calamity Ridge. Turn right (south) there, onto Road 103. Follow this undulating, single-lane dirt road for 27 miles, atop a ridge that presides over a landscape of colossal scale and stark beauty. Some 40 million years ago, during Eocene time, the rising Rocky Mountains blocked the eastward drainage of rivers and streams, while the Uintas blocked drainage to the north. Thus was formed Lake Uinta, which inundated much of what is now western Colorado, eastern Utah and southern Wyoming. For 6.5 million years sediments that washed down from the mountains ran into the lake, laying down the thin layers of mud that became today's Green River Shale. Upper parts of this shale are rich in oily kerogen, a fossil fuel so far too expensive and environmentally damaging to exploit. Volcanic ash later blanketed western Colorado. Uplifting and erosion followed. Sticking with Road 103, keeping right at each fork, you will enter the Piceance Basin-East Douglas Creek Wild Horse Management Area. Then you'll reach the edge of Cathedral Bluffs, dramatic pastel-hued cliffs. At about mile 40, where the road nears the edge, walk out to the rocky exposure to the right, where you can look closely at the bluffs' thin layers of sediment, known for preserving fossil impressions of even the small parts of plants and insects. At Road 26 go right toward the state wildlife area. The road ends in about 7 miles.

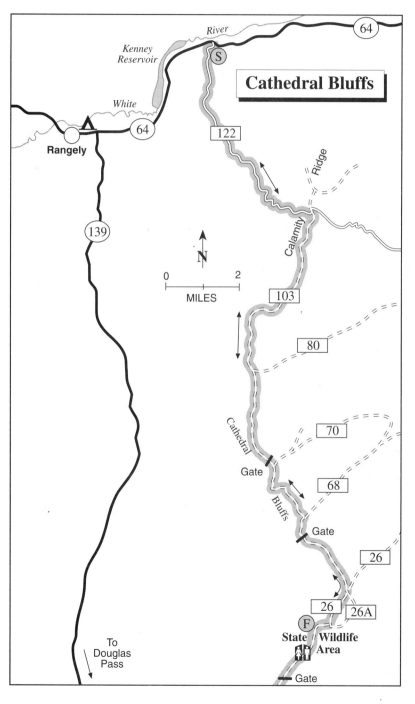

Cathedral Bluffs

Kenney Reservoir

River

64

S

122

Calamity Ridge

White

Rangely

64

139

N

0 2

MILES

103

80

Cathedral

70

Gate

68

Bluffs

Gate

26

26

26A

F

State Wildlife Area

To Douglas Pass

Gate

Sleepy Cat–East Beaver Loop

LOCATION: Northwestern Colorado, northeast of Meeker; White River National Forest; Rio Blanco County.

HIGHLIGHTS: Dense aspen, spruce and fir forest; meadows; great vistas, including the Flat Tops Wilderness. The battlefield at Thornburg, 4.6 miles north of the Sleepy Cat Trail turnoff on Yellowjacket Pass, is worth a visit. It commemorates the 1879 battle on Milk Creek, in which U.S. troops fought Ute Indians who refused to submit to Indian agent Nathan Meeker's efforts to force them into an agrarian lifestyle. The Indians killed Meeker and 11 other whites at the Indian agency, near the junction of state Highways 13 and 64.

DIFFICULTY: Easy to moderate. Segments can become extremely muddy or impassable. Avoid this drive during the fall hunting season, when it's busy and early snows can make the road very muddy. It's generally best from July 1 through September.

TIME & DISTANCE: 24.8 miles; 2 hours.

MAPS: White River National Forest. DeLorme pp. 24–25.

INFORMATION: White River National Forest, Blanco Ranger District.

GETTING THERE: From Meeker, take Highway 13 east and north about 2.3 miles. Turn right (east) onto Thornburg Road, county Road 15. At Yellowjacket Pass (7,538 feet) 11.1 miles from Highway 13, turn right (east) through the gate onto Sleepy Cat Trail, county Road 48 (forest Road 250). Follow Road 250 for the entire drive.

REST STOPS: Anyplace that appeals to you. Meeker and vicinity have many lodging options. I like the Meeker Hotel and Cafe, where Teddy Roosevelt stayed during a bear hunting trip. Built in 1896, it's on the National Register of Historic Places.

THE DRIVE: The road climbs toward aspen and conifer forest, providing fantastic vistas to the east and north across broad expanses that include plateaus and valleys. In 2.7 miles the road enters the national forest, and becomes a bit rough. After 4.4 miles it enters a narrow meadow, Wilson Park. A half-mile or so further, as you drive through another stand of aspen, watch for elaborate carvings in the bark of the aspens, done by Basque sheepherders. Soon the road becomes rough in places, requiring high clearance and, possibly, 4WD. At mile 9.6, as you cross another grassy park, Road 258 branches to the right. Stay on Road 250. At mile 12.6 you're southwest of Sleepy Cat Peak (10,848 feet). Road 250 angles right (south) at a junction where Road 290 continues east. About 2 miles farther, as the road passes through deep forest, there's a downhill stretch that can be very muddy. During a long, steady descent the road passes through another park, at Windy Bill cow camp, crosses East Beaver Creek, and emerges from the forest to provide views of the White River Valley and surrounding mountains and plateaus. About 22 miles from the start the road exits the national forest and passes a small reservoir, then brings you out on county Road 8. Go right (west) to return to Meeker. You can also go left (east) on the Flat Tops Trail Scenic and Historic Byway (Tour 9).

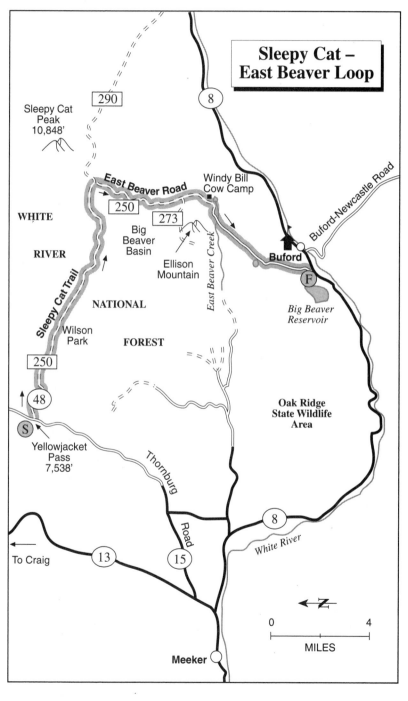

Sleepy Cat – East Beaver Loop

Sleepy Cat
Peak
10,848'

290

East Beaver Road

250

Windy Bill
Cow Camp

WHITE

273

Buford-Newcastle Road

8

Big
Beaver
Basin

Ellison
Mountain

RIVER

East Beaver Creek

Buford

F

Sleepy Cat Trail

NATIONAL

*Big Beaver
Reservoir*

Wilson
Park

FOREST

250

Oak Ridge
State Wildlife
Area

48

S

Yellowjacket
Pass
7,538'

Thornburg

Road

To Craig

13

15

8

White River

N

0   4

MILES

Meeker

43

Flat Tops Trail

LOCATION: Northwestern Colorado between Meeker (Rio Blanco County) and Yampa (Routt County); White River and Medicine Bow-Routt National Forests.

HIGHLIGHTS: A variety of scenic terrain, including valleys and high plateaus, rangelands and woodlands, farmlands, streamside riparian areas, meadows and forests of aspen, lodgepole pine, spruce and fir. This is a U.S. Forest Service and Colorado Scenic and Historic Byway that rises from about 6,400 feet to about 10,400 feet There's a chance you will see wildlife early in the morning or in the evening.

DIFFICULTY: Easy; 42 miles are well-maintained dirt and gravel road, while the rest is paved. Dirt spurs can be impassable when wet. Open June through October. The area, which has the largest elk herd in Colorado, is beautiful but busy during the fall hunting season.

TIME & DISTANCE: 3 hours; 82 miles.

MAPS: White River National Forest. DeLorme pp. 24, 25–26, 34–35. Also get the brochure, *The Flat Tops Trail Scenic Byway.*

INFORMATION: White River National Forest, Blanco Ranger District; Medicine Bow-Routt National Forests, Yampa Ranger District.

GETTING THERE: Begin in Meeker or Yampa. **From Meeker,** take state Highway 13 east, then go right onto county Road 8 at the Flat Tops Trail Scenic Byway information kiosk. **From Yampa,** take county Road 17 west from state Highway 131. Follow Forest Rds. 8 and 16, over Ripple Creek Pass (10,343 feet) and Dunkley Pass (9,763 feet).

REST STOPS: Meeker and Yampa have all services. You'll find a variety of lodging (I like the Meeker Hotel and Cafe, where Teddy Roosevelt once stayed. Built in 1896, it's on the National Register of Historic Places.) There are a number of campgrounds along the way, particularly at Trapper's Lake. Also check out the cabins and restaurant at Trapper's Lake Lodge and Resort. A number of structures, including the lodge, burned in the Big Fish Fire in August 2002, but have been rebuilt.

THE DRIVE: Uplifted seabeds, vast lava flows, ice-age glaciers and rivers have shaped this region over the last 50 million years into a landscape the Ute Indians called the "Shining Mountains." It was occupied by Native Americans for more than 10,000 years, until white settlers arrived. In 1879, the Indians rebelled when Indian Agent Nathan Meeker tried to force them into an agrarian lifestyle. The Indians killed 14 soldiers in a battle along Milk Creek. They also killed Meeker and 11 other whites at the agency, near the junction of Highways 13 and 64. By the early 1880s all of the Utes had been removed from the region and forced onto reservations. Named for 10,000- to 12,000-foot mountains that appear to have been sliced off, the Flat Tops region was given a place in conservation history in 1891, when President Benjamin Harrison established the White River Plateau Timber Reserve, the first in the state and the second in the nation. That laid the foundation for the national forest system. In 1919, Arthur H. Carhart, the first landscape architect for the new U.S. Forest Service, convinced the agency to protect Trapper's Lake, at the end of a 10-mile spur from the byway, from development. That was the genesis of today's wilderness system, to which the 235,230-acre Flat Tops Wilderness (south of the byway) was added in 1975.

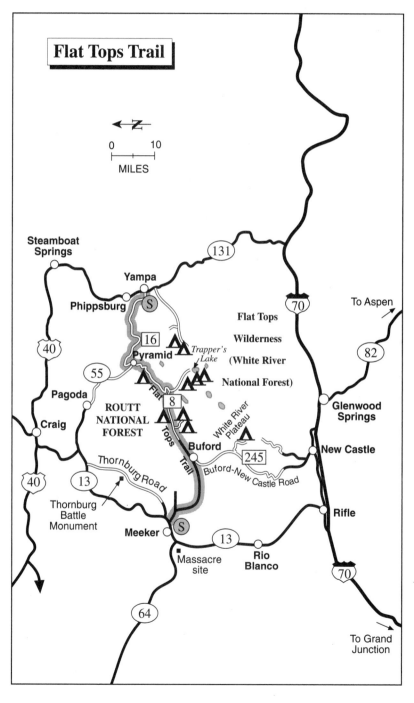

Meeker Hotel *(Tour 8)*

Buckskin Joe *(Tour 22)*

Buford-New Castle Road

LOCATION: In White River National Forest between New Castle, in Garfield County on I-70 west of Glenwood Springs, and Buford, in Rio Blanco County on Flat Top Road/county Road 8 southeast of Meeker. Skirts the west end of Flat Tops Wilderness.

HIGHLIGHTS: This is a pastoral cruise at the meeting place of the Rockies and the western plateau region. There are fantastic vistas of distant mountains, canyons, valleys, mesas and plateaus as you cross a range of environments, including irrigated farmlands, piñon-juniper woodlands, vast meadows and forest of pine, aspen, spruce and fir.

DIFFICULTY: Easy on a well-maintained dirt-and-gravel road.

TIME & DISTANCE: 2 hours; 38.7 miles. The spur to Meadow Lake adds about 11.5 miles.

MAPS: White River National Forest. DeLorme pp. 34–35.

INFORMATION: White River National Forest, Blanco and Rifle ranger districts.

GETTING THERE: To go north (as is described in The Drive)**:** Take exit 105 from I-70 to New Castle. Go right from the off-ramp, then left at the stop sign onto U.S. 6. At the west end of New Castle watch for a national forest access sign on the right, indicating the way to Buford-New Castle Road. Turn right there, onto 7th Street. In 4.8 miles turn north onto Buford-New Castle Road, No. 245. **To go south:** Take Flat Tops Road, county Road 8, east from state Highway 13 near Meeker for about 22 miles. Just before Buford go right (south) onto Buford-New Castle Road.

REST STOPS: There is a pleasant picnic area and fee campground at Meadow Lake, a scenic spur off the main road from Hiner Spring, via roads 601 and 823. There's also a campground in the Oak Ridge State Wildlife Area, at the north end on the South Fork of the White River. If you visit Meeker, you'll enjoy a stay at historic Meeker Hotel, which can honestly boast that "Teddy Roosevelt slept here."

THE DRIVE: From New Castle, the road climbs toward the White River Plateau and The Flat Tops, mountains formed by uplifted seabeds, vast lava flows, ice-age glaciers and rivers. Just north and west of New Castle rises the Grand Hogback, a ridge that marks the western edge of the Rockies and eastern edge of Colorado's semiarid plateau region. The road, paved at the south end, winds into sedimentary hills whiskered with piñon pines and junipers. The pavement ends when you enter White River National Forest. Soon you will be driving past stands of large aspens. Beyond that, the road crosses Triangle Park, a broad, grassy and very pretty meadow bordered by aspen and pine forest. At Hiner Spring, about 29 miles from New Castle and 15 from Buford, the scenic road to Meadow Lake branches east. It's a worthwhile detour, with excellent views of The Flat Tops Wilderness, including the canyon of the South Fork of the White River. From this junction the road begins a long, steady, serpentine descent toward the picturesque farmlands of the White River Valley, with more vistas of distant hills, plateaus and valleys. In the valley, the road crosses the South Fork, then crosses the North Fork to end at Flat Tops Road. Buford is right, as is the Flat Tops Trail (Tour 9). Meeker is left (west).

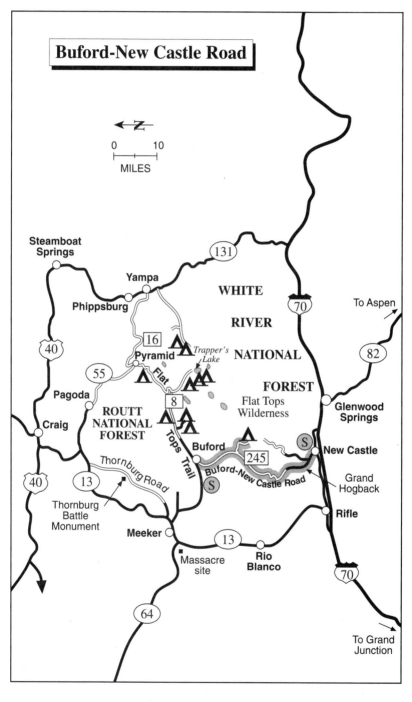

Buford-New Castle Road

Moffat (Rollins Pass) Road

LOCATION: East of Winter Park, from U.S. 40 to the Continental Divide at Rollins Pass (11,660 feet). Arapaho and Roosevelt National Forests. Boulder, Gilpin, and Grand counties.

HIGHLIGHTS: You will travel on the grade of the old Moffat Railroad, a.k.a. Denver, Northwestern and Pacific Railway, to Rollins Pass. Sights include old wooden trestles, the site of Corona Station and Hotel, and spectacular views of Indian Peaks Wilderness, glacial canyons and tundra basins. You can't cross to the east side because the Needle's Eye Tunnel is closed due to falling rock.

DIFFICULTY: Easy to Rollins Pass. The 1.5-mile Old Boulder Wagon Road, which ends at a parking area near the deteriorating Devil's Slide trestles (now closed) and Needle's Eye Tunnel (also closed), is easy, but it is a narrow mountainside track that warrants caution. The railroad grade has blind curves and is rocky in places. You should be able to get through by mid-June.

TIME & DISTANCE: 3 hours; 30 miles round-trip.

MAPS: Arapaho and Roosevelt National Forests; Trails Illustrated's No. 103 (Winter Park, Central City, Rollins Pass). Get a copy of the brochure *The Moffat Road*, available locally. DeLorme p. 39.

INFORMATION: Arapaho and Roosevelt National Forests, Sulphur Ranger District. Winter Park/Fraser Valley Chamber of Commerce and Visitor Center.

GETTING THERE: From U.S. 40 a half-mile south of Idlewild Campground (south of Winter Park), turn east onto county Road 80/forest Road 149, a.k.a. Rollins Pass/Corona Pass Road.

REST STOPS: There are no facilities or services.

THE DRIVE: In the mid-1860s John Quincy Adams Rollins built a toll road along this route over what was known then as Boulder Pass. In 1903–05, Denver banker and mining mogul David H. Moffat replaced it with the Denver, Northwestern and Pacific Railway Company line, which he controlled. The tortuous 23-mile "hill route," always difficult and costly to maintain, declined and was abandoned after 1928, when the 6.2-mile Moffat Tunnel beneath the Continental Divide opened. In 1956 the old grade opened to auto traffic. In the past, adventuresome motorists could drive over the Divide and down to Rollinsville via the two old trestles at Devil's Slide and through Needle's Eye Tunnel. But the trestles are now unsafe and closed. Falling rock inside the tunnel has forced its closure, as well. You can drive up the east side, stopping short of the tunnel. But this way takes you to the pass. The road climbs through forest, where old ties lie scattered about and the soil remains blackened by the soot from steam-powered locomotives. It passes a large trestle and several old log cabins, then rises above timberline. The road is rocky higher up, but you can gaze down into Fraser Valley and across the stunning peaks of the Divide and beyond. On the Divide is the site of Corona, which had a railroad station, hotel, restaurant and workers' quarters. Before the parking area, the Old Boulder Wagon Road (149) branches right, runs along the mountainside above the pass and ends in 1.5 miles at a parking area a short hike from the Devil's Slide trestles (above the gulch) and Needle's Eye Tunnel, to the right (south).

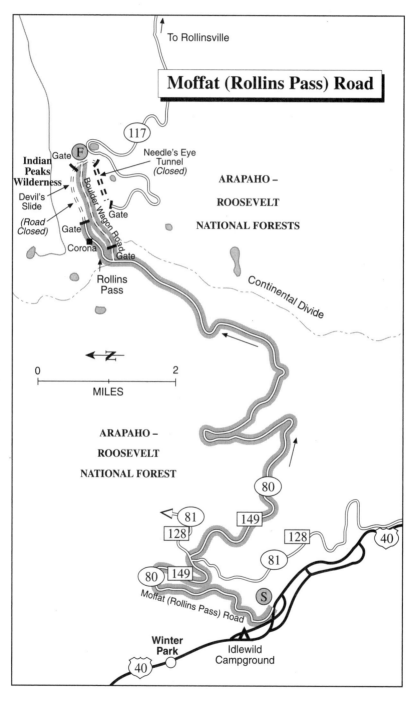

To Rollinsville

Moffat (Rollins Pass) Road

117

Needle's Eye Tunnel (Closed)

Gate F

Indian Peaks Wilderness

Devil's Slide

(Road Closed)

Gate

Boulder Wagon Road

Gate

Corona

Gate

Rollins Pass

ARAPAHO – ROOSEVELT NATIONAL FORESTS

Continental Divide

0   2
MILES

N

ARAPAHO – ROOSEVELT NATIONAL FOREST

80

81

128

149

128

40

81

80   149

Moffat (Rollins Pass) Road

S

Winter Park

40

Idlewild Campground

Wild Horse Trail

LOCATION: West of DeBeque (off I-70 northeast of Grand Junction). Mesa and Garfield counties.

HIGHLIGHTS: The wild horses of the Little Bookcliffs Wild Horse Area, one of four designated wild horse management areas in Colorado; beautiful canyons and plateaus; the bizarre sandstone figures at The Goblins. Best May 1–Labor Day. Colts and fillies are born in spring. Watch for coyotes, eagles and other wildlife.

DIFFICULTY: Easy when the roads are dry. They can become impassable, even with 4WD, when wet. Watch out for ATVs.

TIME & DISTANCE: 2.5 hours; 46 miles. Exploring side routes will add substantial time and distance.

MAPS: Get the brochures *Wild Horse Trail; A Visitor's Guide to Wild Horse Herd Management Area*; and *Little Bookcliffs Wild Horse Area.* DeLorme p. 43.

INFORMATION: BLM, Grand Junction. Town of DeBeque.

GETTING THERE: From I-70, take Exit 62 to DeBeque, about 34 miles northeast of Grand Junction. Drive to DeBeque, and turn left onto Fourth Street at the sign for the Little Bookcliffs Wild Horse Area. Turn left (south) on Minter Street. Cross Third Street, and soon you will angle right, on Second Street. Follow the signs for Deer Park, Winter Flats and Little Bookcliffs Wild Horse Area. Head west on Road V2.

REST STOPS: There are primitive campsites along the way. DeBeque has public restrooms, showers, food, fuel, etc.

THE DRIVE: This high-desert drive is gorgeous whether or not you see any wild horses, which, like most wildlife, are most active mornings and evenings. Spaniards brought the modern horse to the New World in the 1500s. Some escaped into the wild and bred. But today's wild herds are primarily descended from animals that escaped from or were turned loose by Indians, ranchers and farmers. Human presence in this area goes back thousands of years. In the 1880s, whites began arriving in what had long been important hunting grounds for Ute Indians. In 1917, the first oil shale distillation plant in the country was located here. An expected oil shale boom in the 1980s never materialized, but you will pass through a natural gas field. The road crosses colorful badlands of sculpted sandstone, ravines, terraced hills, sagebrush flats and boulder fields. In about 14 miles it reaches Winter Flats, below South Shale Ridge. Although you will see manure piles, called "stud piles" (which studs deposit to mark their territories) and hoof prints in the road, the official wild horse area is to the south. You can access it via the turnoffs for Indian Park and North Soda, two of the best viewing areas. Upwards of 120 horses roam the 30,261-acre refuge. They are most often spotted in the "parks," or large meadows. Winter Flats Road climbs some as it bends north at the west end of South Shale Ridge. At mile 25 is The Goblins, where soft sandstone has been eroded into strange shapes. The road edges around a canyon, then becomes South Dry Fork Road on the north side of the ridge. Here it runs along the base of Horse Mountain. By mile 36 it is good two-lane dirt and gravel, and by mile 43 it's paved.

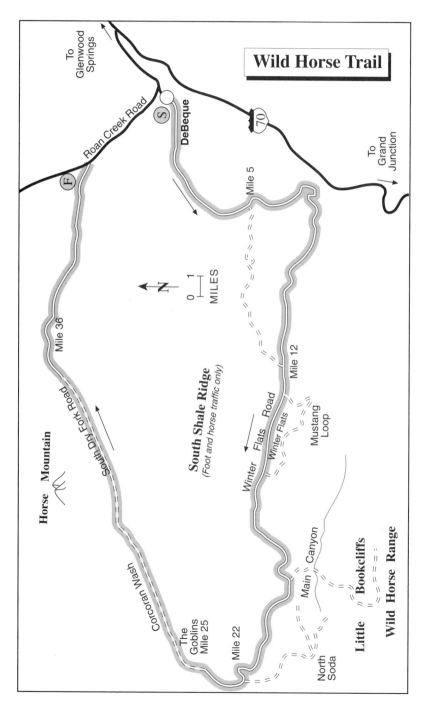

Wild Horse Trail

To Glenwood Springs

Roan Creek Road

F

S

DeBeque

70

To Grand Junction

Mile 5

N

0   1
MILES

Mile 36

South Shale Ridge
(Foot and horse traffic only)

South Dry Fork Road

Horse   Mountain

Mile 12

Winter   Flats   Road

Winter Flats

Mustang Loop

Corcoran Wash

The Goblins
Mile 25

Mile 22

Main   Canyon

Little   **Bookcliffs**

Wild Horse Range

North Soda

Devil's Slide (closed) *(Tour 11)*

Mill Creek Road *(Tour 13)*

Mill Creek Road

LOCATION: East of Vail, south of I-70. Eagle County. White River National Forest.

HIGHLIGHTS: This is a convenient yet very rewarding tour at one of Colorado's most famous resort communities. It will take you up the ski slopes and under the lifts to the 11,816-foot summit of Red Peak for a spectacular 360-degree vista.

DIFFICULTY: Easy as far as a great overlook at mile 8.7, which is 1.2 miles below the summit of Red Peak. From there I rate this drive moderate, because there is a narrow, muddy and rutted section just beyond the overlook. (It might be best to wait until later in the season to drive this final section.) Lower down, watch out for hikers, mountain bikers, trucks and other traffic. Don't expect to see directional signs.

TIME & DISTANCE: At least 2 hours; 19.8 miles round-trip.

MAPS: White River National Forest; Trails Illustrated No. 108 (Vail, Frisco, Dillon). DeLorme p. 37.

INFORMATION: White River National Forest, Holy Cross Ranger District.

GETTING THERE: Take exit 176 from I-70, at Vail. Follow Vail Road from the roundabout on South Frontage Road. Where it bends and dips to the left, continue straight on what looks like a service road and parking area behind the Lodge Tower. Drive toward the Vista Bahn Express lift. Take a hard right immediately after driving under the first lift. Follow forest Road 710.

REST STOPS: There are places to stop along the way, particularly at the overlook at the point where the road becomes rough. There is plenty of parking space on the flat-topped summit.

THE DRIVE: The road is quite good as it climbs through aspen and conifer forest, crossing ski slopes and passing under a lift a number of times to follow Mill Creek into the mountains. 3.3 miles from the bottom of the ski hill you will reach a Y, where a gated road on the right descends to lift 10, Highline Express. The single-lane dirt and rock road straight ahead is your route. In another 3.6 miles continue north (directly ahead) where another road branches right. Now Mill Creek Road makes its way north and then east along a shelf high above Vail Valley and I-70. You will have some fine views across the valley to the spectacular Gore Range. Go up a few more switchbacks, and the road will become rougher, with some dips, ruts and mudholes. Eventually you will reach an overlook where you can gaze at the Gore Range, in the Eagles Nest Wilderness. A moderately difficult section, narrow, rutted and muddy in places, lies ahead in the forest, but once beyond it you will climb to the summit of Red Peak for a panorama that includes Mt. of the Holy Cross, Battle Mountain, the Gore Range and the back bowls of Vail Mountain.

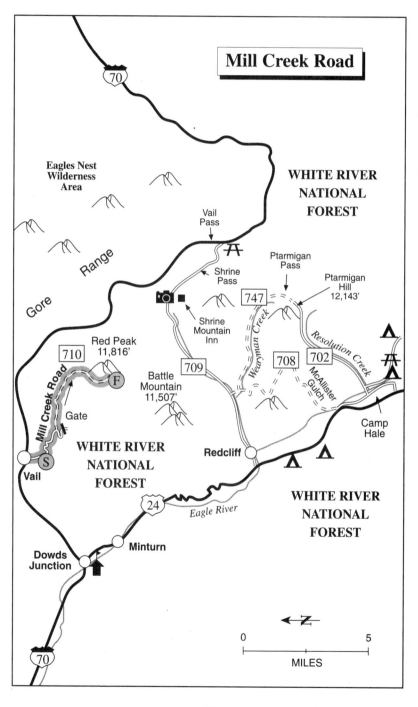

Mill Creek Road

Eagles Nest
Wilderness
Area

**WHITE RIVER
NATIONAL
FOREST**

Gore

Range

Vail
Pass

Shrine
Pass

Shrine
Mountain
Inn

Ptarmigan
Pass

Ptarmigan
Hill
12,143'

747

Wearyman Creek

Resolution Creek

Red Peak
11,816'

710

Mill Creek Road

709

708

702

McAllister Gulch

F

Battle
Mountain
11,507'

Gate

S

**WHITE RIVER
NATIONAL
FOREST**

Vail

Redcliff

Camp
Hale

**Dowds
Junction**

24

Minturn

Eagle River

**WHITE RIVER
NATIONAL
FOREST**

70

70

0   5

MILES

57

Horseshoe Basin

LOCATION: On the western side of the Continental Divide east of Dillon Reservoir and Keystone; south of I-70. White River National Forest. Summit County.

HIGHLIGHTS: You will drive up a long and beautiful glacial gulch with plenty of reminders of bygone days of gold and silver mining. It's a convenient and highly scenic outing if you're in the Keystone area. If you're up to it, you can make the 2-mile hike up to Argentine Pass, an exposed ascent of 2,000 feet on a footpath that is all that remains of the old road over the pass from Waldorf. Or you can drive up to the pass from the other side of the Divide (Tour 15).

DIFFICULTY: Easy for the first 4.6 miles; moderate due to rockiness for the next 1.2 miles. Watch for hikers and mountain bikers.

TIME & DISTANCE: 1.5 hours; 11.6 miles round-trip; longer if you explore side routes and places of interest.

MAPS: White River National Forest. Trails Illustrated No. 104 (Idaho Springs, Georgetown, Loveland Pass). DeLorme p. 38.

INFORMATION: White River National Forest, Dillon Ranger District.

GETTING THERE: East of Keystone, turn south off Loveland Pass Road onto Montezuma Road. Drive 4.3 miles along the Snake River. Where the road bends left, turn left into a large parking area. Go through the gate ahead, and follow Road 214 along Peru Creek.

REST STOPS: The end of the road, in a glacial cirque at almost 11,900 feet, is a great place to stop. The old mine sites are interesting.

THE DRIVE: The rocky little road follows Peru Creek through forest for almost 3 miles. Then, just when you start feeling that the trees may be blocking the view of what you correctly suspect is great Rocky Mountain scenery, things open up. Around you rise the walls of a long gulch, a glacial pathway that gradually bends north below the great wall of the Continental Divide. Here and there are the remains of old mine operations. At mile 3.7 you'll see on the slope to the right the ruins of the Pennsylvania Mine, up Cinnamon Gulch. Soon you will be able to see on the talus wall of the Divide the faint impression of the once-important road over Argentine Pass from Waldorf. The road, completed in 1871, was built by Commodore Stephen Decatur to link Georgetown, east of the Divide, to the gold and silver mines along Peru Creek. But the dangerously steep and unstable terrain up there doomed it in favor of safer routes. Not far beyond the tailings pile at Shoe Basin Mine is the Argentine Pass trailhead. The road becomes much rougher here, and continues for another 0.8 mile or so, ending near the head of the gulch in a beautiful glacial cirque.

ALSO TRY: Webster Pass (Tour 18), Santa Fe Peak (Tour 20).

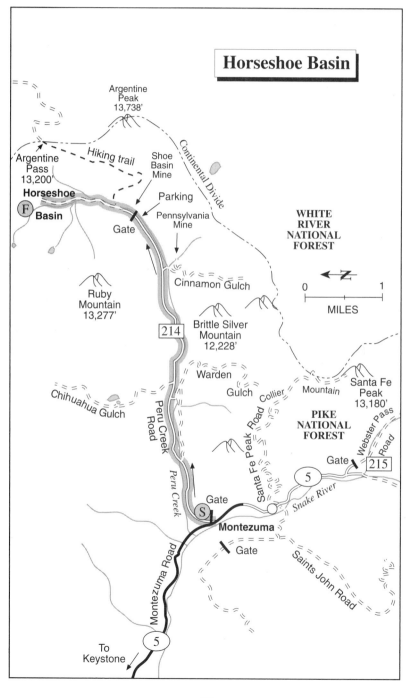

Horseshoe Basin

Argentine
Peak
13,738'

Hiking trail

Shoe
Basin
Mine

Continental Divide

Argentine
Pass
13,200'

Horseshoe

Ⓕ **Basin**

Parking

Pennsylvania
Mine

Gate

WHITE
RIVER
NATIONAL
FOREST

N

0   1

MILES

Cinnamon Gulch

Ruby
Mountain
13,277'

214

Brittle Silver
Mountain
12,228'

Warden

Gulch

Collier

Mountain

Santa Fe
Peak
13,180'

Chihuahua Gulch

Peru Creek
Road

Santa Fe Peak Road

PIKE
NATIONAL
FOREST

Webster Pass

Road

Gate

215

Peru Creek

5

Gate

Ⓢ

Snake River

Montezuma

Gate

Saints John Road

Montezuma Road

5

To
Keystone

Argentine Pass

LOCATION: This spur off beautiful Guanella Pass Scenic and Historic Byway is on the Continental Divide in Clear Creek County, southwest of Georgetown (on I-70). Arapaho and Roosevelt National Forests.

HIGHLIGHTS: Visit historic Georgetown, Colorado's first "silver queen." The drive up a glacial gulch to Argentine Pass (about 13,200 feet) on the Continental Divide is exhilarating, as is the white-knuckler up McClellan Mountain. Watch for bighorn sheep.

DIFFICULTY: Easy, though rocky, to the site of Waldorf, which is usually accessible by late May. The narrow mountainside roads beyond Waldorf leave no margin for error. They are narrow with tight switch-backs; I rate them moderate. A snowbank can block the road to Argentine Pass into August or September.

TIME & DISTANCE: 3 hours. It's 6 miles to the site of Waldorf from Guanella Pass Road. From Waldorf, it's 2.3 miles to Argentine Pass, and 4.7 miles to the overlook on McClellan Mountain.

MAPS: Arapaho and Roosevelt National Forests. Trails Illustrated No. 104 (Idaho Springs). DeLorme pp. 38–39.

INFORMATION: Arapaho and Roosevelt National Forests, Clear Creek Ranger District.

GETTING THERE: Take I-70 to Georgetown, 47 miles west of Denver. Go west into the old town and follow the signs for Guanella Pass. At the edge of town, where the road makes a U and climbs, watch your odometer. 2.5 miles from there the turnoff to Waldorf, on Leavenworth Road (248.1), is on the right. Watch for a small sign.

REST STOPS: Anywhere. A waterfall early on the drive is pleasant. On Guanella Pass Road, there is a picnic area at Clear Lake, and camp-grounds near Upper Cabin Creek Reservoir and Guanella Pass.

THE DRIVE: The rocky road climbs through forest as it courses along a ledge high above Leavenworth Creek. You'll cross timberline before Waldorf, where little remains but tailings. Silver was found here in 1867. The road over Argentine Pass, completed in 1871, was built by Commodore Stephen Decatur to link Georgetown, east of the Divide, to the gold and silver mines west of the Divide. But the steep and unsta-ble roadbed on the west side doomed it, and safer routes were found. In about 1900 mining company owner (and minister) Edward J. Wilcox established the town of Waldorf, which claimed the nation's highest post office (11,666 feet). In 1905–06 Wilcox built the Argentine Central Railroad to haul silver ore to Silver Plume. He later extended the world's highest narrow-gauge steam railway to take tourists to the top of McClellan Mountain, 3,000 feet above Georgetown. From there they could gaze over the sheer drop-off into Stevens Gulch, 2,000 feet below, visit an icy mine touted as an ice cave, and view a mountain panorama. You can relive the unnerving experience of inching up McClellan Mountain by angling right at Waldorf. Carefully follow the narrow mountainside track (No. 248.1) to a heart-stopping drop-off below a cut in the ridge. Turnaround space is tight. From here, you can hike southwest to the 14,270-foot summit of Grays Peak. To reach Argentine Pass, at Waldorf continue across the nail-strewn tailings pile and wind up the head of the gulch toward an old A-frame structure. There, you can gaze down at Horseshoe Basin and Peru Creek (Tour 14). The old road is now a faint foot trail down the west side of the Divide.

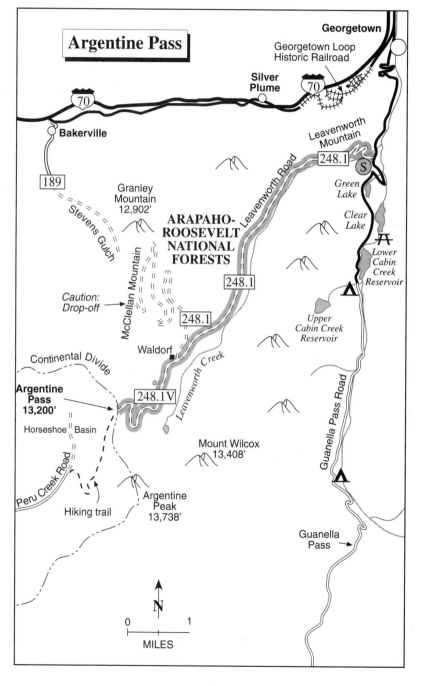

Shrine Pass Road

LOCATION: Between U.S. 24 at Redcliff (also Red Cliff), and I-70 at Vail Pass. White River National Forest. Eagle County.

HIGHLIGHTS: This is a beautiful, if busy, road in the Vail area that gradually ascends to 11,089 feet at Shrine Pass, with views (especially if you drive east to west) of the peaks of the Sawatch Range and Holy Cross Wilderness, including Mt. of the Holy Cross (14,003 feet).

DIFFICULTY: Easy, although the roadbed can have rocks and pot-holes. This pass is usually open by Memorial Day weekend.

TIME & DISTANCE: 1 hour; 12 miles.

MAPS: White River National Forest. Trails Illustrated No. 108 (Vail, Frisco, Dillon). DeLorme pp. 37–38.

INFORMATION: White River National Forest, Holy Cross Ranger District.

GETTING THERE: From I-70, take exit 190 on Vail Pass, between Vail and Frisco. Shrine Pass Road is west of the interstate. **From U.S. 24,** exit to Redcliff and drive beneath the arched highway bridge. Drive into the rustic little town, nestled in a narrow canyon. At the post office go left onto Eagle Street, then immediately turn right onto Shrine Pass Road.

REST STOPS: There is a vista point (wheelchair accessible) and rest area on the pass, from which you can view Mt. of the Holy Cross. Shrine Mountain Inn, just west of the pass, is part of the 10th Mountain Division Hut Association's hut and trail system. It operates a restaurant in summer (call ahead for information and reservations).

THE DRIVE: Though it involves an 11-mile detour via U.S. 24 (the Top of the Rockies Scenic and Historic Byway), if you're not in a hurry this little mountain road (forest Road 709) offers a lovely alternative to I-70. Along the way are mountain vistas, meadows, wildflowers, and the steep, rocky and forested walls of the canyon of Turkey Creek. West of the pass you can stroll along a paved walkway to look out at Mt. of the Holy Cross, where snow sheltered in the dark rock's northeast-facing crevices forms a huge natural cross. About 4 miles from Redcliff the road passes a couple of old roadside cabins, the site of Benson's Cabin. (They mark the start of a separate, rugged 2-mile jeep trail.) Near Redcliff, an intriguing little town that occupies an improbable site in a narrow canyon, you can link up with the Wearyman Road (Tour 17) to Ptarmigan Pass.

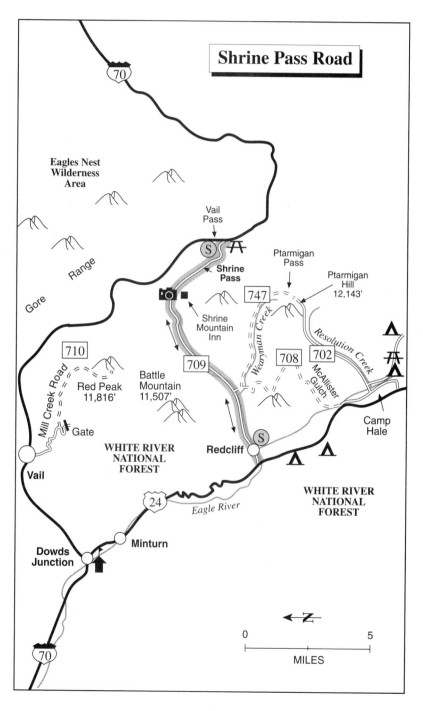

Shrine Pass Road

Eagles Nest Wilderness Area

Gore Range

Vail Pass

S

Shrine Pass

Shrine Mountain Inn

Ptarmigan Pass

Ptarmigan Hill 12,143'

747

Wearyman Creek

Resolution Creek

710

Mill Creek Road

Red Peak 11,816'

Battle Mountain 11,507'

709

708

702

McAllister Gulch

Camp Hale

Gate

WHITE RIVER NATIONAL FOREST

Redcliff

S

Vail

24

Eagle River

WHITE RIVER NATIONAL FOREST

Dowds Junction

Minturn

70

N

0   5

MILES

Horseshoe Basin *(Tour 14)*

Camp Hale *(Tour 17)*

Wearyman Creek/Camp Hale

LOCATION: White River National Forest. East of U.S. 24 between Redcliff (also Red Cliff) and historic Camp Hale. Eagle County.

HIGHLIGHTS: You will enjoy a beautiful mix of forest and meadows with views of the Gore Range, Sawatch Range and Continental Divide, especially on the descent from 11,777-feet Ptarmigan Pass on Resolution Road (702). Wearyman Road (747) can involve real four-wheeling, depending on conditions. Camp Hale is where the U.S. Army's famed 10th Mountain Division trained during World War II.

DIFFICULTY: Moderate on Wearyman Road, a narrow 4WD route that follows Wearyman Creek. There are a number of stream crossings and muddy areas, best crossed later in the summer, and you should be prepared to remove fallen branches and trees from the roadway. Easy on Resolution Road, a good road along Resolution Creek between Camp Hale and Ptarmigan Pass.

TIME & DISTANCE: 1.5 hours; 13.8 miles.

MAPS: White River National Forest. Trails Illustrated Nos. 108 (Vail, Frisco, Dillon) and 109 (Breckenridge, Tennessee Pass). DeLorme pp. 37, 47.

INFORMATION: White River National Forest, Holy Cross Ranger District.

GETTING THERE: Depending on which direction you want to take, you can begin either at Redcliff or Camp Hale, both along U.S. 24, the Top of the Rockies Scenic and Historic Byway. **To go south,** drive through Redcliff to the intersection at Eagle Street, and go left. Then immediately go right, onto Shrine Pass Road. About 2.5 miles from town Wearyman Road branches right, crossing Turkey Creek on a small bridge near the confluence with Wearyman Creek. **To start at Camp Hale and go north,** watch for the sign for Resolution Road (702) along U.S. 24. Turn into Camp Hale and cross the valley of the Eagle River. Take Resolution Road from the northeast side of the valley into the mountains toward Ptarmigan Pass.

REST STOPS: There is a picnic area and fee campground at Camp Hale, and primitive campsites along the way.

THE DRIVE: From Shrine Pass Road, Wearyman Road is a rocky forest two-track route that makes a number of small stream crossings. There is a substantial fording about a half-mile from the start. Beyond it are some boggy areas where the roadbed has been firmed up with timbers. You may encounter some stretches narrowed by brush. Soon the road begins to climb steadily up a forested little vale, through a large meadow on a hillside above Wearyman Creek. There will be some muddy spots that could be difficult early in the season. After crossing more meadows, where wildflowers may be blooming, the road enters an alpine basin at about 11,500 feet, below bald mountaintops. Ahead is the pass. From there on down you'll have excellent views of jagged peaks and basins. From the pass to Camp Hale, Road 702 along Resolution Creek is much better, making for a swift descent. At Camp Hale you can wander among crumbling foundations in a small river valley where about 14,000 soldiers trained for mountain and winter warfare. Nearly 1,000 died and more than 4,000 were wounded fighting in the Italian Alps. You can make a loop by returning via McAllister Gulch Road (708).

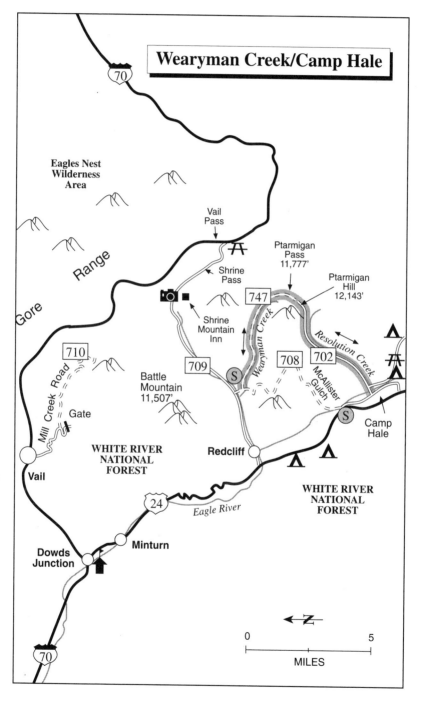

Webster Pass

LOCATION: On the Continental Divide west of Denver, southeast of Keystone and Montezuma. White River and Pike national forests. Summit and Park counties.

HIGHLIGHTS: From Montezuma the road goes up a lush, beautiful glacial trough to the pass, at 12,096 feet. This route's short length and exceptional beauty in both directions make it a rewarding drive. Fording the little Snake River is fun, too. Watch for Rocky Mountain bighorn sheep and mountain goats.

DIFFICULTY: Moderate, but only because it's quite rocky. I stop at the pass, which is usually accessible by early July. The track on the east side of the pass, down into Handcart Gulch, can be blocked by snow into August. Just below the pass it is very narrow, off-camber and, for the average sport-utility vehicle at least, too hazardous. In Handcart Gulch the road is rocky and boggy for 3.4 miles below the pass, and not as scenic as this drive up the west side. The next 5.1 miles to U.S. 285 via Hall Valley are very scenic, on well-maintained county Road 60/forest Road 120. It comes out at the old town site of Webster.

TIME & DISTANCE: 1.5 hours and 8.2 miles round-trip from Montezuma Road.

MAPS: Trails Illustrated No. 104 (Idaho Springs, Georgetown, Loveland Pass). White River National Forest. DeLorme pp. 38, 48–49.

INFORMATION: White River National Forest, Dillon Ranger District; Pike and San Isabel national forests, South Park Ranger District.

GETTING THERE: From Loveland Pass Road east of Keystone, take Montezuma Road 5 miles to the village of Montezuma (also the starting point of the Santa Fe Peak drive, Tour 20). Drive through town for about a mile, then turn left onto forest Road 285.

REST STOPS: There are many places to stop along the way, including the pass.

THE DRIVE: The rocky road passes through a gate, and in about 1.3 miles crosses the Snake River, which actually is a large creek, though it can be deep. Beyond the crossing the roadbed is rocky, but the scenery in the verdant gulch is excellent. Soon you'll reach a Y. Webster Pass is left. The right branch is the Radical Hill Jeep Trail (narrow, precipitous, twisting, tight switchbacks and probably blocked by snow). From here you'll begin climbing the wall of the glacial basin, and the scenery just gets better. Five miles from Montezuma the road reaches the pass, named for brothers William and Emerson Webster, who opened this old toll road in 1878. The red peak there is 12,801-foot Red Cone, marked by an extremely steep, one-way (downhill) jeep trail for experts. To the south is 12,518-foot Handcart Peak. There's room to park, so you can get out and scan the slopes for bighorn sheep or hike down to Handcart Gulch.

ALSO TRY: Horseshoe Basin (Tour 14), Santa Fe Peak (Tour 20).

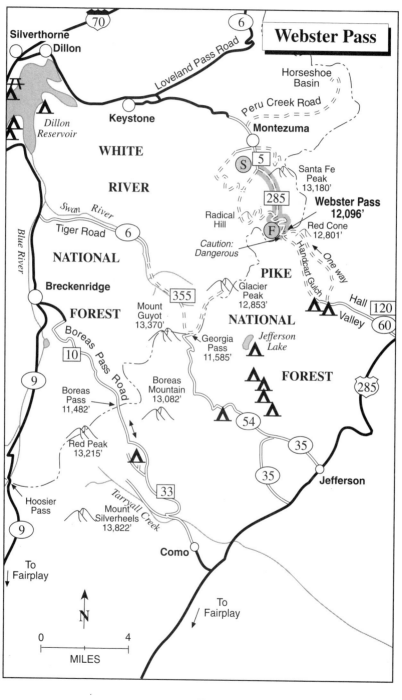

Webster Pass

70

6

Silverthorne
Dillon

Loveland Pass Road

Horseshoe
Basin

Peru Creek Road

Keystone

Montezuma

Dillon
Reservoir

WHITE

S 5

Santa Fe
Peak
13,180'

RIVER

Swan River

285

**Webster Pass
12,096'**

Tiger Road 6

Blue River

Radical
Hill

Red Cone
12,801'

F

Caution:
Dangerous

One way

Handcart Gulch

NATIONAL

PIKE

Breckenridge

355

Glacier
Peak
12,853'

Hall

120

Mount
Guyot
13,370'

NATIONAL

Valley

60

FOREST

Georgia
Pass
11,585'

Jefferson
Lake

285

10

Boreas Pass Road

FOREST

9

Boreas
Pass
11,482'

Boreas
Mountain
13,082'

54

Red Peak
13,215'

35

35

Hoosier
Pass

33

Tarryall Creek

Jefferson

9

Mount
Silverheels
13,822'

To
Fairplay

Como

To
Fairplay

N

0   4

MILES

Georgia Pass

LOCATION: On the Continental Divide between Highway 9 north of Breckenridge (Summit County) and Jefferson (Park County), on U.S. 285. The east side is in Pike National Forest; the west side is in White River National Forest.

HIGHLIGHTS: This is an adventuresome day trip out of Breckenridge that lets you make a loop. I recommend starting in Jefferson, on the east side, because it's easier to go downhill on the rough road below the pass on the west side. At the 11,585-foot pass there are great vistas of South Park, 13,370-foot Mt. Guyot, and beyond.

DIFFICULTY: Easy to moderate. The east side follows a 2WD road. The poorly marked route on the west side is rough near the pass.

TIME & DISTANCE: 2 hours; 23 miles.

MAPS: Pike and White River national forests. DeLorme pp. 38, 48.

INFORMATION: White River National Forest, Dillon Ranger District; Pike and San Isabel national forests, South Park Ranger District.

GETTING THERE: To go west, the direction I recommend, take U.S. 285 to Jefferson. Turn west toward the mountains on county Road 35 at the sign for Jefferson Lake Road and Michigan Creek Road In 2.8 miles angle right, onto county Road 54, and follow it to the pass. **From Highway 9:** About 3 miles north of Breckenridge, turn east on Tiger Road (county Road 6) toward the golf course. Follow it along the Swan River for 5.7 miles, then turn right at the confluence of the river's north and south forks, following the south fork. In another half-mile turn right. About 9 miles from the highway take Road 222.

REST STOPS: Food, fuel, etc., are available at Breckenridge and Jefferson. There is camping on both sides of the Divide.

THE DRIVE: The supply road from South Park over the Divide at Georgia Pass served mines in the Breckenridge area after the discovery of gold in 1859. Easier crossings at Hoosier Pass, on today's Highway 9, and Boreas Pass (Tour 23) northwest of Como, later replaced it. From Jefferson, you will pass through rangelands and spruce/aspen forest. By mile 11 the road climbs steeply, narrows and becomes a bit rougher, and at mile 12 it's a shelf as it crosses timberline. This vantage point just below the pass provides vistas across South Park. On the pass, atop the Continental Divide below Mt. Guyot, roads go in three directions. (To the right is a spur that goes into the trees and winds around to the east and south, ending in 1.8 miles at a rocky knoll with a spectacular vista.) To go to Breckenridge, angle left at the pass sign, and follow the middle route. In about 75 yards the road descends steeply through a badly chewed up stretch. Low-range gears will be helpful. In another 75 yards go through the intersection, continuing the rough descent. A mile from the pass go right at the T (left, if you're headed uphill). In 0.3 mile you'll go through a gate, then reach a Y. The forks connect shortly, but the left branch (right branch on the way up) is easiest. There are many spurs, so follow the most-used track as you work your way downhill, and stay with the South Fork of the Swan River. 1.7 miles from the pass keep right and cross the stream. Soon you will pass a private residence, and the road will become much better. When you cross the river, heavily dredged for gold, go left to reach Highway 9.

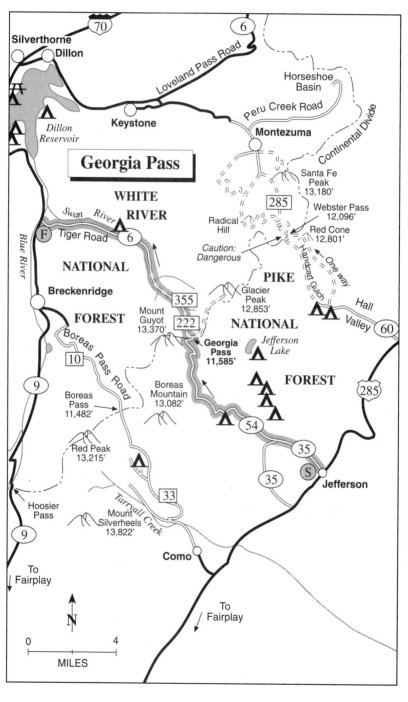

Santa Fe Peak

LOCATION: On the Continental Divide west of Denver, southeast of Keystone and Montezuma. Summit County. White River National Forest.

HIGHLIGHTS: A white-knuckler that ends just shy of a 13,180-foot summit. Astounding panoramic views.

DIFFICULTY: Moderate to difficult. It's steep in places with tight switchbacks, narrow shelf segments and unnerving sidehill spots. Extra caution is due on this drive. I had no problems with a Toyota 4Runner, but the narrow roadway and tight switchbacks may make this unsuited for some larger vehicles. This route usually doesn't open until mid-July.

TIME & DISTANCE: 1.5 hours; 8.8 miles round-trip.

MAPS: Trails Illustrated No. 104 (Idaho Springs, Georgetown, Loveland Pass). White River National Forest. DeLorme p. 38.

INFORMATION: White River National Forest, Dillon Ranger District.

GETTING THERE: From Loveland Pass Road east of Keystone, turn south onto Montezuma Road. Drive 5 miles to Montezuma, then go left at the stop sign onto Morgan Gulch/Santa Fe Peak Road.

REST STOPS: The summit.

THE DRIVE: Montezuma, a 10,400-foot-high hamlet tucked against the ramparts of the Continental Divide, was named for the last Aztec emperor. It's the kind of village where you might have to stop to let a wandering horse cross the street. It isn't unique for being the offspring of 1860s silver mining, but it is unique for surviving busts, fires and time to remain occupied into the 21st century. However, since it's so close to popular ski areas and the heavily populated Front Range, one has to wonder how much longer its quiet, rustic character will last. Dirt and gravel Morgan Gulch/Santa Fe Peak Road climbs steeply out of town through pine forest. In half a mile it's rocky and steep. It makes a few easy switchbacks, then becomes a single-lane shelf road. Through the trees, you'll get views west to spectacular Glacier Mountain and other peaks and glacial basins across the valley of the Snake River. 2.8 miles from town the road crosses timberline. As you ascend Collier Mountain, you'll maneuver over some off-camber spots, around tight switchbacks, and pass an old mine. From the crest of Collier Mountain you will also have outstanding vistas east. (In case you're wondering about the road far below, along Geneva Creek, a private property owner has closed it with a massive locked gate.) More sidehills and steep, tight switchbacks lie ahead as the climb continues. At about mile 3.9 the road will enter a basin. Go left at two posts marking a two-track road that goes up the hill ahead. In a half-mile you will arrive at a flat-topped summit, the end of the drive, where the panorama is fantastic.

ALSO TRY: Webster Pass (Tour 18) and Horseshoe Basin (Tour 14).

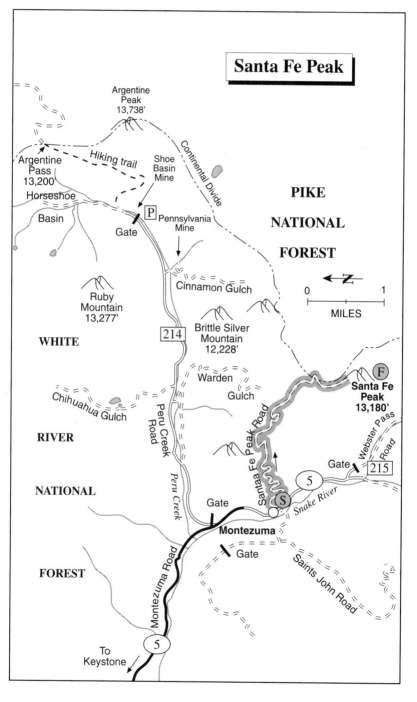

Santa Fe Peak

Argentine
Peak
13,738'

Hiking trail

Shoe
Basin
Mine

Continental Divide

Argentine
Pass
13,200'

Horseshoe

Basin

P

Gate

Pennsylvania
Mine

PIKE

NATIONAL

FOREST

Cinnamon Gulch

Ruby
Mountain
13,277'

Brittle Silver
Mountain
12,228'

N

0   1

MILES

WHITE

214

Warden

Gulch

F

**Santa Fe
Peak
13,180'**

Chihuahua Gulch

RIVER

Peru Creek
Road

Santaa Fe Peak Road

Webster Pass
Road

215

Gate

NATIONAL

Peru Creek

Gate

5

S

Snake River

Montezuma

Gate

FOREST

Montezuma Road

Saints John Road

To
Keystone

5

Mosquito Pass Road

LOCATION: Mosquito Range between Leadville, on U.S. 24, and Alma, on Highway 9. Pike and San Isabel national forests. Lake and Park counties.

HIGHLIGHTS: This road crosses historic Mosquito Pass, the highest (13,186 feet) vehicular pass in the country. The glaciated alpine views are outstanding, particularly to the west, where the peaks of the Sawatch Range include Colorado's highest, 14,433-foot Mt. Elbert. Contestants in the arduous annual pack burro race between Leadville and Fairplay, held on the last full weekend in July, cross this pass.

DIFFICULTY: Moderate, with spots that may be difficult. There are very rocky, narrow and steep segments with long drop-offs, as well as tight switchbacks. Snowbanks can block the road at the top and on the east side into late summer, or even all summer, so call ahead. It's a great drive even if you can't go all the way across.

TIME & DISTANCE: 2 hours; 15 miles.

MAPS: Trails Illustrated No. 109 (Breckenridge, Tennessee Pass). Pike National Forest and San Isabel National Forest. DeLorme pp. 47–48.

INFORMATION: Pike and San Isabel national forests, Leadville and South Park Ranger Districts. Get the auto tour brochure *Mosquito Pass; Mining Madness, the Lore and Legend*, available locally.

GETTING THERE: From Leadville, go east from Highway 24 on 7th Street East, up Evans Gulch. In 3.5 miles you'll see the Diamond Shaft ahead; turn left, and follow primitive Road 438, Mosquito Pass Road, to the pass. **From Highway 9** about 0.9 mile south of Alma, turn west onto county Road 12, at the sign for Mosquito Gulch. There may be a sign stating whether the pass is open or closed.

REST STOPS: There are no facilities. But you can stop on the pass, or at the old mine and mill sites along the way.

THE DRIVE: With the lure of silver drawing hordes of fortune seekers to Leadville, this old toll road was busy indeed between 1879, when it opened, and 1880, when railroad lines reached Leadville. In the summer of 1879, for example, more than 100 wagons crossed the pass daily. Before then the route was an Indian footpath. In the 1860s, the Rev. John Dyer, a Methodist minister, author and missionary, carried his message, and eventually the mail, through the gap, trudging along on 10-foot-long Norwegian snowshoes in winter. Once the railroad offered easier transport, the harrowing pass crossing was abandoned. Local residents reopened it after World War II. Today, it is a thrilling and popular 4WD route. From the west, make the easy drive up Evans Gulch past numerous old tailings piles and diggings to the 1,000-foot-deep Diamond Shaft. From there, a rough and steep road climbs above a beautiful glacial gulch along a narrow shelf, making tight switchbacks on the way to the pass. On the east side, the good county road passes through rustic old Park City and past the London Mine. There it becomes rougher as it climbs above timberline to the head of Mosquito Gulch, to the North London Mine. A snowbank might be blocking the road here. The pass is beyond the roadcut up ahead, but there may be yet another snowbank between the roadcut and the pass.

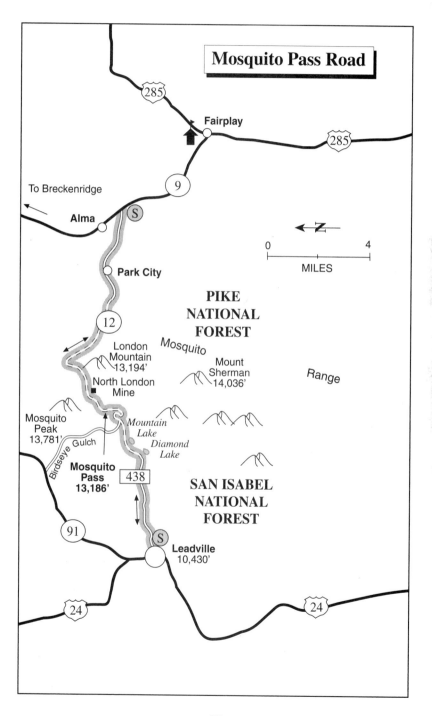

Mosquito Pass Road

285

Fairplay

285

To Breckenridge

9

Alma   S

Park City

PIKE
NATIONAL
FOREST

0   4
MILES

12

London
Mountain
13,194'

Mosquito

Mount
Sherman
14,036'

Range

North London
Mine

Mosquito
Peak
13,781'

Mountain
Lake

Diamond
Lake

Birdseye Gulch

Mosquito
Pass
13,186'

438

SAN ISABEL
NATIONAL
FOREST

91

S   Leadville
10,430'

24   24

Mt. Bross/Kite Lake

LOCATION: Near the Continental Divide south of Breckenridge, northwest of Fairplay. Park County. Pike and San Isabel national forests.

HIGHLIGHTS: You will drive onto the 14,172-foot summit of Mt. Bross for a spectacular vista. Along the way is the Bristlecone Pine Scenic Area, home to centuries-old trees. The road up Buckskin Gulch passes the town site of Buckskin Joe, an old cemetery and other historic sites. It ends at pretty Kite Lake, a trailhead for hikers out to top four of Colorado's famous 14ers: (Mt. Democrat, 14,148 feet; Mt. Lincoln, 14,286 feet; Mt. Cameron, 14,239 feet; and Mt. Bross).

DIFFICULTY: Easy, with one chewed-up (moderate) spot. The road up Mt. Bross is on a shelf with long drop-offs. The summit can be swarming with hikers on weekends, so be careful and considerate. I would put this one off until mid-July.

TIME & DISTANCE: From Alma: 5.5 miles to Kite Lake; 6.4 miles to the bristlecones; 10.3 miles to the top of Mt. Bross. You can spend anywhere from a couple of hours to most of a day.

MAPS: Trails Illustrated No. 109 (Breckenridge, Tennessee Pass). Pike National Forest. DeLorme p. 48.

INFORMATION: Pike and San Isabel national forests, South Park Ranger District. Get the brochure *Buckskin Gulch: The Personalities Behind the Pans*.

GETTING THERE: From Breckenridge or Fairplay, take state Highway 9 to Alma. In the middle of town, turn west at the little wooden sign for Buckskin and Kite Lake (county Road No. 8).

REST STOPS: There is a pleasant, though shadeless, campground at Kite Lake. You'll find food, fuel and lodging in Alma and Fairplay.

THE DRIVE: To fully appreciate the drive to Kite Lake, refer to the informational brochure, which you can get at the Forest Service office in Fairplay. The road up Buckskin Gulch passes through the town site of Buckskin Joe, the county seat from 1862 to 1867. The short-lived mining town was named for buckskin-clad Joe Higgenbottom. About 1.4 miles from Alma, at a tour marker noting the site of Buckskin Joe, a little road goes into the woods on the right, to the cemetery. Other sights include an arrastra, or stone ore-crushing facility, along Buckskin Creek at mile 2.5, and a mill a short distance farther up the beautiful glacial canyon, before you reach Kite Lake. At mile 2.8 from Alma is the right turn onto Road 787, to Windy Ridge, where the gnarled Rocky Mountain bristlecone pines grow, and the summit of Mt. Bross. While similar trees in California's White Mountains are as old as 4,600 years, the oldest here dates back more than 800 years. (The oldest tree in Colorado is a South Park bristlecone that apparently sprouted about 442 B.C.) The road to the grove has one rough spot at a mine site. Beyond the grove the road switchbacks up Mt. Bross' eastern and northern faces, providing breathtaking vistas across South Park and down into Cameron Amphitheater, below Mt. Lincoln (the road down there is closed beyond the lake). Your route passes private mining claims and arrives at a flat. A loose and steep stretch angles left toward the summit, from which you can gaze out at three neighboring peaks that exceed 14,000 feet.

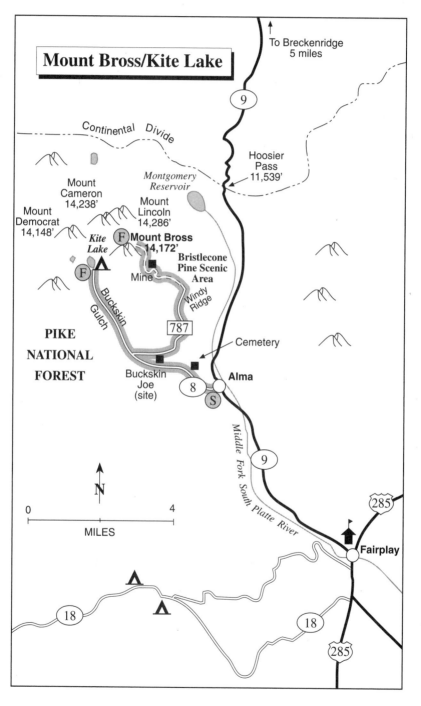

Mount Bross/Kite Lake

To Breckenridge
5 miles

9

Continental Divide

Hoosier
Pass
11,539'

Montgomery Reservoir

Mount
Cameron
14,238'

Mount
Democrat
14,148'

Mount
Lincoln
14,286'

Kite Lake

F

F

Mount Bross
14,172'

Bristlecone Pine Scenic Area

Mine

Windy Ridge

Buckskin Gulch

787

Cemetery

PIKE

NATIONAL

FOREST

Buckskin
Joe
(site)

8

S

Alma

9

Middle Fork South Platte River

285

N

0   4

MILES

Fairplay

18

18

285

Boreas Pass

LOCATION: On the Continental Divide between Breckenridge, on Highway 9, and Como, on U.S. 285. White River and Pike national forests. Summit and Park counties.

HIGHLIGHTS: This beautiful drive across the Divide, on the bed of an old narrow-gauge railroad, is rich in historic sites. The 11,481-foot pass, notorious for brutal winters and cold winds, was named for the Greek god of the north wind. At the west end, there are high-elevation views of Breckenridge, the valley of the Blue River and surrounding summits from the narrow, sinuous shelf road. At the west end, there are equally outstanding vistas across the high basin of South Park. Since it's easy to make a loop on Highways 9 and 285 via Fairplay, this is a great outing from Breckenridge.

DIFFICULTY: Easy, on a well-maintained dirt-and-gravel road with some rocky spots. There are long drop-offs on the west end, and many blind curves. You may encounter mountain bikers, joggers, even folks on horseback. The road is usually open by June.

TIME & DISTANCE: 2 hours; 21.5 miles.

MAPS: Trails Illustrated No. 109 (Breckenridge, Tennessee Pass). *Recreational Map of Colorado*. DeLorme p. 48.

INFORMATION: White River National Forest, Dillon Ranger District; Pike and San Isabel national forests, South Park Ranger District. Get the brochure for Boreas Pass, *Iron Rails: From Bust to Rust*, which explains the history along the way.

GETTING THERE: From the east: Take U.S. 285 to the junction with county Road 33, 10 miles north of Fairplay. Go northwest through Como. **From the south end of Breckenridge:** Turn east off Highway 9 onto Boreas Pass Road, county Road 10 (paved for the first 3.5 miles).

REST STOPS: At Rocky Point, near Halfway Gulch east of the Divide, walk to the short stretch of the original railroad grade that remains unaltered. You can camp at waterless Selkirk Campground, east of the Divide along North Tarryall Creek. On the pass, stop at the restored two-story log building that was Boreas Station. On the second Saturday in September you can also join the Boreas Pass Railroad Days celebration.

THE DRIVE: From the amenities of today's Breckenridge to the former tent town of Como, this scenic drive lets today's explorers experience the range of Colorado history. Gold was first found in Tarryall Creek in 1805, but it wasn't until 1859 that a major discovery occurred there and along the Blue River west of the Divide. By 1880 Leadville, across more high mountains southwest of Breckenridge, was a booming silver town. Opportunity was ripe for railroaders. By 1882 the Denver, South Park and Pacific Railroad was operating from Denver to Como and Breckenridge, hauling people and supplies in and the region's riches out along what had been a pack trail and wagon road over Boreas Pass, originally known as Breckenridge Pass. In December 1884 the line reached Leadville. It became the Colorado and Southern in 1889. But by 1937 a variety of problems, from poor management to high costs and mining industry downturns, brought railroading here to an end. In 1938 the tracks were removed. In 1956 the old grade was converted to an auto route.

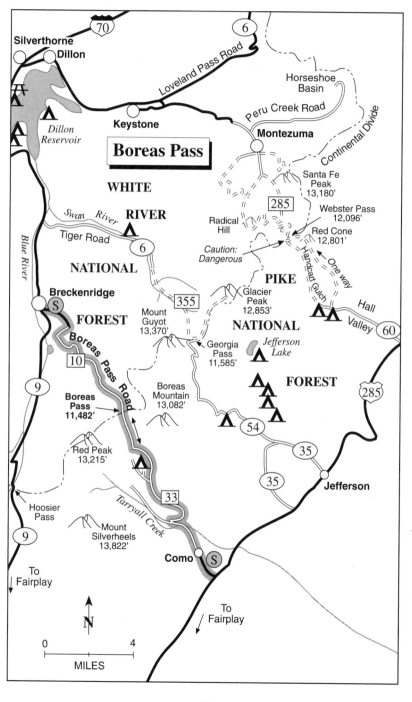

Peak 10 Road *(Tour 24)*

Peak 10 *(Tour 24)*

Peak 10

LOCATION: Southwest of Breckenridge, in the Tenmile Range. White River National Forest. Summit County.

HIGHLIGHTS: This convenient yet highly scenic drive from Breckenridge will take you directly up some of the ski area's famous runs — without a lift ticket or skis! The road provides fantastic views of the mountains framing the Blue River Valley. It ends at about 13,360 feet, but you can continue on foot to the pointy 13,633-foot summit of Peak 10 for a magnificent 360-degree, top-of-the-world view.

DIFFICULTY: Easy to moderate. Staying on course can be tricky because of all the forks, side roads and new construction. The last few hundred feet are on steep, narrow and rocky switchbacks. Watch for mountain bikers, hikers and, while you're on the ski runs, work crews and equipment. A snowbank may block the road about a mile below the end of the road until late July or even early August, but you can park and hike the rest of the way.

TIME & DISTANCE: Less than an hour, and 6.6 miles one way.

MAPS: Trails Illustrated No. 109 (Breckenridge, Tennessee Pass). White River National Forest. DeLorme p. 48.

INFORMATION: White River National Forest, Dillon Ranger District.

GETTING THERE: At the traffic light at Main and South Park Avenue, at the south end of town, take the latter west. Where South Park curves north, go left onto Village Drive. Turn left into the Beaver Run Resort parking lot. Drive across the lot to the ski run. Exit the parking lot, set your odometer at 0, and immediately turn right.

REST STOPS: The summit. Breckenridge has it all.

THE DRIVE: Driving beneath ski lifts in summer is weird. You might even find it difficult to stop watching out for skiers as you traverse the runs. Almost 0.4 mile from the parking lot, angle left, following the road south across the ski hill. The road will angle right at about mile 0.65 and pass under the lifts. At mile 1.3 make a hard left, then in a short distance a hard right. Keep zigzagging up the mountain, taking in the views of the Blue River Valley and the surrounding mountains. At about mile 3.1 you will pass Peak 9 Restaurant, on your right. Follow the road left, continuing up the mountain. Here you will have great views down into Sawmill Gulch, just to the north. Eventually the road will pass behind a reddish-brown building (on your left), the ski patrol house. Then it passes the Mercury Superchair. The road leaves the ski area here and becomes quite rocky and steep in places as it crosses timberline, then climbs to a meadow at about mile 5.5. Here you might encounter a large patch of snow blocking the road. Beyond the meadow the rocky road climbs steeply past the old Briar Rose Mine to end at an electronic site. Now you are on a divide between two glacial basins, and the views are spectacular. But for even more thrills — if you can handle looking down long and precipitous drop-offs on either side of you — scale the narrow, rocky spine behind the electronic site to the tip of Peak 10.

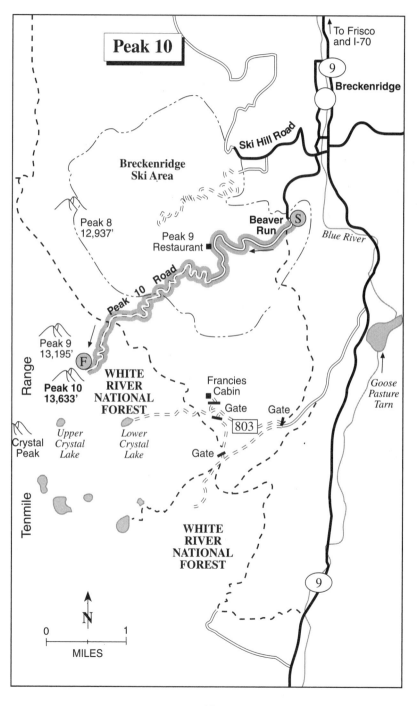

Peak 10

To Frisco
and I-70

9

Breckenridge

Ski Hill Road

Breckenridge
Ski Area

Peak 8
12,937'

Peak 9
Restaurant

Beaver
Run

S

Blue River

Peak 10 Road

Peak 9
13,195'

F

Peak 10
13,633'

WHITE
RIVER
NATIONAL
FOREST

Francies
Cabin

Gate

Gate

Goose
Pasture
Tarn

Range

Crystal
Peak

Upper
Crystal
Lake

Lower
Crystal
Lake

803

Gate

Tenmile

WHITE
RIVER
NATIONAL
FOREST

9

N

0   1

MILES

Hagerman Pass

LOCATION: On the Continental Divide between Turquoise Lake (west of Leadville), and Basalt, on state Highway 82 southeast of Glenwood Springs. Holy Cross Wilderness lies to the north, Hunter-Fryingpan and Mt. Massive wildernesses lie to the south. White River and San Isabel national forests. Pitkin and Lake counties.

HIGHLIGHTS: 11,925-foot Hagerman Pass; great scenery and railroad history. In the 1880s, James Hagerman extended the Colorado Midland Railroad from Colorado Springs to Aspen under the Divide here, via a 2,164-foot tunnel. But at 11,528 feet high it was a troublesome route. Hagerman eventually sold out. The tunnel, opened in 1887, was closed in 1893 and replaced by lower 9,398-foot-long Busk-Ivanhoe Tunnel. But the railroad fell on hard times, and was sold again. The tracks were removed during World War I. The lower tunnel was open to autos in the 1920s and 1930s, but it was abandoned in 1943.

DIFFICULTY: Easy, but the road up to and over the pass is rocky. A snowbank can block the road just below the east side of the pass.

TIME & DISTANCE: 2.5 to 3 hours; 54 miles.

MAPS: White River National Forest; Trails Illustrated No. 126 (Holy Cross, Ruedi Reservoir). DeLorme pp. 46–47.

INFORMATION: White River National Forest, Sopris Ranger District; Pike and San Isabel national forests, Leadville Ranger District.

GETTING THERE: From the west, take Highway 82 to Basalt, midway between Glenwood Springs and Aspen. Turn east on Fryingpan Road (county Road 104) toward Ruedi Reservoir. **From the east,** drive west from Leadville along the south shore of Turquoise Lake. As you approach the lake's west end, angle southwest (left) onto forest Road 105, the road over the pass.

REST STOPS: There are campgrounds at Ruedi Reservoir and Chapman Reservoir (on the west side along the Fryingpan River) and Turquoise Lake. You will see places to stop for a picnic or primitive camping along the way. The old charcoal kilns are worth a visit, too.

THE DRIVE: From Turquoise Lake, Hagerman Pass Road makes an easy climb up the canyon of Busk Creek. At the head of the canyon it makes a sharp bend, then becomes more rudimentary as it climbs to the Divide. The views across the Turquoise Lake Valley are outstanding. From the west, the 32-mile drive along the canyon of the Fryingpan River, past huge Ruedi Reservoir to the end of the pavement, is pretty and relaxing. When the pavement ends, continue a short distance, make a left, then hook left again. Continue on unpaved, single-lane Road 105. About 3 miles from where the pavement ends is a large meadow, Sellar Park. There's a line of old charcoal kilns across the meadow, to the right. You'll drive along a shelf above Ivanhoe Creek, and the road will become increasingly rocky as you climb. At a Y near a gate, with Ivanhoe Lake ahead, angle left. It's 3.9 miles from here to the pass. The road will get rougher, but remain easy, as it follows power lines above timberline to the Divide. Eventually you'll come to a sign noting the pass. Then the road makes a beautiful descent to Turquoise Lake.

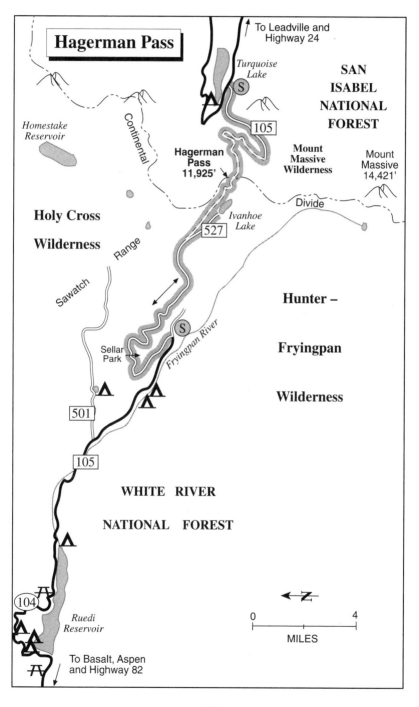

Hagerman Pass

To Leadville and Highway 24

Turquoise Lake

SAN ISABEL NATIONAL FOREST

Homestake Reservoir

Continental

105

Hagerman Pass 11,925'

Mount Massive Wilderness

Mount Massive 14,421'

Holy Cross Wilderness

Range

Sawatch

Ivanhoe Lake

Divide

527

Hunter –

Fryingpan

Wilderness

Fryingpan River

Sellar Park

501

105

WHITE RIVER

NATIONAL FOREST

104

Ruedi Reservoir

To Basalt, Aspen and Highway 82

N

0   4

MILES

85

McDonald Creek Canyon

LOCATION: Just east of the Utah/Colorado line, south of I-70; in the Rabbit Valley Recreation Area. Mesa County.

HIGHLIGHTS: If you're patient, observant and lucky, you will see mysterious rock art left by Fremont Culture Indians perhaps 1,000 years ago, in a beautiful canyon with walls of layered, multicolored sedimentary rock. There also are dramatic sandstone features and distant views of Utah's La Sal Mountains. The famous Mygatt-Moore Dinosaur Quarry, where many important fossils have been uncovered, is just north of the interstate. Spring weekends can be busy. Fall is probably best. Note: Do not touch rock art.

DIFFICULTY: Easy, with blind curves. Parts of the route follow a wash. The hike is along a dry, gently sloping canyon streambed. There are no facilities or developed water sources. Carry water, and insect repellent to ward off gnats in May–June. Mechanized travel, fires and camping are not allowed in the canyon.

TIME & DISTANCE: It's about 3.1 miles to the parking area at McDonald Creek Canyon, and you can spend as much time as you'd like exploring the canyon. It's a hike of about 1.5 miles to its mouth at the Colorado River. Allow several hours, and carry water.

MAP: DeLorme p. 42.

INFORMATION: Colorado Welcome Center, just off the freeway at Fruita. BLM's Grand Junction Field Office. Get the flyer *McDonald Creek Cultural Resource Area*.

GETTING THERE: From Grand Junction, take I-70 west for 30 miles to Rabbit Valley (Exit #2). Cross the interstate on the overpass and go south through a large parking area for the Rabbit Valley Recreation Area. Cross the cattle guard; follow the road ahead.

REST STOPS: There is a six-site, waterless campground with toilets just beyond the first large parking area. There are picnic tables and a toilet near the turnoff to the canyon.

THE DRIVE: The little road passes stands of piñon pines and junipers and impressive sandstone rock outcrops that recall great dunes, seas and rivers. Then it follows a wash, or streambed, through a low canyon of terraced walls. About 2.7 miles from that large parking area you will arrive at a huge, blob-like sandstone boulder (on the right) that looks like a gumdrop or a Hershey Kiss. Here, at Castle Rocks, go left (there may be a sign and arrow), or east, and follow a two-track along another canyon wash for 0.3 mile to a parking area, where you will find a sign-in box. The hike begins here. To spot the pictographs (painted figures) and petroglyphs (pecked figures), look on cliffs and rock overhangs. They are difficult to find, but a sign at the parking area and the brochure vaguely explain their locations. The first of four panels is about 100 yards down the streambed on the canyon's west-facing (left) wall. Stop at a slab of sandstone in the faint trail, and scan the rock about 15 feet above the streambed for red pictographs. Two more panels are located about a half-mile from the start, just below the drop-off. On the east side of the canyon is a panel of petroglyphs and some historic names and dates. On the west side is a panel of pictographs. The last panel is high on the wall in a large alcove near the mouth of McDonald Creek. Good luck!

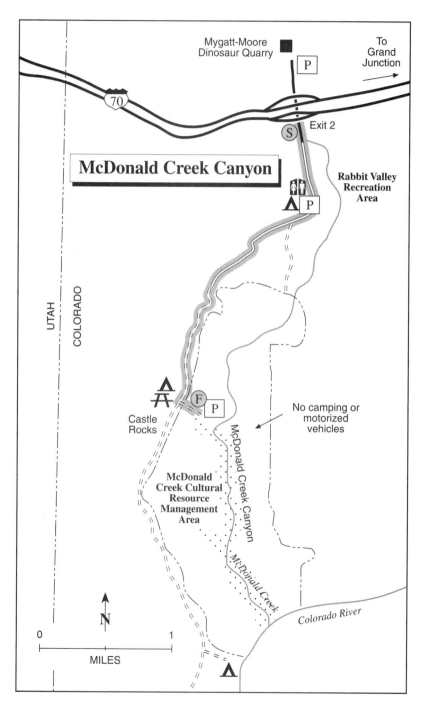

To Grand Junction

Mygatt-Moore Dinosaur Quarry

P

70

S   Exit 2

McDonald Creek Canyon

Rabbit Valley Recreation Area

P

UTAH   COLORADO

Castle Rocks

F   P

No camping or motorized vehicles

McDonald Creek Canyon

McDonald Creek Cultural Resource Management Area

McDonald Creek

N

0   1

MILES

Colorado River

Black Ridge Road

LOCATION: Mesa County just west of Colorado National Monument. South of I-70 and 10 miles west of Grand Junction.

HIGHLIGHTS: This sandstone canyon country includes views of the Uncompahgre Plateau, Grand Mesa, the national monument, Grand Valley, the Book Cliffs, the Colorado River and the Black Ridge Canyons Wilderness Study Area. Day-hiking is popular in Rattlesnake Canyon, which has the largest concentration of natural arches (11) outside of Utah. Near the end of the drive, some arches can be seen from the road.

DIFFICULTY: Easy when dry, impassable when wet. The last two miles are rocky and rutted.

TIME & DISTANCE: 3 hours; 22 miles round-trip.

MAPS: Get the brochure for the Black Ridge Canyons Wilderness Study Area. DeLorme p. 42.

INFORMATION: BLM's Grand Junction Field Office.

GETTING THERE: Take I-70 to Fruita. Drive south to Colorado National Monument. 10.7 miles beyond the entrance, turn west (right) toward Glade Park. In 0.2 mile turn right (north) onto Black Ridge Road, and zero your odometer.

REST STOPS: There are some primitive campsites along the road, but no facilities or water. Fruita has all services. There are campgrounds and picnic areas in the national monument and elsewhere in the area.

THE DRIVE: The eroded canyons, cliffs, spires and arches of Black Ridge Canyons and Colorado National Monument could not be more different from Colorado's famous Rocky Mountain peaks. This semi-arid landscape of sprawling, deeply incised plateaus is part of the vast uplift called the Colorado Plateau, named for the river that drains it. Here, as in Utah's famous canyon country, various types of multihued sandstone tell of archaic dunes, deserts, seas, marshes and tidal flats from the Jurassic and Triassic periods, 144 to 245 million years ago. The road courses along at over 6,500 feet elevation, high above Grand Valley and the Colorado River. Early on it crosses a small wash, then runs along a low, narrow, winding canyon flanked by hills dotted with piñon pines and junipers. Keep right at the Y at mile 1.3. At mile 1.7 go right, up a small road to a peak topped by electronic towers. From about 7,300 feet you will have a fantastic view of the region. The main road will likely be rutted in places. After angling right (north) at mile 10, the road descends and becomes quite rocky. You'll see several pullouts on the left where you can gaze down into Rattlesnake Canyon and scan the canyon walls for arches. The road will end soon at a trailhead parking area (day use only) overlooking the canyons and the Grand Valley. Mountain bikes aren't allowed on the hiking trails.

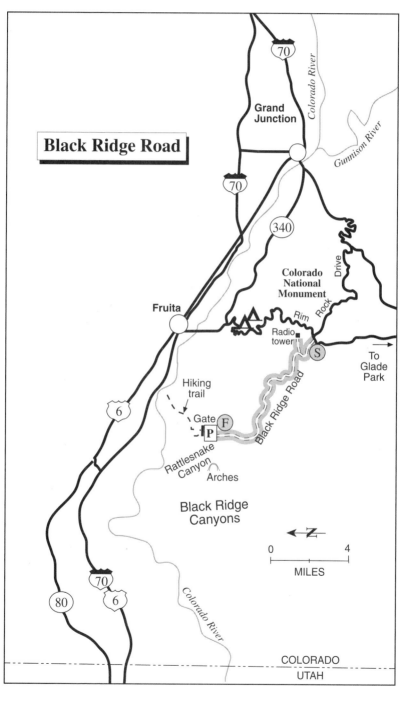

Black Ridge Road

70

Colorado River

Grand
Junction

Gunnison River

70

340

Colorado
National
Monument

Rock Drive

Fruita

Rim

Radio
tower

S

Black Ridge Road

To
Glade
Park

Hiking
trail

6

Gate

F

P

Rattlesnake
Canyon

Arches

Black Ridge
Canyons

N

0   4
MILES

70

80   6

Colorado River

COLORADO
UTAH

Grand Mesa/Land's End Road

LOCATION: East of Grand Junction; Grand Mesa National Forest. Mesa County.

HIGHLIGHTS: This drive includes much of the 55-mile Grand Mesa Scenic and Historic Byway, a fine tour of one of the world's largest (368,418 acres) flat-topped mountains, more than 11,000 feet high. Look for wildflowers in late spring and summer. It's a fine autumn drive, too. The vistas take in the Grand Valley, San Juan Mountains, Uncompahgre Plateau, Book Cliffs and Utah's La Sal Mountains. The mesa's 300 lakes provide good trout fishing.

DIFFICULTY: Easy. State Highway 65 is open year-round; dirt-and-gravel Land End's Road is closed in winter. Best May–October.

TIME & DISTANCE: 3 hours and 63 miles.

MAPS: Grand Mesa National Forest; DeLorme pp. 43–44, 55.

INFORMATION: Grand Mesa Byway Association. GMUG, Grand Valley Ranger District, Collbran. Land's End and Grand Mesa visitor centers.

GETTING THERE: From I-70 about 17 miles east of Grand Junction, take exit 49 toward Mesa, via paved Highway 65. After about 30 miles turn west (right) onto dirt-and-gravel Land's End Road. Or take U.S. 50 about 13 miles south of Grand Junction, or 27 miles north of Delta, then turn east onto Kannah Creek Road. In about 3 miles angle northeast (left) at the Y onto Land's End Road.

REST STOPS: Refer to the Forest Service map for campgrounds and picnic sites. Tables, toilets, books and information are available at the Land's End Visitor Center, where chipmunks will entertain you. There are toilets at the Land's End Road/Highway 65 junction.

THE DRIVE: Millions of years ago, geologic forces began to lift layers of sedimentary rock. When fissures formed, molten magma, or basalt, flowed up and outward. When the flows cooled, they formed a hard, erosion-resistant cap atop the more easily eroded sediments. As erosion wore away the unprotected sedimentary rock, the basalt-protected expanse remained. Later, ice-age glaciers flowed out from the center. When they melted, they left behind hundreds of sumps. The softer underlying sedimentary rock also shifted and slumped under the weight of the lava cap over time. Thus were formed the mesa's many lakes and ponds. Driving from the base, one ascends through four life zones, from a semiarid upper Sonoran zone to the mountain shrub zone, then the spruce and fir forests of the montane zone, and finally, above 10,000 feet, the sub-alpine zone. Human history reaches back some 8,000 years here, across the cultures of the Folsom, Uncompahgre and Ute peoples. In the 19th century cattle and sheep ranchers battled over grazing. The highway from I-70 begins between the terraced sandstone walls of Plateau Canyon, then climbs through aspen and conifer forests. Land's End Road branches west from Highway 65, though you can take the highway to the mesa's lake country. It crosses rolling meadows splashed with wildflowers, passes restored Raber Cow Camp Cabins, and edges along the brink of the mesa. At the top of the switchbacks stands the Land's End Visitor Center, a rustic building, originally intended to be an observatory, built by the Depression-era Civilian Conservation Corps. The switchbacks are easy and scenic. From Land's End, there are 12.4 miles of maintained dirt and gravel, then 8.4 miles of asphalt to U.S. 50.

Lead King Basin *(Tour 29)*

Sundeck, Aspen Mountain *(Tours 30, 31)*

Crystal City/Lead King Basin

LOCATION: Gunnison County east of Marble, between Maroon Bells-Snowmass and Raggeds wildernesses. White River National Forest.

HIGHLIGHTS: This fascinating 4x4 loop starts at the old quarry town of Marble and passes one of Colorado's most picturesque sites, the Crystal Mill, built in 1893. It follows the Crystal River through the quasi-ghost town of Crystal, then circles Sheep Mountain. The scenery ranges from deep river canyons to alpine meadows and glaciated peaks.

DIFFICULTY: Moderate to difficult, with tight switchbacks and narrow shelf segments with long drop-offs. The road to Crystal is busy; yield to uphill traffic. Passing will be impossible in places, so you might have to back up for substantial distances to pullouts. Lead King Basin Road (No. 315) is slick and dangerous when wet, so avoid it under those conditions. It also has sidehill sections, and tight switchbacks that make long-wheelbase vehicles inadvisable.

TIME & DISTANCE: 4 hours; 17 miles.

MAPS: Trails Illustrated No. 128 (Maroon Bells, Redstone, Marble). White River National Forest. DeLorme pp. 45–46.

INFORMATION: White River National Forest, Sopris Ranger District.

GETTING THERE: Take state Highway 133 south from Carbondale for 22 miles to the Marble turnoff, 3.4 miles southeast of McClure Pass. Turn east onto county Road 3/forest Road 314 and drive to Marble.

REST STOPS: Crystal has a tiny store with limited inventory. You will see many scenic places to stop, as well as primitive campsites.

THE DRIVE: Marble was named for the rock that was quarried and milled here from 1892 to 1942. (Production resumed in 1990.) The quarry yielded marble for the Lincoln Memorial, the Tomb of the Unknown Soldier (a single 100-ton block) and the state Capitol. From Marble, the road follows the Crystal River up a narrow, forested canyon. About 1.3 miles from the center of Marble, the 4WD road begins. In another 0.8 mile Lead King Basin Road (315) branches left. (You'll return that way, or you can go left here and take the loop in the opposite direction.) Continue on Road 314 toward Crystal, 4 miles farther. The narrow shelf road descends steeply to the river, passing Lizard Lake, and becomes very rocky. In a few miles you will see the historic Crystal Mill perched above the Crystal River. The 1880s village of Crystal is just beyond that. Drive through it, and follow the road as it bends left. Almost a mile from Crystal, go left where dangerous Schofield Pass Road (317), on which 14 people have died, goes straight, up Crystal Canyon. Here, Lead King Basin Road climbs along the gorge of the North Fork of the Crystal River. At one point it becomes a very narrow ledge, pinched between a cliff and the gorge. When you reach a private cabin, cross the bridge on the left. The road passes the Geneva Lake trailhead, at the lower portion of Lead King Basin, and bends west. As you drive high above Lost Trail Creek, the views of the Raggeds Wilderness, to the southwest, are fabulous. The road switchbacks as it climbs, then descends via more switchbacks, crosses the creek, passes the Colorado Outward Bound school and returns to the road to Crystal and Marble. Go right, toward Marble.

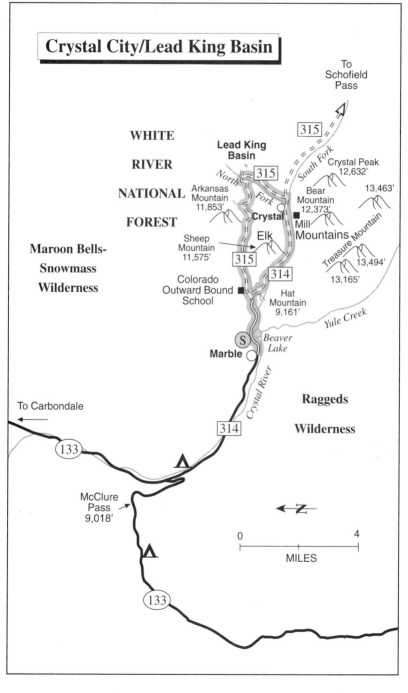

Crystal City/Lead King Basin

To Schofield Pass

315

WHITE

RIVER

NATIONAL

FOREST

Lead King Basin

315

Arkansas Mountain 11,853'

North Fork

South Fork

Crystal Peak 12,632'

Bear Mountain 12,373'

13,463'

Crystal

Elk

Mill Mountains

Sheep Mountain 11,575'

Treasure Mountain

13,494'

315

13,165'

314

Maroon Bells-Snowmass Wilderness

Colorado Outward Bound School

Hat Mountain 9,161'

Yule Creek

S

Beaver Lake

Marble

Crystal River

To Carbondale

Raggeds

Wilderness

314

133

McClure Pass 9,018'

0   4

MILES

133

Aspen Mountain Loop

LOCATION: On the mountain that looms above the old silver mining town, now home to the super-rich. Pitkin County.

HIGHLIGHTS: Exploring this famous mountain isn't just for wintertime skiers. In summer and fall, you can explore its mix of adventure roads and Rocky Mountain scenery, with the comforts and amenities of Aspen close by. The views along the way are outstanding.

DIFFICULTY: Easy, but the road can be rough in places. Watch out for hikers, mountain bikers and motorcyclists on the summit.

TIME & DISTANCE: 2 hours. It's about 5.3 miles to the Sundeck via Midnight Mine Road. Aspen Mountain Summer Road (a.k.a. Summer Road) is 4.4 miles. Add another 2.5 miles or so for roads around the summit, and 2.4 miles down Little Annie Road to Castle Creek Road, if you choose to go that way.

MAPS: USGS' Aspen, Hayden Peak and New York Peak. White River National Forest. Trails Illustrated No. 127 (Aspen and Independence Pass), although it omits the road between Richmond Hill Road and Little Annie and Midnight Mine roads, which makes this a loop. DeLorme p. 46.

INFORMATION: White River National Forest, Aspen Ranger District.

GETTING THERE: This loop follows either Aspen Mountain Summer Road (which traverses the ski slopes), or Midnight Mine Road (which climbs from paved Castle Creek Road) to the Sundeck restaurant atop 11,212-foot Aspen Mountain. **To start on Midnight Mine Road:** At the traffic light about a half-mile west of Aspen on Highway 82, turn south onto Maroon Creek Road, then immediately turn left onto Castle Creek Road. In 2.7 miles turn left onto Midnight Mine Road (118). **To take Summer Road:** Follow Main Street (Highway 82) to Original Street, at the southeast corner of town, then take Original to Ute Avenue. Where Original and Ute meet and Ute bends left, go straight, onto a little street that climbs behind the condos. This road will become Summer Road at a gate at the ski hill. Summer Road can be closed temporarily for ski hill maintenance and construction.

REST STOPS: The Sundeck, a restaurant on Aspen Mountain.

THE DRIVE: Aspen Mountain Summer Road ascends the ski slopes toward the Sundeck, passing under Silver Queen gondola and Little Nell lift and providing excellent views of the Roaring Fork Valley. If you start on Midnight Mine Road, you might see a sign stating whether the Summer Road is open, or closed for ski hill work. Midnight Mine Road descends to a bridge over Castle Creek. Soon it becomes a narrow single-lane mountainside road as it climbs up Queen's Gulch. After 2.3 miles you will pass the Midnight Mine. 1.8 miles farther go left at the fork, and in just over a mile you'll reach the Sundeck. If the Summer Road gate at the gondola is open, then take Summer Road back to town. If it's closed, go right at the gondola, onto Richmond Hill Road. In about 0.7 mile the road angles sharply right, up a steep section, to the top of Richmond Hill. Then it descends to an intersection.

There, Richmond Hill Road goes left toward Taylor Pass (Tour 31). For this loop, go right, and in a mile you will reach another intersection. Here you can go left on Little Annie Road, or right on Midnight Mine Road. Either way will take you to Castle Creek Road and back to Aspen.

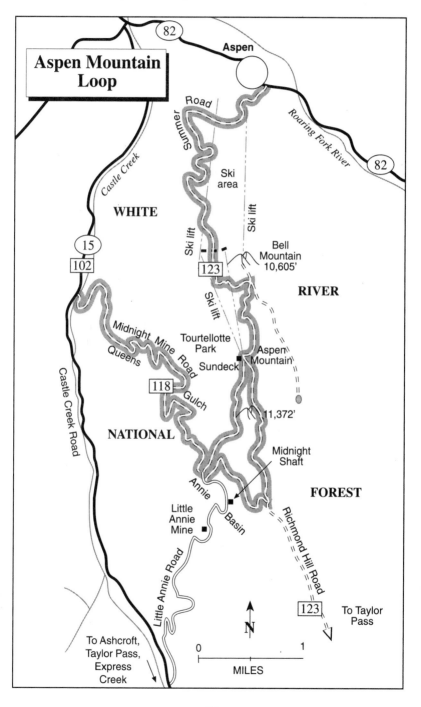

Aspen Mountain Loop

82

Aspen

Summer Road

Roaring Fork River

82

Castle Creek

WHITE

15
102

Ski area

Ski lift

Ski lift

Ski lift

Bell Mountain 10,605'

123

RIVER

Midnight Mine Road

Queens

118

Tourtellotte Park

Sundeck

Gulch

Aspen Mountain

11,372'

Castle Creek Road

NATIONAL

Annie

Little Annie Mine

Basin

Midnight Shaft

FOREST

Richmond Hill Road

123

To Taylor Pass

Little Annie Road

N

0   1

To Ashcroft, Taylor Pass, Express Creek

MILES

Taylor Pass *(Tour 31)*

Aspen Mountain Summer Road *(Tour 31)*

Taylor Pass Loop

LOCATION: South of Aspen; Pitkin County. White River National Forest, between the Collegiate Peaks and Maroon Bells-Snowmass wilderness areas.

HIGHLIGHTS: This convenient day-trip out of Aspen provides fine Rocky Mountain four-wheeling. The alpine scenery, especially views of the Maroon Bells-Snowmass Wilderness, is stunning as the road climbs to and then descends from more than 12,000 feet. The 1880s ghost town of Ashcroft, once a silver mining town near the confluence of Castle and Express creeks, is one of the more interesting such sites in Colorado. The town died when Aspen boomed and silver was devalued in 1893.

DIFFICULTY: Moderate. Snowbanks can block the road, especially along Express Creek Road (122) and on the southern slope of Taylor Pass, well into summer.

TIME & DISTANCE: 3 hours; about 20 miles, including mileage getting to the top of Aspen Mountain.

MAPS: White River National Forest. Trails Illustrated No. 127 (Aspen, Independence Pass). DeLorme p. 46.

INFORMATION: White River National Forest, Aspen Ranger District.

GETTING THERE: Get to the top of Aspen Mountain, via either Summer Road (if it's open), Midnight Mine Road or Little Annie Road. See Tour 30, Aspen Mountain Loop.

REST STOPS: Ashcroft has toilets and a creekside picnic area. You also can refresh at the Sundeck restaurant atop Aspen Mountain.

THE DRIVE: From the gondola and Sundeck restaurant on Aspen Mountain, Richmond Hill Road (123) runs south along its namesake hill, into forest. This segment can be rough and rutted in places, with many dips and bumps. Soon it enters a large meadow, where it runs along the edge of Collegiate Peaks Wilderness, to the east. Eventually you will emerge from the forest, climb above timberline and edge along alpine tundra in a treeless landscape with fantastic views of the jagged peaks and glacial basins of Maroon Bells-Snowmass Wilderness. There will be some switchbacks and steep segments from here as you climb to a crest at about 12,260 feet. Here, you will be able to look down on Taylor Pass and Taylor Lake. When you reach the pass, do not go south on difficult Taylor Pass Road (761). Instead, angle northwest onto Express Creek Road (122), which is a mere shelf just below the pass. It follows Express Creek down a long, beautiful gulch, ending at paved Castle Creek Road. To visit nearby Ashcroft, turn south (left) on Castle Creek Road. To return to Aspen, turn north (right).

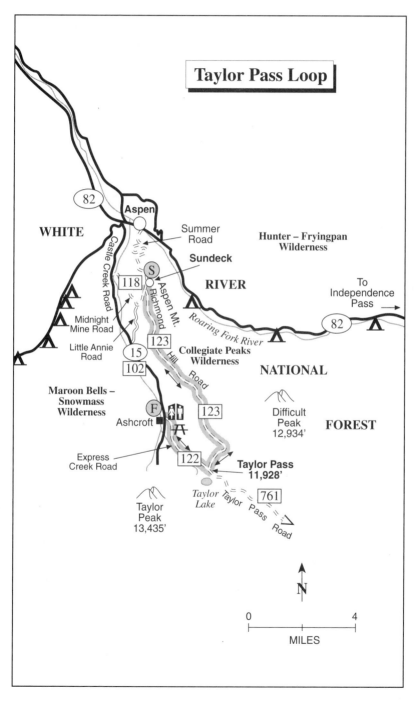

Taylor Pass Loop

Aspen

WHITE

Summer
Road

Sundeck

RIVER

Hunter – Fryingpan
Wilderness

To
Independence
Pass

82

82

118

S

Castle Creek Road

Aspen Mt. Richmond Hill Road

Roaring Fork River

Midnight
Mine Road

Little Annie
Road

15

123

102

Collegiate Peaks
Wilderness

NATIONAL

Maroon Bells –
Snowmass
Wilderness

F

Ashcroft

123

Difficult
Peak
12,934'

FOREST

Express
Creek Road

122

Taylor Pass
11,928'

Taylor Peak
13,435'

Taylor
Lake

Taylor Pass Road

761

N

0   4
MILES

Lincoln Creek Road

LOCATION: Lincoln Gulch, a corridor through the Collegiate Peaks Wilderness southeast of Aspen. White River National Forest. Pitkin County.

HIGHLIGHTS: Lincoln Creek Road is a great day-trip from Aspen with outstanding scenery and history, in a high glacial furrow. A number of old log buildings recall mining silver, gold, lead, zinc, iron, graphite and molybdenum in the Lincoln Mining District during the late 19th and early 20th centuries. (Many of the old mine properties and structures remain privately owned.)

DIFFICULTY: Easy for 6.7 miles, to Portal Campground. Moderate (due to the rocky roadbed) for the remaining 4.4 miles.

TIME & DISTANCE: 4 hours; 22 miles. Allow more time (1.5–2 hours) to hike up to pretty Anderson and Petroleum lakes.

MAPS: White River National Forest. Trails Illustrated No. 127 (Aspen, Independence Pass). DeLorme pp. 46–47.

INFORMATION: White River National Forest, Aspen Ranger District.

GETTING THERE: Take state Highway 82 southeast from Aspen toward Independence Pass. In 9.1 miles turn south (right) onto Lincoln Creek Road. Cross the bridge over the Roaring Fork River, and follow county Road 23/forest Road 106 along Lincoln Creek.

REST STOPS: You can camp at Lincoln Gulch Campground at the start of the drive, and Portal Campground about midway. There are a number of designated primitive campsites early in the drive as well.

THE DRIVE: The bumpy road along Lincoln Creek bisects the Collegiate Peaks Wilderness, where mechanized travel is otherwise prohibited. After a couple of miles, park and walk over to the creek, which has eroded an impressive gorge in the bedrock. After about 4 miles the road becomes very good as it parallels two canals and approaches Grizzly Reservoir. When you reach a cluster of buildings at the reservoir, angle left. The one-lane road is rougher from here, and in 0.3 mile you will reach Portal Campground, at the south end of the lake. The road, which becomes even rockier from here, continues up the spectacular gulch. In another 2.9 miles it passes Frenchman's Cabin, built about 1894. This signals your entry into the Lincoln Mining District, established in 1880 after several silver veins were discovered. (The road is flanked by private property from here.) Production was good, but the ore had to be hauled over Red Mountain (on the eastern flank of the gulch) and then to Leadville. In 1900 the Ruby Mines and Development Company began operating in the gulch, and the town that had sprouted up ahead was christened Ruby. Soon you will see, on the right, the trailhead for the easy hike up to Petroleum and Anderson lakes, which occupy glacial basins at about 11,500 feet. The road passes a few more old structures, then ends in a basin at the head of the gulch, at the site of Ruby and the Ruby Mine.

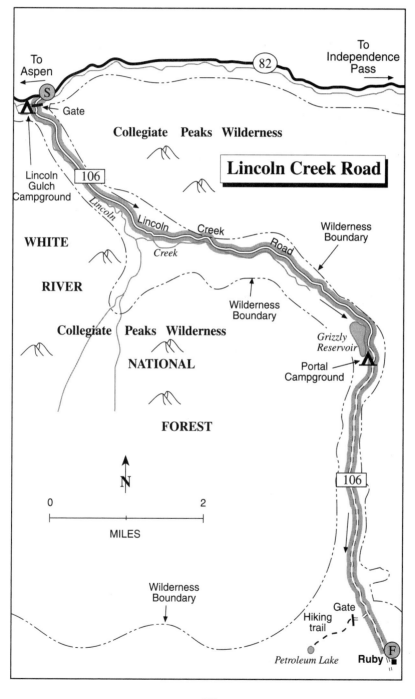

To Aspen

To Independence Pass

82

S

Gate

Collegiate   Peaks   Wilderness

Lincoln Creek Road

Lincoln Gulch Campground

106

Lincoln

Lincoln   Creek

Creek

Road

WHITE

RIVER

Wilderness Boundary

Wilderness Boundary

Collegiate   Peaks   Wilderness

Grizzly Reservoir

NATIONAL

Portal Campground

FOREST

N

0   2

MILES

106

Wilderness Boundary

Gate

Hiking trail

Petroleum Lake

Ruby

F

Weston Pass Road

LOCATION: Between U.S. 24 south of Leadville and U.S. 285 south of Fairplay. Pike and San Isabel national forests. Lake and Park counties.

HIGHLIGHTS: You'll find excellent alpine, meadow and forest scenery on the way up to and over 11,921-foot Weston Pass, on a road that evolved from a Ute Indian trail and wagon route to the motorway it is today.

DIFFICULTY: Easy to moderate on the west side between U.S. 24 and the pass, on a roadbed that is rocky and rough in places; easy on the east side, on a very good graded road from U.S. 285 to the pass. This pass is usually open by June 1.

TIME & DISTANCE: 2 hours; 27 miles.

MAPS: Trails Illustrated No. 110 (Leadville, Fairplay). Pike National Forest and San Isabel National Forest. Bring the brochure *Weston Pass: Road of Dreams, The Miner's Turnpike*, available locally. DeLorme pp. 47–48.

INFORMATION: Pike and San Isabel national forests, Leadville and South Park Ranger Districts.

GETTING THERE: To go east, turn east off U.S. 24 about 5.5 miles south of Leadville, continue south for less than a mile, then turn east again onto county Road 7/forest Road 425. **To go west,** take U.S. 285 about 11.2 miles south of Fairplay, then turn west onto county Road 22 just south of where the highway crosses the South Fork of the South Platte River.

REST STOPS: Weston Pass Campground, on the east side.

THE DRIVE: This drive is particularly rich in both history and scenery. On the west side, the rather primitive road passes through glacial hummocks forming Mt. Massive Lakes, and climbs along Big Union Creek into a picturesque gulch to the pass. On the east side it's a well-maintained dirt and gravel road. The tour includes vistas across the upper Arkansas River Valley to the Sawatch Range to the west, where Mt. Elbert, Colorado's highest, ascends to 14,433 feet. To the south rise the summits of the Buffalo Peaks. And to the east sprawls a vast, 9,500-foot-high mountain-rimmed basin, South Park. You will see many reminders of the role this wagon road played in regional mining and commerce from 1862, when the Territorial Legislature authorized a toll road over the pass, to 1880, when the railroad reached Leadville and use of the pass road declined. Among the sights are old log structures (particularly interesting are those of the Ruby Mine, at the summit), mining scars, countless stumps that are all that remain of Engelmann spruce stands logged by miners, and beaver ponds that recall the French and American trappers who preceded the miners and settlers. During its peak in 1878–79, the road could be jammed with wagon traffic. One September day in 1879, 225 freight and stagecoach teams were counted going over the summit. And who was Weston? Two men with that last name factor in local history. One was Algernon S. Weston, a pioneer, lawyer and rancher who became a judge and senator. The other was Philo M. Weston, who also owned ranch land in the area. Low on the east side the road forks, but both legs connect Weston Pass Road with U.S. 285 in about 7 miles.

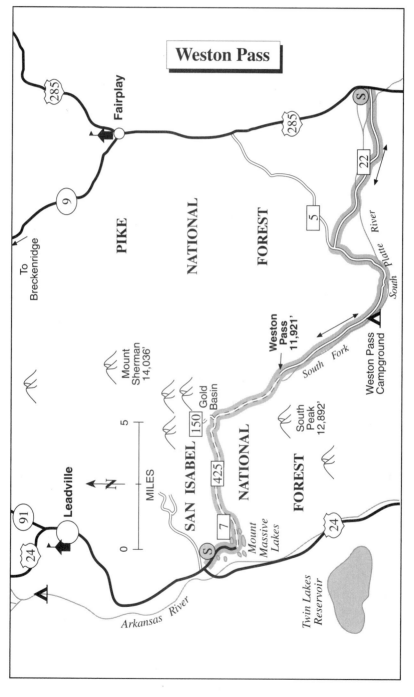

Paradise Divide *(Tour 34)*

Paradise Divide *(Tour 34)*

Paradise Divide

LOCATION: North of Crested Butte, Gunnison County. Gunnison National Forest.

HIGHLIGHTS: A convenient and fun loop around Anthracite Mesa from Crested Butte, in an old mining area with terrific Rocky Mountain scenery.

DIFFICULTY: Easy. Watch out for mountain bikers, joggers and walkers. The crossing at Paradise Divide can be blocked by late-summer snowbanks.

TIME & DISTANCE: 2.5 hours; 22 miles.

MAPS: Gunnison Basin Area; Trails Illustrated No. 131 (Crested Butte, Pearl Pass) and No. 133 (Kebler Pass, Paonia); DeLorme pp. 46, 58.

INFORMATION: GMUG, Gunnison Ranger District.

GETTING THERE: From Crested Butte, take Gothic Road north toward the ski area, and turn left (northwest) onto Washington Gulch Road, No. 811.

REST STOPS: There is a primitive BLM camping area with a pit toilet along Slate River Road (734) at Oh-Be-Joyful Creek. There also are Gothic Campground and Avery Peak picnic area, along Gothic Road. Of course, Crested Butte has it all.

THE DRIVE: Easy Washington Gulch Road (811) passes pretty meadows and stands of aspen and pine below Gothic Mountain. You may not even need to shift into 4WD as you head up the gulch, which becomes ever more spectacular. After about 8 miles the road goes over a crest and dips into another gulch, with the Slate River far below. In another mile or so you will reach a shelf road, No. 734. Go right. It will become a bit rougher as it takes you above timberline to Paradise Divide, a crest separating two beautiful glacial gulches. From there you can drive down into Paradise Basin, in White River National Forest (Sopris Ranger District) to Schofield Pass Road. (**Note:** Do not attempt the dangerous 4x4 trek to Crystal via Schofield Pass Road, on which 14 people have been killed, unless you are in a short-wheelbase vehicle and you are an experienced four-wheeler.) At Schofield Pass, you can angle south on beautiful Schofield Pass/Gothic Road (317), past Emerald Lake and the old town of Gothic (now occupied by the Rocky Mountain Biological Laboratory). Or from Paradise Divide you can hike the trail to Yule Pass, then backtrack on Road 734 and descend through the old mining camp of Pittsburg, on the west side of Anthracite Mesa. Then follow Slate River Road back to Crested Butte.

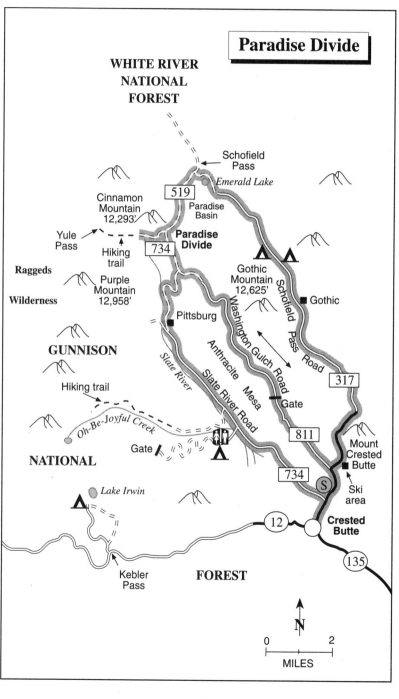

Paradise Divide

WHITE RIVER
NATIONAL
FOREST

Schofield
Pass

Emerald Lake

519

Cinnamon
Mountain
12,293'

Paradise Basin

Yule
Pass

Hiking
trail

Paradise
Divide

734

Raggeds

Purple
Mountain
12,958'

Gothic
Mountain
12,625'

Gothic

Wilderness

Pittsburg

GUNNISON

Slate River

Washington Gulch Road

Schofield Pass Road

Hiking trail

Anthracite Mesa

317

Oh-Be-Joyful Creek

Slate River Road

Gate

811

Gate

Mount
Crested
Butte

NATIONAL

Lake Irwin

734

S

Ski
area

12

Crested
Butte

Kebler
Pass

FOREST

135

N

0   2
MILES

Dominguez Road

LOCATION: At the northern end of the Uncompahgre Plateau in western Colorado; west of Delta, south of Grand Junction. Uncompahgre National Forest. Mesa County.

HIGHLIGHTS: This is an exquisite little road along Big Dominguez Creek. It provides beautiful examples of the plateau's varied scenery, from semiarid canyons and piñon-juniper woodlands to sagebrush and wildflower meadows, scenic draws and small valleys. You'll get views of the Book Cliffs, Grand Valley and Grand Mesa. This is a leg of the 142-mile Tabeguache (pronounced Tab-a-watch) mountain bike trail. It links up with Divide Road (Tour 36).

DIFFICULTY: Easy. May be impassable when wet. Avoid this area during hunting season. Watch out for mountain bikers.

TIME & DISTANCE: 1.5 hours; 18.2 miles.

MAPS: Uncompahgre National Forest. USGS' Delta map. DeLorme pp. 54–55.

INFORMATION: GMUG, Ouray Ranger District. BLM's Grand Junction Field Office.

GETTING THERE: Both ends of Dominguez Road (408) are on Divide Road, the plateau's primary north-south road. The north end is 6 miles up Divide Road from state Highway 141 (in Unaweep Canyon about 15 miles southwest of Whitewater). The south end is 16 miles farther up Divide Road. I think it's more scenic to begin at the south end, but it's great either way.

REST STOPS: The BLM's 9-site Big Dominguez Campground is along the way, but it has no drinking water. Divide Fork and Carson Hole campgrounds are on Divide Road.

THE DRIVE: Starting from the south end, on Divide Road, pass Road 409 and follow Dominguez Road across a cattle guard. In a little more than a mile the route arrives at a cow camp tucked among a stand of aspens. (This is private property.) Then the road, named for 18th-century Spanish missionary and explorer Fray Francisco Atanasio Dominguez, makes a long descent along a beautiful draw along Big Dominguez Creek, where sagebrush is interspersed with wildflowers. Toward the southern end, before you begin the steep descent into Dominguez Canyon, the road may be deeply rutted in places from folks who've driven on it while it was muddy. Soon you'll see exposed sandstone "slickrock," and then the shelf road drops into the surprisingly verdant, colorful and narrow canyon where the campground and restrooms are. After crossing the creekbed, the narrow road climbs to connect in about 5 miles with Divide Road.

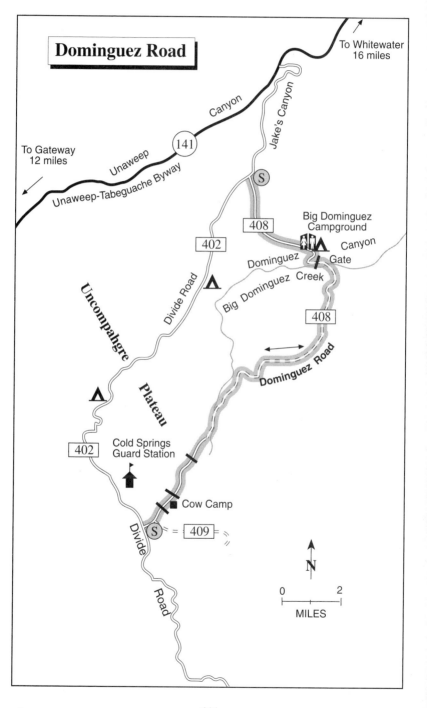

Dominguez Road

To Whitewater
16 miles

Canyon

Jake's Canyon

141

Unaweep

To Gateway
12 miles

Unaweep-Tabeguache Byway

S

408

Big Dominguez
Campground

402

Canyon
Gate

Divide Road

Dominguez

Big Dominguez Creek

408

Uncompahgre

Dominguez Road

Plateau

402

Cold Springs
Guard Station

Cow Camp

Divide

S

409

N

0   2

MILES

Road

Divide Road

LOCATION: On the Uncompahgre Plateau in western Colorado. Uncompahgre National Forest. Mesa and Montrose counties.

HIGHLIGHTS: This multifaceted 10,000-foot-high uplift is a particularly intriguing place to visit, with its deeply incised canyons and gorges, bucolic grasslands, aspen-and-pine forests, lush riparian meadows and vistas from plateau country to alpine peaks. To the south rise the San Juan Mountains; to the west, Utah's La Sals. You can easily link up with Dominguez Road (Tour 35).

DIFFICULTY: Easy on a well-maintained dirt-and-gravel road. Watch out for mountain bikers along the northern half, where Divide Road is part of the 142-mile-long Tabeguache Trail (pronounced Tab-a-watch).

TIME & DISTANCE: Since there are a number of ways to get up to Divide Road atop the plateau, time and distance can vary quite a bit. Plan on 100 miles and 4–5 hours to drive between state Highway 141 southwest of Whitewater and state Highway 145 east of Norwood.

MAPS: Uncompahgre National Forest. *Recreational Map of Colorado.* DeLorme pp. 54–55, 65–66.

INFORMATION: GMUG, Norwood and Ouray ranger districts.

GETTING THERE: Many roads, each with something to recommend it, reach Divide Road (402) from the base of the plateau. For example, you can drive up from Nucla, Norwood, Montrose, Delta, Dry Mesa or state Highway 62 west of Dallas Divide. My favorite accesses are beautiful Unaweep Canyon, where Divide Road ascends the south wall; and Sanborn Park Road (510), which climbs from Highway 145 at the San Miguel River just east of Norwood to reach Divide Road in about 21 miles.

REST STOPS: Refer to the map for campgrounds; not all have water. Waterless Big Dominguez is operated by the BLM.

THE DRIVE: 300 million years ago, thick layers of primordial rock were raised skyward, only to be eroded away and lowered. More sediments were laid down over time. Then, 10 million to 28 million years ago, tectonic forces in the Earth's crust lifted the region again. Water coursing down its increasingly steep slopes eroded deep, long and dramatic canyons and gorges in the horizontal layers of sandstone, just as it does today. Dinosaur bones lie fossilized in the sediments (see Tour 37). Human beings began leaving their mark about 10,000 years ago. First came the Fremont people, later the Tabeguache Utes who named the plateau, still later Spanish explorers, then ranchers, then prospectors searching for the mineral carnotite, which contains radium, uranium and vanadium. In fact, more than 60 percent of the uranium used by the Manhattan Project in World War II came from this area. Today, people come for the hunting (you'll probably see deer), the mountain biking, the exploring, the fantastic vistas—a wide range of outdoor pleasures.

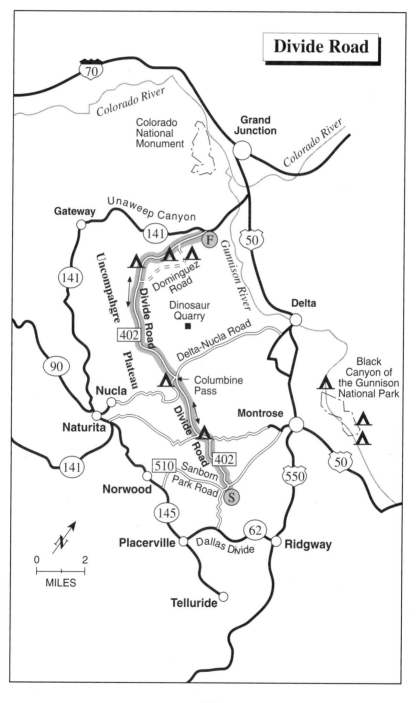

Divide Road

70

Colorado River

Colorado National Monument

Grand Junction

Colorado River

Gateway

Unaweep Canyon

141

F

50

Gunnison River

Uncompahgre

Dominguez Road

Divide Road

Delta

Dinosaur Quarry

141

402

Plateau

Delta-Nucla Road

90

Columbine Pass

Black Canyon of the Gunnison National Park

Nucla

Naturita

Divide Road

Montrose

141

402

S

510

Sanborn Park Road

550

50

Norwood

145

N

0   2

MILES

Placerville

Dallas Divide

62

Ridgway

Telluride

Dinosaur Quarry Loop

LOCATION: Western Colorado's Uncompahgre Plateau, southwest of Delta. Delta, Mesa and Montrose counties.

HIGHLIGHTS: Dry Mesa Dinosaur Quarry; the rugged and beautiful canyon along Escalante Creek; a Ute Indian rock art site.

DIFFICULTY: Easy to moderate with one stream crossing. Roads can be impassable when wet. Flash flooding is possible during storms.

TIME & DISTANCE: 4 hours; 60 miles.

MAPS: Uncompahgre National Forest. DeLorme pp. 55–56.

INFORMATION: BLM's Uncompahgre Field Office; GMUG, Ouray Ranger District.

GETTING THERE: To end in Delta: About 11 miles north of town turn southwest off U.S. 50 to a rest area. **To start in Delta:** Take Fifth Street west from the stop light on Main Street. In about 6.8 miles, where the paved road bends southeast toward the Delta Correctional Center, continue west toward the plateau on unpaved Cabin Bench Road, No. 501 on the Forest Service map.

REST STOPS: Rock tables and a toilet at the shady parking area.

THE DRIVE: Despite the name of the canyon you'll be driving through, 18th century Spanish missionaries Fray Francisco Atanasio Dominguez and Fray Silvestre Velez de Escalante didn't come this way in 1776, when they were searching for a route between Santa Fe, New Mexico, and Monterey, California. They traveled east of Grand Mesa. But they did explore more unknown territory than Lewis and Clark. So geologists with the 1875 Hayden Survey named one Gunnison River tributary Rio Escalante, and another downstream Rio Dominguez. From the rest area, a graded road descends into a draw among desert hills. 3.6 miles after crossing the Gunnison River, turn left at the sign for Escalante Rim Road. This is the confluence of Escalante Creek and Dry Fork Escalante Creek. Ford the stream, then go right at the Y, following Dry Mesa Road (502) toward the fenced-off Ute Indian petroglyphs (symbols pecked into the rock). The vandalized rock art site is on the right, a short way up the wooded canyon. Dry Mesa Road continues up a scenic little canyon, then climbs out of it, providing beautiful views down the canyon and beyond to Grand Mesa. It soon reaches a boulder-strewn bench with piñon pines and junipers. In another mile you'll be on Dry Mesa, a finger of the Uncompahgre Plateau where the views reach southeast to the San Juan Mountains. As the road angles south, about 10 miles from the canyon, Road 502.1a branches north (right). It ends in 2.3 miles at a short foot trail to a dinosaur quarry where you can watch paleontologists work one of the best sites in the world for Jurassic Period (208-144 MYA) specimens. Among the fossil bones found here, in the Brushy Basin Member of the Morrison Formation, are those of some of the world's largest sauropods (gigantic plant-eaters), including 120-foot-long Supersaurus. Meat-eaters found here include Allosaurus and the only known specimen of Torvosaurus. 3.4 miles from this turnoff, go left at the junction with Cabin Bench Road (501). It descends along the plateau's east slope to reach Delta in 28 miles.

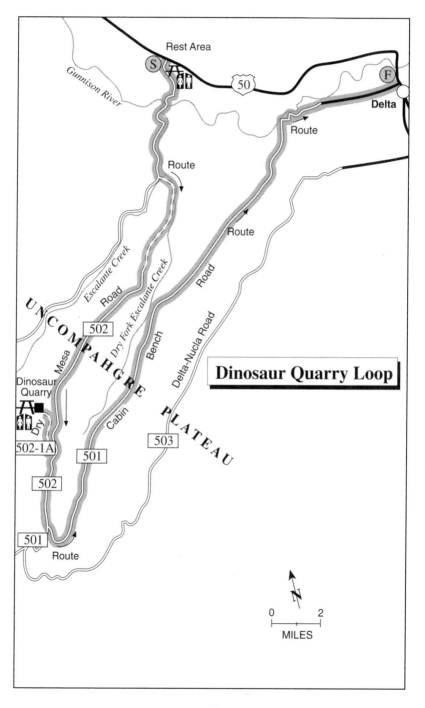

Dinosaur Quarry Loop

Rest Area

S

50

F

Delta

Gunnison River

Route

Route

Route

Escalante Creek

Dry Fork Escalante Creek

UNCOMPAHGRE

Road

Road

502

Mesa

Bench

Delta-Nucla Road

Dinosaur
Quarry

Dry

Cabin

PLATEAU

503

502-1A

501

502

501

Route

N

0   2

MILES

Dry Mesa Dinosaur Quarry *(Tour 37)*

Soap Creek Road *(Tour 38)*

Soap Creek Road

LOCATION: The road follows Soap Creek north from the west end of Blue Mesa Reservoir (on U.S. 50 west of Gunnison) to the southern boundary of the West Elk Wilderness. Gunnison County.

HIGHLIGHTS: Although this drive dead-ends at a trailhead for hikers headed into the West Elk Wilderness, it remains an exceptionally beautiful tour in both directions. The road courses through green volcanic mountains along a canyon that wind and water have eroded into intricate cliffs and spires. It passes through two beautiful mountain parks, Little Soap Park and then Big Soap Park. You may see meadows splashed with the colors of wildflowers, too.

DIFFICULTY: Easy to moderate, but it can be muddy in places.

TIME & DISTANCE: 5.5 hours; about 40 miles round-trip.

MAPS: Trails Illustrated No. 134 (Black Mesa, Curecanti Pass). Gunnison Basin Area. DeLorme pp. 57, 67.

INFORMATION: GMUG, Gunnison Ranger District.

GETTING THERE: At the west end of Blue Mesa Reservoir (west of Gunnison), turn north from U.S. 50 onto state Highway 92, at Blue Mesa Dam, toward Hotchkiss and the north rim of the Black Canyon of the Gunnison. Drive across the dam. At mile 0.7 from the dam turn right, onto Soap Creek Road, which becomes forest Road 721 and, toward the end, Road 443.

REST STOPS: Soap Creek, Ponderosa and Commissary campgrounds are along the way.

THE DRIVE: The all-weather road edges along the reservoir for miles, providing outstanding views of long canyons and cliffs of erodable volcanic rock amid tall ponderosa pines. Almost 7 miles from the start you'll pass Ponderosa Campground. In another mile is the turnoff to Soap Creek Campground. There, the road diminishes to a single-lane dirt road through rumpled and imposing mountains that long ago were the source of great lava flows and layers of pumice that blanketed the landscape. Just beyond Commissary Campground the road becomes a 4WD route, at least according to the sign. There is a steep, rocky and loose pitch ahead. At the top you will be on the rim of a canyon, with excellent views of erosion's handiwork. A steep descent perhaps 75 yards long follows, and beyond that the scenery really opens up. The road will skirt lovely Little Soap Park, go over a rise and then deliver you to the magnificently wild-looking landscape of Big Soap Park, rolling sagebrush and grass flanked by hummocky mountain slopes forested with vast stands of aspen. Ahead and on both sides of you rise the peaks of the West Elk Wilderness, with little Soap Creek running down from its heights. At about mile 16.3 the road will bend left at a large cottonwood grove toward a couple of small private cabins (much of this area is private land). Here, Road 443 crosses West Soap Creek and continues for a couple of miles along Soap Creek to the Soap Creek trailhead at the wilderness boundary, beyond which mechanized travel is prohibited.

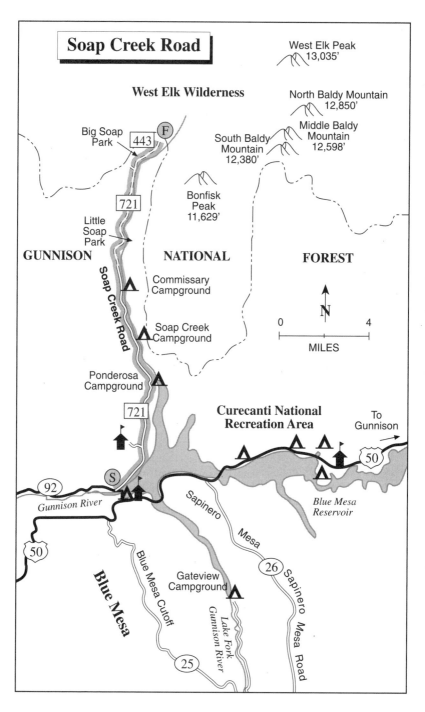

Soap Creek Road

West Elk Peak
13,035'

West Elk Wilderness

North Baldy Mountain
12,850'

Big Soap Park
443 (F)

Middle Baldy Mountain
12,598'

South Baldy Mountain
12,380'

721

Bonfisk Peak
11,629'

Little Soap Park

GUNNISON   NATIONAL   FOREST

Soap Creek Road

Commissary Campground

N

Soap Creek Campground

0   4
MILES

Ponderosa Campground

721

Curecanti National Recreation Area

To Gunnison

92

50

Gunnison River

Sapinero

Mesa

Blue Mesa Reservoir

50

26

Blue Mesa Cutoff

Gateview Campground

Sapinero Mesa Road

Blue Mesa

Lake Fork Gunnison River

25

St. Elmo to Tincup

LOCATION: Continental Divide; Sawatch Range; Gunnison, San Isabel national forests; southwest of Buena Vista. Gunnison and Chaffee counties.

HIGHLIGHTS: Great mountain scenery, especially from 12,154-foot Tincup Pass atop the Divide; the historic towns of St. Elmo and Tincup; fording Mirror Lake.

DIFFICULTY: Moderate. The roads to St. Elmo and Tincup are good. The old wagon road over the pass is rough. There is a chewed-up section below the pass on the Tincup side. A snowbank can block the road just below the pass on the St. Elmo side into August. At the south end of Mirror Lake, stay at water's edge on the east bank. Do not drive straight between where the road appears to enter and exit the lake, because the lake can be deep.

TIME & DISTANCE: 2 hours; 13 miles from St. Elmo to Tincup.

MAPS: Trails Illustrated No. 130 (Salida, St. Elmo, etc.) and No. 129 (Buena Vista, Collegiate Peaks). Gunnison Basin Area. DeLorme p. 59.

INFORMATION: GMUG, Gunnison Ranger District; Pike and San Isabel national forests, Salida Ranger District.

GETTING THERE: From the west, take Cumberland Pass Road (765) to Tincup, southeast of Taylor Park Reservoir. In Tincup, go left at the old town hall, and take Road 267 toward Mirror Lake. **From the east,** take U.S. 285 south of Buena Vista to Nathrop. Turn west on state Highway 162 toward the mountains, St. Elmo and Tincup Pass. Beyond the store in St. Elmo turn right, onto the bridge, then angle left. Soon you'll see where Tincup Pass Road enters the forest.

REST STOPS: Stop at the rustic country store in St. Elmo, near the chipmunk crossing. There are a number of campgrounds, including those at Mirror Lake on the west side and St. Elmo on the east side. You will find many primitive campsites along the Tincup Pass Road.

THE DRIVE: St. Elmo was named Forest City when it was incorporated in 1880. But it was subsequently renamed after the 1866 novel by Augusta Wilson to avoid confusion with a Forest City in California. Once a thriving mining town and railroad stop, today it remains isolated, authentic, even occupied, although five historic structures burned in 2002. (Note: it was an electrical fire, not wildfire.) The name Tincup has various purported origins: gold was found in a tin cup, near a tin cup, or was weighed in tin cups. Wild in its heyday, three of its marshals met their ends here: one was killed by a saloon keeper, another died by suicide, and a third died in a shootout. Named Virginia City when it was incorporated in 1880, its name was changed to avoid confusion with Virginia City, Nevada. (Montana also has a Virginia City.) Tincup became the hub of a rich mining district after a silver strike in 1879. Some estimates put its peak population at 6,000, others at 600. The rough road (267) over Tincup Pass was used to haul ore and supplies between the two towns straddling the Divide. Mirror Lake is about 3 easy miles from Tincup. At the lake's south end, the route edges along the east bank. From there it crosses East Willow Creek, then climbs almost 3 miles to the pass. There are rocky, muddy and deeply rutted sections. The east side from St. Elmo is easier but rough as it climbs for 6.2 miles to the pass. But once out of the forest the views of the gulch that leads to the pass are fantastic.

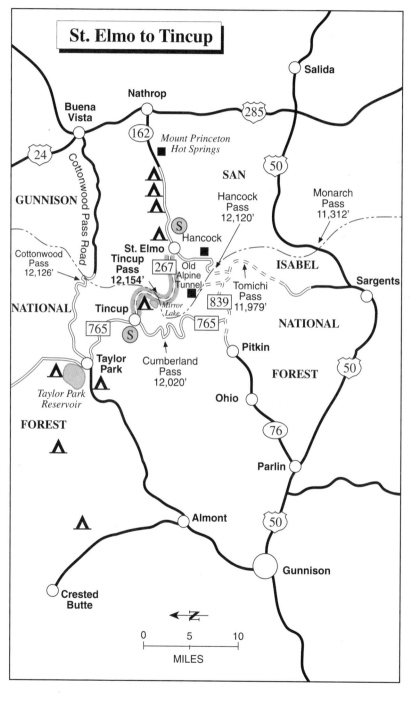

St. Elmo to Tincup

Alpine Tunnel/Hancock Pass

LOCATION: Continental Divide, between Gunnison and Buena Vista. Gunnison and San Isabel national forests. Gunnison and Chaffee counties.

HIGHLIGHTS: You'll experience Colorado's railroad history while driving on soot-blackened old grades to the first train tunnel beneath the Divide. The road over Hancock Pass includes some genuine four-wheeling on the way to historic St. Elmo, a "living" ghost town.

DIFFICULTY: Easy to the Alpine Tunnel from Cumberland Pass Road (765), and from St. Elmo to the site of Hancock. Crossing Hancock Pass is moderate. It should open up by early July.

TIME & DISTANCE: About 3 hours (excluding time spent at the tunnel); 20 miles.

MAPS: Trails Illustrated's No. 130 (Salida, St. Elmo, Shavano Peak). Gunnison Basin Area. San Isabel National Forest. DeLorme p. 59.

INFORMATION: GMUG, Gunnison Ranger District; Pike & San Isabel National Forests, Salida Ranger District. Get a copy of the flyer *Alpine Tunnel Historic District.*

GETTING THERE: From the west, the direction I describe: Take U.S 50 to Parlin. Then take Road 76 northeast to Pitkin. From Pitkin, take Cumberland Pass Road (765) northeast for about 2.5 miles. Turn right (southeast) onto Road 839, my starting point. (If you're taking Cumberland Pass Road from Taylor Park, Road 839 is 8.1 miles south of the pass). **From the east:** Take U.S. 285 to Nathrop. Turn west on state Highway 162, toward St. Elmo and Tincup Pass. Just before St. Elmo, turn left (south) onto Road 295.

REST STOPS: There are numerous campgrounds in the area.

THE DRIVE: Today's single-lane road is an old railroad grade high above Middle Quartz Creek. It takes you past the site of Woodstock, where an avalanche in 1884 killed 13 people. A bit farther, Road 888 branches right, to Hancock and Tomichi passes. You'll return to it. For now, continue on Road 839 for another 2.3 miles, eventually traversing a masonry section dubbed The Palisades. At road's end is an old railroading center that bustled when trains began running beneath the Continental Divide through the 1,772-foot Alpine Tunnel here in 1882. The tunnel was difficult to maintain, and train use ended in 1910. Its portals have since collapsed. From there, return to Road 888 and make the short, rocky climb to a Y. Go left, on Road 266, to Hancock Pass. (The Forest Service rates Tomichi Pass, to the right via Road 888, difficult and hazardous.) The mile to Hancock Pass is rough. About 2.1 miles from the pass is a junction; go left, through the parking area for the trail to the tunnel's eastern portal, and continue through the site of Hancock. Follow Road 295 to the junction with 267 and 292. St. Elmo and Tincup (Tour 39) are to the left; Mt. Antero (Tour 41) and U.S. 285 are to the right.

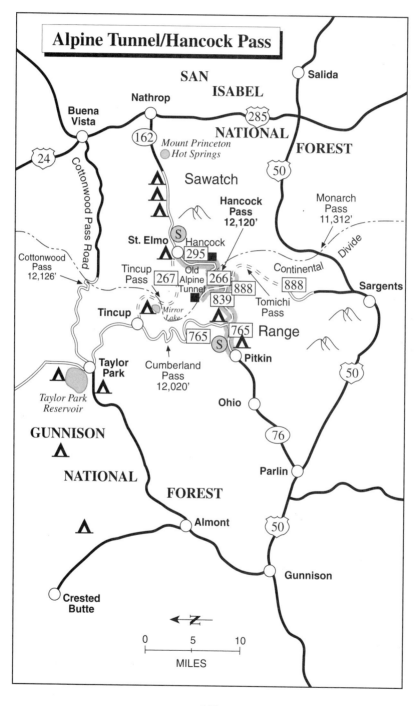

Alpine Tunnel/Hancock Pass

SAN ISABEL NATIONAL FOREST

Salida

Nathrop

Buena Vista

285

162

Mount Princeton Hot Springs

24

Sawatch

Cottonwood Pass Road

50

Hancock Pass 12,120'

Monarch Pass 11,312'

St. Elmo

S

Hancock

295

Cottonwood Pass 12,126'

Tincup Pass

267

Old Alpine Tunnel

266

Continental

Divide

Sargents

888

Tincup

Mirror Lake

839

888

Tomichi Pass

765

765

Range

50

Taylor Park

Cumberland Pass 12,020'

S

Pitkin

Taylor Park Reservoir

GUNNISON

Ohio

NATIONAL

76

Parlin

FOREST

Almont

50

Gunnison

Crested Butte

0   5   10

MILES

Mt. Antero

LOCATION: Sawatch Range in Chaffee County, southwest of Buena Vista; San Isabel National Forest.

HIGHLIGHTS: The 14,269-foot summit of Mt. Antero, one of the Upper Arkansas River Valley's 15 "14ers." One stream crossing. Rock and mineral collecting at the highest gem field in the United States, and the third-highest gem field in the world.

DIFFICULTY: Moderate to difficult. There are narrow shelf segments and tight switchbacks. Near the top the switchbacks are steep, loose and hazardous. I recommend parking lower down and hiking to the summit, which ultimately is reached on a foot trail anyway. Be prepared for unpredictable weather, including storms. The road is usually open by mid-June.

TIME & DISTANCE: 4–5 hours; about 14 miles round-trip. The drive to Brown's Lake adds roughly 6 miles and 3 hours.

MAPS: Trails Illustrated No. 130 (Salida, St. Elmo, Shavano Peak); San Isabel National Forest. DeLorme pp. 59–60.

INFORMATION: Pike and San Isabel national forests, Salida Ranger District.

GETTING THERE: Take U.S. 285 to Nathrop, south of Buena Vista. Turn west on county Road 162 to Mt. Princeton Hot Springs, St. Elmo and Tincup Pass. Drive 12.6 miles into the Sawatch Range. Near a parking area, go left (south) on Baldwin Creek Road (277).

REST STOPS: Refer to your map for campgrounds in the area.

THE DRIVE: Baldwin Creek Road is steep, rocky and slow, with substantial potholes to crawl over as it takes you through forest along the pretty gorge of Baldwin Creek. Sightseers, hikers, all-terrain-vehicle riders, four-wheelers and rock hounds share this surprisingly busy road, which provides access to Baldwin Lake as well as Mt. Antero. At mile 2.8 you will be rewarded with a spectacular view of lofty peaks. Here, the road up Mt. Antero (278) goes left, crossing Baldwin Creek. Road 277.2 continues ahead to Baldwin Lake. Beyond the creek the road, still rocky and steep, climbs toward timberline, providing great views of canyons and high peaks. At mile 4, at a talus slope, the narrow mountainside shelf road begins to switchback up the flanks of Mt. Antero, named for a Uinta Ute Indian chief. There are some particularly steep and tight switchbacks; most have pullouts. The road becomes less rocky, but there will be some off-camber spots that can be disconcerting, especially if the road is wet. Eventually the route, Road 1A, bends eastward around the south side of the mountain, then angles north on a rolling expanse crisscrossed by a number of side roads. (From the bend at 1A, Road 278 continues south and then east to pretty Brown's Lake, which has good trout fishing.) The views to the east of the Arkansas River Valley are awesome. But the "road" up Mt. Antero deteriorates into steep, loose and hazardous switchbacks that end on a saddle with room to park and turn around. I recommend parking lower down and hiking to the saddle. There you'll see the rocky foot path north to the summit, a 45-minute (one-way) trek that is not for the fainthearted. Watch for developing storms.

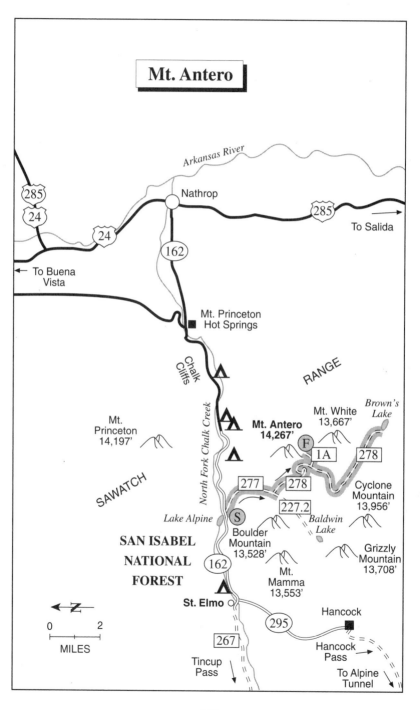

Mt. Antero

285

24

285

To Salida

Nathrop

24

162

← To Buena
Vista

Arkansas River

■ Mt. Princeton
Hot Springs

Chalk
Cliffs

RANGE

Mt. White
13,667'

Brown's
Lake

Mt.
Princeton
14,197'

**Mt. Antero
14,267'**

F

1A

278

North Fork Chalk Creek

277

278

Cyclone
Mountain
13,956'

SAWATCH

227.2

Lake Alpine

S

Baldwin
Lake

Grizzly
Mountain
13,708'

**SAN ISABEL
NATIONAL
FOREST**

Boulder
Mountain
13,528'

162

Mt.
Mamma
13,553'

N

St. Elmo

Hancock

0   2

295

MILES

267

Tincup
Pass

■ Hancock

Hancock
Pass

To Alpine
Tunnel

Shelf Road/Gold Belt Tour

LOCATION: South of Cripple Creek, north of Cañon City. Fremont and Teller counties.

HIGHLIGHTS: This old toll road, which Cañon City built in 1892, is the rough middle leg of the Gold Belt Tour, a Colorado Scenic and Historic Byway and a National Back Country Byway (see Tour 43, Phantom Canyon). The third leg is mostly paved High Park Road, to the west. It was the first wagon and stage route to link the Cripple Creek and Victor gold fields with the Arkansas River Valley and cities of the Front Range. Points of interest include Window Rock, a hole eroded into 1.7 billion-year-old rock; The Shelf, a rough one-lane section above Fourmile Creek; the site of the toll collector's cabin (private land); the limestone cliffs of the Shelf Road Recreation Area, popular among rock climbers; Red Canyon Park's sandstone figures; Garden Park Fossil Area, an important dinosaur graveyard discovered in 1876; the site of the West's first oil well; possibly Rocky Mountain bighorn sheep. The road through the canyons of Fourmile and Cripple creeks involves an elevation change from 5,330 feet at Cañon City to 9,395 feet at Cripple Creek, and passes through differing life zones. Add Phantom Canyon for a loop.

DIFFICULTY: Easy when dry, but it is a more rudimentary and remote backcountry road than Phantom Canyon Road.

TIME & DISTANCE: 2 hours; 26 miles; longer with the scenic spurs through Red Canyon Park and Shelf Road Recreation Area.

MAPS: Trails Illustrated No. 137 (Pikes Peak, Cañon City). Bring *The Gold Belt Tour*, a widely available brochure. DeLorme pp. 62, 72.

INFORMATION: BLM's Royal Gorge Field Office.

GETTING THERE: From Cripple Creek, take Second Street south for 0.3 mile. Angle right onto Teller County Road 88. From the north side of Cañon City, follow Fields (a.k.a. Field) Avenue north. It becomes the Shelf Road (Fremont County Road 9).

REST STOPS: There are toilets, tables and interpretive signs at Garden Park. Red Canyon Park also has toilets and tables. The Bank Campground (fee; no water) is at the Shelf Road Recreation Area.

THE DRIVE: In the late 19th and early 20th centuries, when this gold mining district on Pikes Peak's western flank was out-producing the combined output of the California and Alaska gold rushes, a trip along the Shelf Road took six hours northbound, four hours southbound. Tolls ranged from 30 cents for a horse and rider to $1.75 for a six-horse stagecoach. Since this little dirt road gets less than half the traffic of well-maintained Phantom Canyon Road, you'll have the solitude to imagine those days. From the town of Cripple Creek the road descends through a narrow canyon. 5.5 miles from town, look high up the cliff for a small arch, Window Rock. (Also watch for bighorn sheep.) 9.6 miles from town the road crosses Fourmile Creek, then climbs up the canyon wall on The Shelf, a crude one-lane segment with a long drop-off on one side. From The Shelf you can look down at a small log outbuilding in the meadow where the toll collector once lived. At Garden

Park, near the rest area, are several famous quarries where paleontologists found the fossilized bones of Tyrannosaurus, Stegosaurus, Diplodocus, Allosaurus and other large dinosaurs. About a mile farther south is the site of the first oil well (1862) west of the Mississippi River.

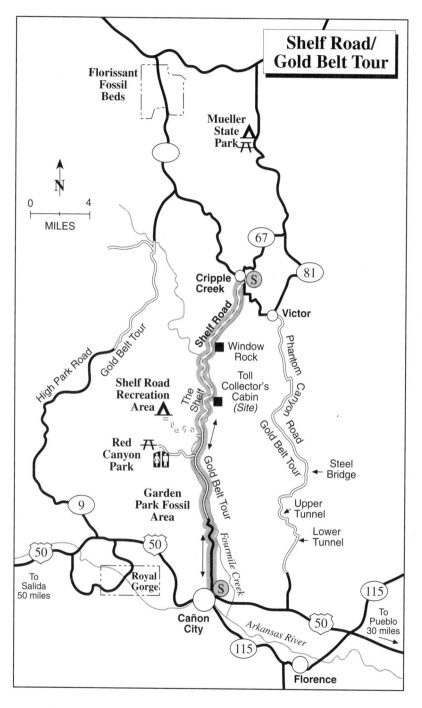

Phantom Canyon Road/ Gold Belt Tour

LOCATION: Southeast of Cripple Creek, northeast of Cañon City, between Victor and U.S. 50. Fremont and Teller counties.

HIGHLIGHTS: This is the eastern leg of the Gold Belt Tour (also see Tour 42, Shelf Road), a Colorado Scenic and Historic Byway and a BLM National Back Country Byway. (The westernmost leg is the mostly paved High Park Road.) It snakes along the bed of the old narrow-gauge Florence and Cripple Creek Railroad (the "Gold Belt Line"), which served the Cripple Creek and Victor Mining District, created by the rush that followed Bob Womack's discovery of gold in 1890. The road passes through two tunnels, and crosses a historic steel trestle. While it is not as rough and remote as the Shelf Road, its high-walled canyon, dramatic cliffs, varied ecosystems and beauty make it a first-rate tour. Victor seems an authentic old mining town. Cripple Creek, a tourist mecca, has limited-stakes gambling.

DIFFICULTY: Easy, on a well-maintained but serpentine gravel road that narrows to a single lane in many places. This is a popular drive with many blind curves, so be careful. The road parallels Eightmile Creek, and heavy rains can cause flash floods.

TIME & DISTANCE: 2 hours; 31 miles. Combine it with the more rugged Shelf Road for a fabulous loop.

MAPS: Trails Illustrated No. 137 (Pikes Peak, Cañon City). Bring the widely available brochure *The Gold Belt Tour*. DeLorme pp. 62, 72.

INFORMATION: BLM's Royal Gorge Field Office.

GETTING THERE: To begin at the south end, turn north on Phantom Canyon Road (Fremont County Road 67) from U.S. 50 about 7 miles east of Cañon City. **To go south from Victor,** take Teller County Road 861, Skaguay Road, southeast, then turn south onto Phantom Canyon Road, Teller County Road 86.

REST STOPS: There are two rest areas with toilets and tables along the way. There is primitive camping at the site of McCourt, 9.5 miles from the south end, and elsewhere in the canyon.

THE DRIVE: Soon after Cañon City completed the Shelf Toll Road in 1892, Florence completed the Cripple Creek Free Road between the soaring rock walls of Phantom Canyon. Both linked the Arkansas Valley and Front Range cities with the gold mines at Cripple Creek and Victor, where production—21 million ounces from the 1890s to 1920s—exceeded the California and Alaska gold rushes combined. In 1894, the F&CC Railroad replaced the wagon road. In addition to passengers, including tourists, the rails carried supplies to the mines and ore to the smelters at Florence. Twelve stations existed along the grade (watch for the signs marking town sites), including Adelaide, where a flood in July 1895 washed away part of the town, killing six people. About midway you will cross the canyon on a steel span built in 1897 to replace a wooden trestle that burned in 1896. The drive's elevation changes from 9,730 feet at Victor to 5,180 feet at Florence. Watch how the life zones change, from grassy meadows and piñon-juniper woodlands to lush riparian areas and forest of spruce, fir, ponderosa pine and aspen.

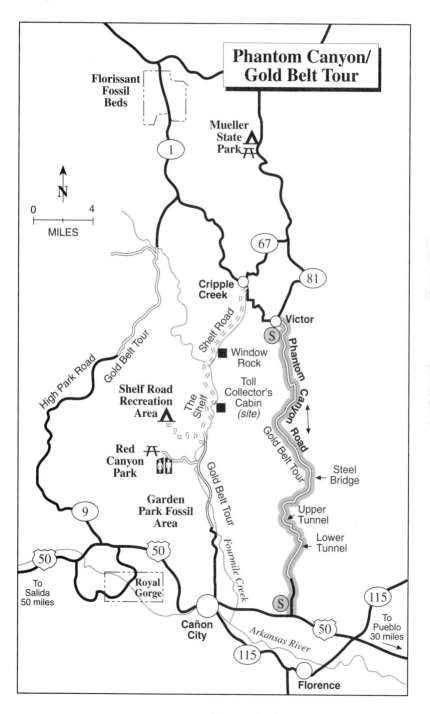

Phantom Canyon/
Gold Belt Tour

Florissant
Fossil
Beds

Mueller
State
Park

N

0   4
MILES

1

67

81

Cripple
Creek

Shelf Road

Victor

S

Window
Rock

Gold Belt Tour

High Park Road

Shelf Road
Recreation
Area

The Shelf

Toll
Collector's
Cabin
(site)

Phantom Canyon Road

Gold Belt Tour

Red
Canyon
Park

Garden
Park Fossil
Area

Gold Belt Tour

Steel
Bridge

Upper
Tunnel

Lower
Tunnel

9

50

50

50

Royal
Gorge

To
Salida
50 miles

Fourmile Creek

Cañon
City

S

115

To
Pueblo
30 miles

50

115

Arkansas River

Florence

Phantom Canyon Road *(Tour 43)*

Owl Creek Pass Road *(Tour 44)*

Owl Creek Pass Road

LOCATION: East of Ridgway, on U.S. 550, and south of U.S. 50 near Cimarron. North of Uncompahgre Wilderness. Uncompahgre National Forest. Ouray, Montrose, Gunnison counties.

HIGHLIGHTS: This beautiful cruise through forest and pastoral landscapes is particularly appealing in late summer or early fall, when the aspens are turning. Great views of high and jagged Cimarron Ridge, the 12,152-foot monolith of Courthouse Mountain and 11,781-foot Chimney Rock. Owl Creek Pass is 10,114 feet. Owl Creek Pass Road should be open by June.

DIFFICULTY: Easy. Spurs can be moderate. The Cow Creek spur can be impassable when wet.

TIME & DISTANCE: 2.5; 42 miles. Optional spurs add substantial time and distance.

MAPS: Gunnison Basin Area. Uncompahgre National Forest. DeLorme pp. 66–67.

INFORMATION: GMUG, Ouray Ranger District. Montrose Public Lands Center.

GETTING THERE: About 2 miles north of Ridgway, turn east from U.S. 550 onto Owl Creek Pass Road (county Road 10), and drive toward that high, dramatic spine up ahead. To go south, take Cimarron Road from U.S. 50 southeast of Cimarron, or Road P77 south from U.S. 50 west of Cimarron. Either way, take forest Road 858 past Silver Jack Reservoir, through Cimarron Forks and over Owl Creek Pass.

REST STOPS: There are three campgrounds north of Silver Jack Reservoir, and one at Cimarron Forks. There's a toilet in a parking area on Owl Creek Pass.

THE DRIVE: You won't bump your head against the sky on this drive, as you might seem to on the much higher pass routes in the San Juans. Nor are you likely to scrape the undercarriage of your vehicle on boulders lurking in the roadbed, or reach for the panic button on eroded shelf roads with long drop-offs to eternity. Instead, as you ascend toward the crossing amid the dramatic sawtooth heights of Cimarron Ridge, you will see pastoral hills and rangelands, serrated ridges and fluted cliffs, and be surrounded by vast stands of aspen that ignite when the chill of late summer and early autumn arrives. Yes, you'll get some magnificent Rocky Mountain views on this easy, relaxing and rewarding backway. But while routes like those over Imogene and Ophir passes overwhelm with beauty of epic scale, the appeal of drives like this one is more subtle. Along the way are three worthwhile side routes that can take you even deeper into the landscape: Road 860 (6.9 miles round-trip) along the West Fork of the Cimarron River; Road 861 (9.2 miles round-trip) along the Middle Fork of the Cimarron River; and the more rugged, potentially muddy 18.5-mile (round-trip) Cow Creek detour on Road 857.

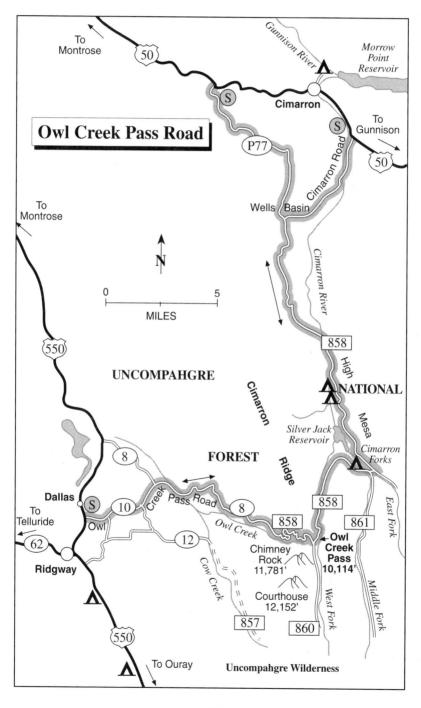

Owl Creek Pass Road

Alpine Plateau

LOCATION: Gunnison County, southwest of Sapinero between U.S. 50 and Colorado Highway 149; north of Uncompahgre (Big Blue on some maps) Wilderness. Partially in Uncompahgre National Forest.

HIGHLIGHTS: Expansive views include canyons, forested mountains, grassy meadows and vast, deeply incised plateaus, all from a friendly little dirt road that climbs to about 11,500 feet atop a broad plateau. This is a wonderful alternative to the highways if you're heading to or from Lake City.

DIFFICULTY: Easy when dry, on a mostly single-lane dirt road that is somewhat rocky and rutted in places.

TIME & DISTANCE: 2 hours; 27.5 miles.

MAPS: *Recreational Map of Colorado*. Uncompahgre National Forest. Trails Illustrated No. 141 (Silverton, Ouray, Telluride, Lake City). DeLorme p. 67.

INFORMATION: GMUG, Gunnison Ranger District.

GETTING THERE: About 11 miles north of Lake City, just north of Narrow Grade Creek, turn north off Highway 149 onto Alpine Road (868), which will soon veer west. In 5.6 miles, on Soldier Summit, go right (north) onto Road 867. Or from U.S. 50 about midway between Cimarron and Sapinero, turn south onto Road 867 and drive toward the Inn at Arrowhead. Follow Road 867 south along the East Fork of Little Blue Creek.

REST STOPS: Big Blue Campground is near the southern end of the drive. There are many campgrounds on Blue Mesa Reservoir, along U.S. 50. The Inn at Arrowhead has lodging, dining, fuel.

THE DRIVE: Going south, start by driving up a narrow canyon on a well-maintained gravel road, and continue south. Going north, the narrow single-lane road climbs out of the beautiful canyon of the Lake Fork of the Gunnison River and edges along a shelf high above a deep side canyon. Either way, you'll climb onto lofty Alpine Plateau, where flaming aspens are interspersed in autumn among dark conifers. The road undulates across broad, open, grassy meadows called "parks," and you just might see a deer lazing among the roadside trees, watching you go by. The vistas are awesome in places, particularly to the north across Curecanti National Recreation Area and the West Elk Wilderness. You could make a grand loop, if you have time, by combining this drive with Blue Mesa Cutoff (Tour 46) or Sapinero Mesa Road (Tour 47).

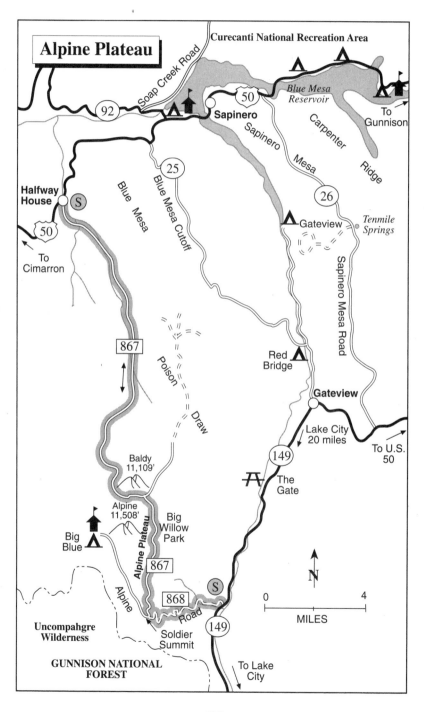

Alpine Plateau

Curecanti National Recreation Area

Soap Creek Road

Blue Mesa Reservoir

92

Sapinero

50

Sapinero Mesa

Carpenter Ridge

To Gunnison

25

Blue Mesa

Blue Mesa Cutoff

26

Halfway House

S

50

To Cimarron

Gateview

Tenmile Springs

Sapinero Mesa Road

867

Poison Draw

Red Bridge

Gateview

Lake City 20 miles

149

To U.S. 50

Baldy 11,109'

Alpine 11,508'

The Gate

Big Willow Park

Big Blue

Alpine Plateau

867

N

0   4

MILES

868

S

Alpine Road

149

Uncompahgre Wilderness

Soldier Summit

To Lake City

GUNNISON NATIONAL FOREST

Blue Mesa Cutoff

LOCATION: Gunnison County. It links U.S. 50 at Curecanti National Recreation Area with state Highway 149 north of Lake City.

HIGHLIGHTS: If you're going to or from the Lake City area, this is a pleasant rural alternative to the highway. The vistas of distant canyons and mountains are wide and engaging from this high mesa. The old Denver and Rio Grande Railroad grade north from Red Bridge Campground through the narrow, high-walled canyon of the Lake Fork of the Gunnison River, is a very worthwhile side trip through history. You can combine this drive with Tours 45 and 47.

DIFFICULTY: Easy, on a well-maintained county road.

TIME & DISTANCE: 1.5 hours; 26 miles, including the intriguing 9.2-mile round-trip drive through Lake Fork Canyon to the Gateview Campground, at the end of the road.

MAPS: Gunnison Basin Area. DeLorme p. 67.

INFORMATION: Gunnison County. Curecanti National Recreation Area.

GETTING THERE: Take U.S. 50 about 3.75 miles west of Sapinero, on Blue Mesa Reservoir, and turn south onto county Road 25. The southern portal is on Highway 149 about 20 miles north of Lake City.

REST STOPS: You can camp at Curecanti National Recreation Area, Red Bridge Campground, and at Gateview Campground (at the end of the old railroad grade in Lake Fork Canyon). There are primitive campsites as well.

THE DRIVE: The mesa is an undulating, hilly landscape of sagebrush, grass, aspen, and pine. All around are sweeping views of distant ranges and dark, faraway canyons. At the north end, the road goes through rocky narrows. At the south end, a good little dirt road edges north along the east bank of the Lake Fork, squeezed between the river and the high wall of a canyon that was occupied by Ute Indians and their predecessors for centuries before whites arrived. The road here once was the bed of a narrow-gauge railway between Sapinero and Lake City. After gold and silver were discovered near Silverton, across the mountains to the south, Lake City served as a gateway to the lodes of the San Juans. From 1875 to 1877, Lake City grew from nothing to a boom town with more than 3,000 residents. They pressed for rail service, which arrived in 1889, and for more than 40 years steam locomotives chugged noisily up and down the canyon. Today, interpretive sites explain the arduous and dangerous task of constructing a railroad between the canyon's sheer walls. The rock foundations of an old work camp can still be seen as well. Gold miners also worked the canyon, scouring the riverbed for placer ore at more than 100 claims.

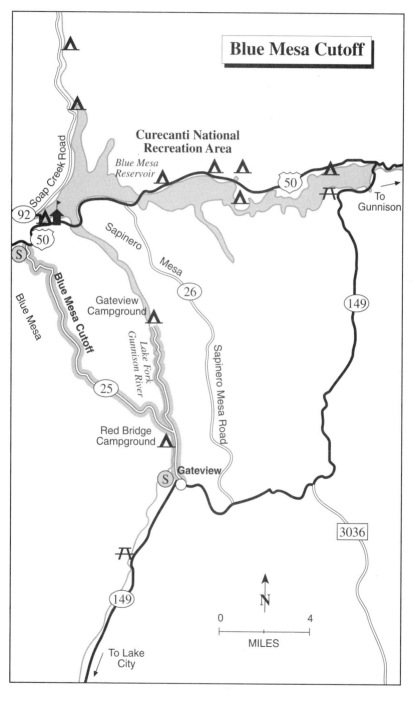

Blue Mesa Cutoff

Curecanti National
Recreation Area

Blue Mesa
Reservoir

Soap Creek Road

Sapinero

Mesa

92

50

S

Blue Mesa

Blue Mesa Cutoff

26

Gateview
Campground

Lake Fork
Gunnison River

25

Red Bridge
Campground

S Gateview

Sapinero Mesa Road

149

3036

50

To
Gunnison

To Lake
City

N

0   4

MILES

Sapinero Mesa Road

LOCATION: On Sapinero Mesa in Gunnison County; between U.S. 50 east of Sapinero and state Highway 149.

HIGHLIGHTS: This is a picturesque and relaxing cruise through rolling sagebrush hills and gullies, with glimpses of the high San Juan Mountains to the south and the Curecanti National Recreation Area and the West Elk Mountains to the north. You can combine this with either Alpine Plateau (Tour 45) or Blue Mesa Cutoff (Tour 46) to make a loop.

DIFFICULTY: Easy on a county-maintained road.

TIME & DISTANCE: 30–45 minutes; 15.3 miles.

MAPS: Gunnison Basin Area. *Recreational Map of Colorado.* DeLorme pp. 67–68.

INFORMATION: Gunnison County.

GETTING THERE: To go south: About 2.5 miles east of Sapinero turn south from U.S. 50 onto county Road 26/Sapinero Mesa Road. **To go north:** About 3.5 miles east of Gateview turn north off Highway 149 onto county Road 26/Sapinero Mesa Road.

REST STOPS: No place in particular, although Curecanti National Recreation Area at the north end has picnicking, camping and other amenities.

THE DRIVE: Even in a region famous for sky-scraping mountain pass roads, it can be rewarding to travel gentle country roads across bucolic landscapes. So it is with Sapinero Mesa Road, which also is known as the Lake City Cutoff, since it is an alternate route to that gateway to the high San Juans. Instead of chiseled peaks and tundra at 13,000 feet, this route traverses open, rolling rangelands that rise from about 7,800 feet at the north end to about 9,000 feet at the south end. Instead of getting your adrenaline pumping, it relaxes you. Even with broad vistas that include distant snowy peaks, it seems a more intimate place than the spectacular passes. It is certainly more fun than the highway.

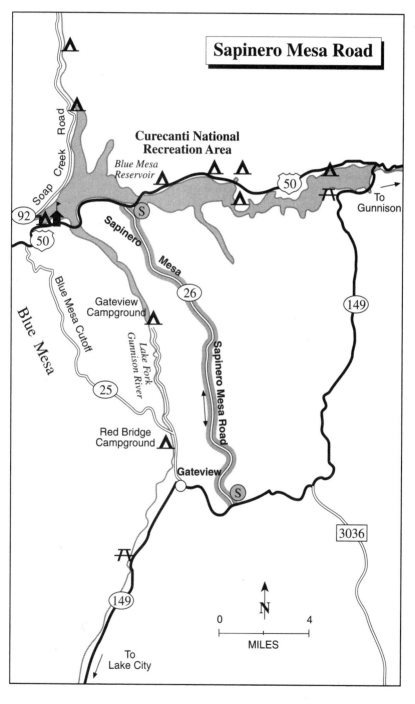

Sapinero Mesa Road

Curecanti National
Recreation Area

Blue Mesa
Reservoir

Soap Creek Road

Sapinero Mesa

Blue Mesa Cutoff

Gateview
Campground

Lake Fork Gunnison River

Sapinero Mesa Road

Red Bridge
Campground

Gateview

Blue Mesa

To
Gunnison

To
Lake City

N

0   4

MILES

Marshall Pass Road

LOCATION: Crosses the Continental Divide between U.S. 50 at Sargents, and U.S. 285 south of Poncha Springs. Gunnison and San Isabel national forests. Saguache and Chaffee counties.

HIGHLIGHTS: This is a picturesque cruise on the serpentine bed of an old toll road that later became a railroad grade, evidenced by the soot-blackened soil along the way. Adding to the fun are great mountain vistas, beaver areas, crossing the Continental Divide at Marshall Pass (10,842 feet), and views of pastoral farmlands along Marshall Creek.

DIFFICULTY: Easy. The road is usually open by June.

TIME & DISTANCE: 2 hours; 31 miles.

MAPS: *Recreational Map of Colorado.* San Isabel National Forest. Gunnison Basin Area. DeLorme pp. 69, 70.

INFORMATION: GMUG, Gunnison Ranger District; Pike and San Isabel national forests, Salida Ranger District.

GETTING THERE: At Sargents, about 36 miles east of Gunnison on U.S. 50, take county Road XX32/forest Road 243 southeast along Marshall Creek. Or from U.S. 285, turn southwest onto county Road 200 at Mears Junction, about 6 miles south of Poncha Springs.

REST STOPS: There is a fee campground at O'Haver Lake, and many primitive campsites along the way. There is a pleasant park in Poncha Springs, as well.

THE DRIVE: Discoveries sometimes stem from the oddest circumstances. Such was the case in 1873, when Lieutenant William L. Marshall of the Wheeler Survey developed a severe toothache while working in the Silverton area. Hoping to find a dentist in Denver, he sought out the shortest way to get there. That turned out to be the pass that today bears his name. After famed toll-road and railroad builder Otto Mears completed a road over Marshall Pass in 1880, it became an important transportation corridor between the Gunnison Valley, west of the Divide, and the Arkansas River Valley, to the east. Mears sold the route to the narrow-gauge Denver and Rio Grande Railroad, which built a line over the pass in 1881. The rail line was abandoned in 1953, and the rails were removed in 1955. Today, the ground along much of the old grade remains blackened by the soot from the old locomotives, and on the eastern side you'll drive through impressive gaps cut through rock outcrops that got in the railroaders' way. This drive also includes the bucolic farmlands along Marshall Creek; riparian areas where beavers appear to be making short work of large aspen stands; long, meandering stretches through spruce-fir forest; the high and bald peaks of the Divide, particularly 13,971-foot Mt. Ouray, just north of the road; broad vistas that reach south to the San Juans; and the old town site of Shirley, a railroad switching station on Poncha Creek near the east end.

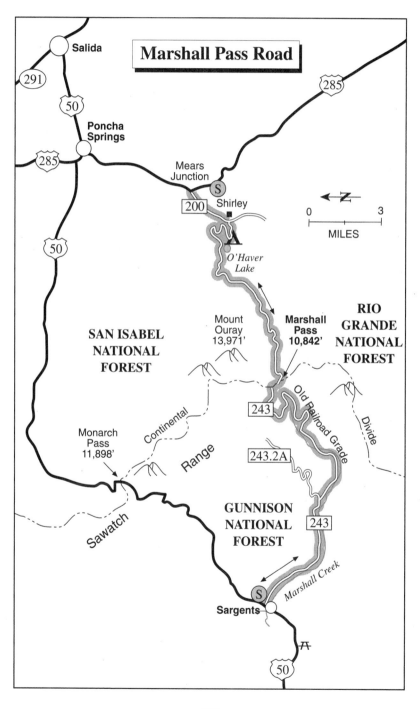

Marshall Pass Road

Salida
291
50
Poncha
Springs
285
285
50

Mears
Junction
S
200   Shirley

N
0   3
MILES

O'Haver
Lake

SAN ISABEL
NATIONAL
FOREST

Mount
Ouray
13,971'

Marshall
Pass
10,842'

RIO
GRANDE
NATIONAL
FOREST

Continental

243

Old Railroad Grade

Divide

Monarch
Pass
11,898'

Range

243.2A

Sawatch

GUNNISON
NATIONAL
FOREST

243

S
Sargents

Marshall Creek

50

Hayden Pass Road

LOCATION: Sangre de Cristo (Spanish for Blood of Christ) Range; Rio Grande and San Isabel national forests. This east-west road links the San Luis Valley at Villa Grove (Saguache County), on U.S. 285, with the Arkansas River Valley at Coaldale (Fremont County), on U.S. 50.

HIGHLIGHTS: There are great vistas across the San Luis and Arkansas River valleys from this 19th-century toll road over 10,709-foot Hayden Pass, named for a Texas Creek settler. Climbing about 2,700 feet, this 4WD road traverses one of Colorado's steepest escarpments, in a mountain range that has 10 of Colorado's 54 "Fourteeners." The range was named for the way it seemed to reflect the blood-red light of the setting sun.

DIFFICULTY: Moderate, on a rocky, steep and narrow road. The east side is a narrow shelf road with a few slightly off-camber spots. The road is wider on the west side, but the roadbed rock is looser. Be prepared to remove snags (dead trees) or branches. Watch for ATVs. The road is usually open by early July.

TIME & DISTANCE: 1.5 hours; 16 miles.

MAPS: Rio Grande and San Isabel national forests. DeLorme pp. 70–71.

INFORMATION: Rio Grande National Forest, Saguache Ranger District; Pike and San Isabel national forests, Salida Ranger District.

GETTING THERE: To go west, take U.S. 50 to Coaldale, about 20 miles southeast of Salida. Follow county Road 6 along Hayden Creek about 5 miles to Hayden Creek Campground, then turn left at the posted 4x4 road to Hayden Pass (about 4 miles). **To go east,** take U.S. 285 to Villa Grove, about 22 miles south of Poncha Springs. Turn east at a small park, Villa Grove Commons, on county Road LL57.

REST STOPS: The summit. Hayden Creek and Coaldale campgrounds, on the east side.

THE DRIVE: The soaring Sangre de Cristo Range, which exceeds 14,000 feet, forms a north-south spine that extends for about 235 miles, from Salida in the north to Santa Fe, New Mexico, in the south. Its western slope, a large fault zone that rises to form the imposing eastern wall of the Connecticut-size San Luis Valley, is particularly steep. In the 1880s, Hayden Pass provided access from the Arkansas River country to the silver mines at Bonanza, west of Villa Grove, and other points west. On the way over the pass, you will see a range of life zones, from grasslands and shrublands to piñon-juniper woodlands, and montane and subalpine forest. From either side, the road is rocky, narrow in places, and steep. I think going from west to east is easier, but the opposite direction provides views across the San Luis Valley to the San Juan Mountains. The views from the summit are obscured by pine forest, and are not the breathtaking sort one so often finds in the Southern Rockies. On the west side, the road is easy dirt for the first 5 miles or so from Villa Grove, then becomes rocky as it climbs. From the east, the road is paved for 1.5 miles from the highway, then maintained dirt and gravel to the 4WD road turnoff at Hayden Creek Campground. From there, the road to the pass is narrow with some roadside brush.

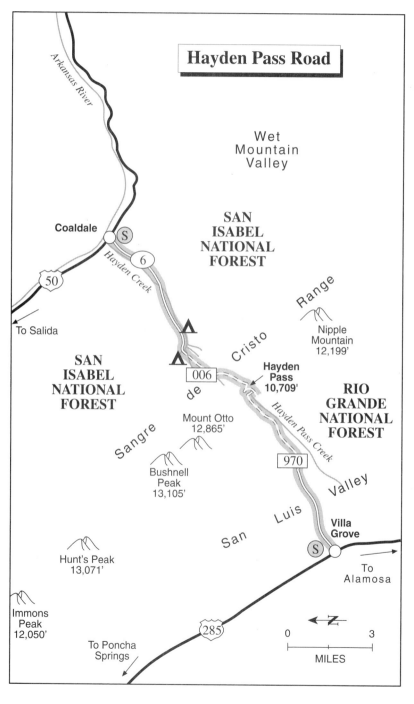

Los Pinos-Cebolla Road

LOCATION: West of the Continental Divide, between state Highway 149 southeast of Lake City, and state Highway 114. Gunnison National Forest. Hinsdale and Saguache counties.

HIGHLIGHTS: For travelers not pressed for time, this little country road along Mill, Cebolla and Los Pinos creeks is one of the prettiest around, with canyons, craggy cliffs, rolling hills and valleys, dense forests, and meadows with grazing deer.

DIFFICULTY: Easy, on a narrow, winding dirt road.

TIME & DISTANCE: 2.5 hours; 43.6 miles. Add 18.9 miles to go over Cochetopa Pass, along the northern segment.

MAPS: Gunnison Basin Area. ACSC's *Indian Country*. DeLorme pp. 67–68, 77.

INFORMATION: GMUG, Gunnison Ranger District.

GETTING THERE: From Highway 149 southeast of Lake City, turn north onto forest Road 788 just west of Slumgullion Pass. The turnoff is 8.9 miles southeast of Lake City. You can access this route from the north at several points along Highway 114 as well.

REST STOPS: There are campgrounds along the southern leg, north of Highway 149, and along the northern leg, south of Highway 114.

THE DRIVE: It was evening when I turned north onto this road after descending from Cinnamon Pass, to the west. With the drama of that sky-scraping crossing (Tour 65) behind me, the gentle meanders of this little road were relaxing and welcome. Instead of gazing anxiously across glaciated peaks and gulches as a September storm headed my way, I followed Mill Creek through the intimate vale between the Powderhorn and La Garita wilderness areas. I descended past ponds, marshes and beaver dams, driving through a picturesque valley and into a narrow canyon of gray-green rock. When night came, I camped at one of the campgrounds along Cebolla Creek, and had it to myself — except for the busy mouse that spent the night hidden somewhere in my 4Runner. The next day was a similar picturesque mix of deep canyons, pastoral valleys, rolling hills, one-lane bridges and forested mountains. I knew I was approaching the pass, which rises to 10,420 feet, when the road began its gentle climb. Just beyond the pass the road winds down through aspens and into a beautiful, open valley. Here, I detoured up Road 790 to Groundhog Park, but I found this spur far less scenic and rewarding than the main road, No. 788. After leaving the national forest, the main road passes the old Los Pinos Indian Agency, now a Forest Service work center. Then it follows Los Pinos Creek to a T intersection. Those who are satisfied can go 4 miles to the left to Highway 114. Those who want more can go right, crossing the Continental Divide at 10,032-foot Cochetopa Pass to reach Highway 114. I was quite satisfied, and went left.

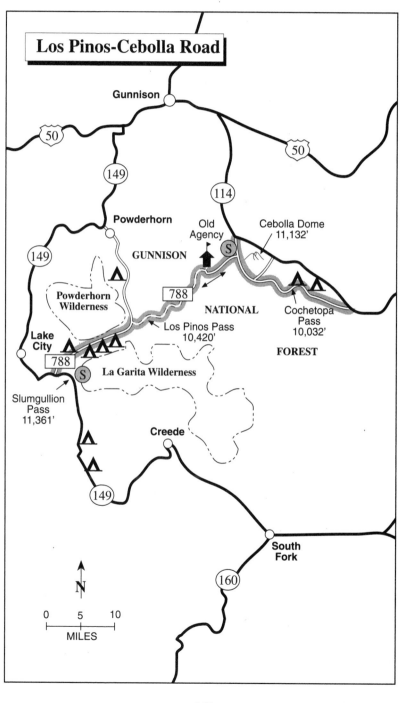

Los Pinos-Cebolla Road

Last Dollar Road

LOCATION: Northwest of Telluride, San Miguel County. Uncompahgre National Forest. Connects state Highways 62 and 145.

HIGHLIGHTS: This is an almost idyllic country road that is especially lovely in late afternoon, so long as rain doesn't turn the dirt to mud, with spectacular views of the San Miguel Mountains, in the Lizard Head Wilderness. There are plenty of wildflowers, too.

DIFFICULTY: Easy when dry; can be impassable when wet, even with 4WD.

TIME & DISTANCE: 1.5 hours; 20.5 miles.

MAPS: Trails Illustrated No. 141 (Silverton, Ouray, Telluride, Lake City). Uncompahgre National Forest. DeLorme pp. 66, 76.

INFORMATION: GMUG, Norwood Ranger District. Montrose Public Lands Center.

GETTING THERE: To end at Telluride: Take Highway 62 west of Dallas Divide. About 12 miles southwest of Ridgway, turn south onto Last Dollar Road (county Road 58P/forest Road 638). **To begin west of Telluride:** Just east of where Highway 145 branches south (at "Society Turn," to which Telluride's upper crust once rode in horse-drawn carriages) take the road north toward the airport. In 1.9 miles turn right, onto the dirt road (T60/638) just before the airport.

REST STOPS: You'll see a number of pleasant places to stop, but it does pass through a lot of privately owned land as well as publicly owned national forest. Telluride has everything.

THE DRIVE: With its meadows, old homesteads, forest corridors and inspiring vistas of chiseled peaks, this pastoral old wagon road seems to have it all. You might even get to stop at a kid's roadside lemonade stand in summer. It is by no means a serious four-wheeling road. But conditions do vary from graded county road to fairly rocky and narrow Forest Service road as it skirts along the southern edge of the Mt. Sneffels Wilderness and Deep Creek Mesa, climbing gradually to about 10,300 feet. I think it's a particularly relaxing and picturesque backway. But my wife and I still talk about the time we drove it, or at least attempted to, one July afternoon during a light rain. The all-season tires on our Toyota 4Runner quickly became clogged with greasy mud. Even with 4WD, the road was treacherous. Once the rain stopped, though, it didn't take long to dry out and become driveable again. I recommend taking it from north to south, ending at Telluride, because of the fantastic views (especially in the golden light of late afternoon) of the mountains.

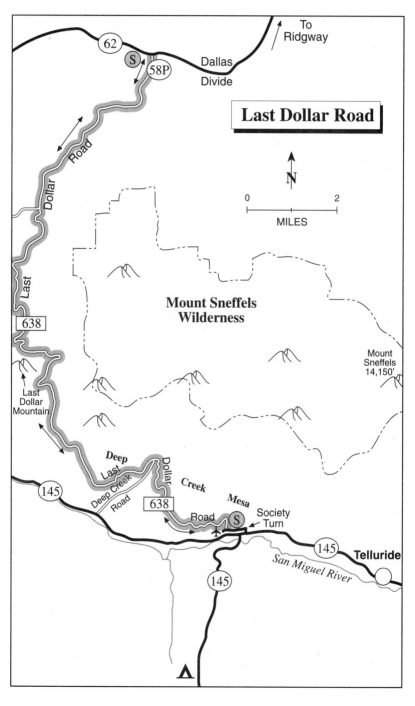

Last Dollar Road

Last Dollar Road *(Tour 51)*

Yankee Boy Basin *(Tour 52)*

Yankee Boy Basin

LOCATION: Southwest of Ouray, Ouray County. San Juan Mountains. Uncompahgre National Forest, although most of Yankee Boy and nearby Governor basins are private land.

HIGHLIGHTS: Spectacular alpine scenery, abundant wildflowers, waterfalls, a high-walled canyon and old town sites in a once-booming mining area. This great drive, which is usually open by mid-June, can be combined with a side trip to Box Canyon Falls and Park early in the drive and the drive over Imogene Pass (Tour 53).

DIFFICULTY: Easy to moderate. Rocky, steep and narrow in places. This is a popular drive, so watch for traffic. There is avalanche danger on Camp Bird Road. Mine sites are dangerous.

TIME & DISTANCE: 2–3 hours; 17 miles round-trip. Longer if you hike from the end of the road to beautiful Blue Lakes, in the Mt. Sneffels Wilderness.

MAPS: Trails Illustrated No. 141 (Silverton, Ouray, Telluride, Lake City); Uncompahgre National Forest; DeLorme pp. 66, 76.

INFORMATION: GMUG, Ouray Ranger District. Montrose Public Lands Center. At about mile 6.7, at the entrance to Yankee Boy and Governor basins, look for a metal box containing informative brochures.

GETTING THERE: About 0.3 mile south of Ouray, at a bend in U.S. 550 (the San Juan Skyway/Million Dollar Highway), turn south onto county Road 361 (Camp Bird Road) at the sign for Camp Bird Mine, Yankee Boy Basin and Box Canyon Falls and Park.

REST STOPS: There are primitive campsites along the way, but much of the land is private. You will find a toilet at mile 7.8 from the highway. This sensitive alpine zone is a popular place, and while there are many places to stop and view the wildflowers, do not pick or trample them. If everyone who visited picked flowers and tramped through the meadows, there soon would be nothing left. You might also visit beautiful Box Canyon Falls and Park, near the start.

THE DRIVE: Very good Camp Bird Road climbs up the deep canyon of Canyon Creek, through pine forest dominated by glaciated peaks and basins that soar well above 13,000 feet. At about mile 2.8, across a one-lane bridge, the asphalt ends and the road becomes a narrow shelf blasted long ago into the dramatic canyon's west wall. Note the waterfalls cascading down from the hanging valleys above the canyon. At mile 6, at the confluence of Sneffels, Imogene and Canyon creeks, you will pass the left turn to Camp Bird, a gold mine named for the food-stealing Canada Jay, and Imogene Pass. From here the little road courses up the canyon of Sneffels Creek. At mile 6.3 it passes through the site of Sneffels, a town founded in 1875 at an elevation of almost 10,400 feet after gold and silver deposits were discovered. Originally called Porter, it once had a population of 2,000. At a fork at mile 6.9, at the site of Ruby City, keep right. (The narrow road left, up to Governor Basin, starts out easy as it climbs and switchbacks to another stunning alpine basin, but it becomes rough and narrow. It is worthwhile, however, to drive up it for 2.1 miles from this junction to a pullout with a terrific view.) The road to Yankee Boy Basin, rocky from here, climbs steeply for another mile or so.

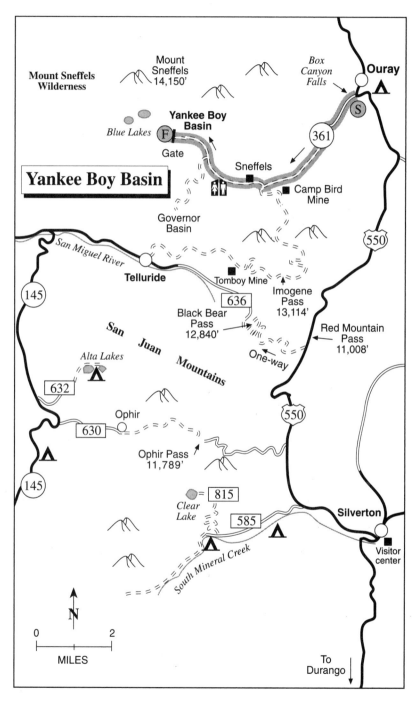

Imogene Pass

LOCATION: Between Ouray and Telluride, in the San Juan Mountains. Uncompahgre National Forest. Ouray and San Miguel counties.

HIGHLIGHTS: This is one of Colorado's top 4WD routes, with some of the best alpine scenery in the state. Named for a prospector's wife, 13,114-foot Imogene Pass links two old mining towns that now rank high on tourists' itineraries. The views of Telluride, Black Bear Pass (Tour 55), Ingram Falls and Bridal Veil Falls are fantastic. Great wildflowers, too, but don't pick them so that other visitors can enjoy them. Tomboy mine and town site, 3,000 feet above Telluride, are interesting. Combine with Yankee Boy Basin (Tour 52).

DIFFICULTY: Moderate. Rocky with stretches of narrow shelf road and drop-offs. It's busy, too. Uphill traffic has the right of way. The road is usually open by July 4th.

TIME & DISTANCE: 3 hours; about 19 miles.

MAPS: Trails Illustrated No. 141 (Silverton, Ouray, etc.). Uncompahgre National Forest. DeLorme pp. 66, 76.

INFORMATION: GMUG, Ouray and Norwood ranger districts. Montrose Public Lands Center.

GETTING THERE: From Ouray: Take U.S. 550, the San Juan Skyway/Million Dollar Highway, about 0.3 mile south of town. Where it bends to the east, turn south onto county Road 361 (Camp Bird Road) at the sign for Camp Bird Mine, Yankee Boy Basin and Box Canyon Falls. In 6 miles turn left (south) at Camp Bird. **From Telluride:** Take Oak Street (a block north of the center of town) north to Tomboy Road, and follow Tomboy Road east up the canyon wall.

REST STOPS: There are many places to stop. The top of the pass, with its terrific mountain views, is a popular place. People like to take photos at the pass sign, so if it's a busy day, don't hog it. At the Ouray end, visit Box Canyon Falls and Park, near U.S. 550.

THE DRIVE: Several rich mines kept the lower portions of this road busy. Above Telluride was the Smuggler-Union silver and gold mine and, in Savage Basin, the mine and town of Tomboy, among the richest gold operations in North America between the 1880s and 1920s. Almost 1,000 people lived there in its heyday. Today you'll see efforts to control its polluted runoff. Above Ouray were Camp Bird and, farther up, Upper Camp Bird, both named for food-stealing Canada Jays. Estimates of that operation's gold production run as high as $50 million. From Telluride, the narrow, rocky road switchbacks up the forested canyon wall above town, passes through a tunnel bored through solid rock, then edges along a narrow shelf with an unnerving drop-off. About 5 miles from Telluride you will reach Tomboy. The pass is another 1.5 miles or so. From Camp Bird, cross Sneffels Creek, follow the rough road through the forest at the brink of a canyon, then cross the creek again. Soon the rocky shelf road starts its long climb through Imogene Basin to the pass. About 3.6 miles from Camp Bird you will see Upper Camp Bird Mine high to the right. In another 3 miles you will reach the pass, where you can park and enjoy fabulous Rocky Mountain scenery.

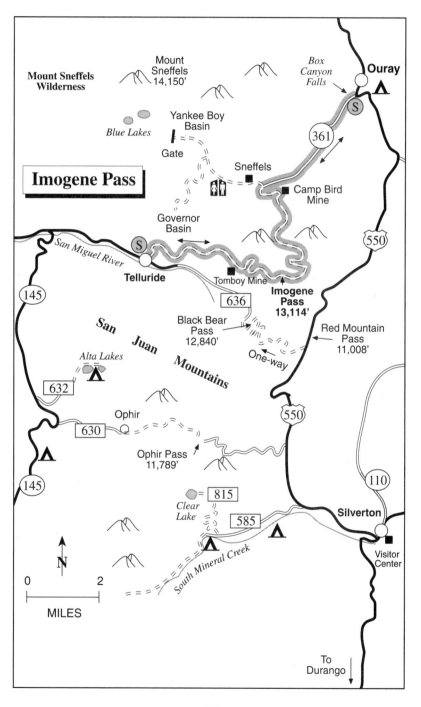

Mount Sneffels Wilderness

Mount Sneffels 14,150'

Box Canyon Falls

Ouray

Blue Lakes

Yankee Boy Basin

Gate

Imogene Pass

Sneffels

361

550

Camp Bird Mine

Governor Basin

San Miguel River

Telluride

Tomboy Mine

Imogene Pass 13,114'

636

145

San Juan Mountains

Black Bear Pass 12,840'

One-way

Red Mountain Pass 11,008'

Alta Lakes

632

Ophir

630

Ophir Pass 11,789'

550

110

815

Clear Lake

585

Silverton

Visitor Center

N

0   2

MILES

South Mineral Creek

To Durango

Imogene Pass *(Tour 53)*

Imogene Pass *(Tour 53)*

Lizard Head Loop

LOCATION: This drive skirts the Lizard Head Wilderness (named for the prominent 13,113-foot spire), from state Highway 145 west of Telluride to Highway 145 southwest of Lizard Head Pass. Uncompahgre and San Juan national forests. San Miguel and Dolores counties.

HIGHLIGHTS: This is a relaxing mountain tour from the Telluride area that climbs to more than 11,000 feet. It loops around the San Miguel Mountains, providing dramatic views from the vast western plateaus to the soaring San Juan Mountains. Aspen stands promise great early-autumn color.

DIFFICULTY: Easy. Road conditions vary from rocky single-lane shelf to well-maintained dirt and gravel. Watch for bicyclists.

TIME & DISTANCE: 3.5 hours; 53 miles.

MAPS: Uncompahgre and San Juan national forests. Trails Illustrated No. 141 (Silverton, Ouray, Telluride, Lake City). DeLorme pp. 75–76.

INFORMATION: GMUG, Norwood Ranger District; San Juan National Forest, Mancos-Dolores Ranger District. San Juan Public Lands Center.

GETTING THERE: From the north: 3 miles southeast of the junction of Highways 145 and 62 (about 1.5 miles west of Sawpit; 10.5 miles west of Telluride), turn south from Highway 145 onto Fall Creek Road (county Road 57P/forest Road 618). **From the south:** Take Highway 145 to Cayton Campground, about 6 miles south of Lizard Head Pass. Turn northwest onto Dunton Road (535) at the sign for Dunton.

REST STOPS: Picnic tables and toilets at Woods Lake (day use only, but there is primitive camping in the adjacent national forest). Burro Bridge Campground on Dunton Road. Cayton Campground on Highway 145 at the south end of the route. Many primitive campsites.

THE DRIVE: South of Highway 145, Fall Creek Road passes through a residential area (go slow), following the creek. The pavement ends in a mile. Continuing toward Woods Lake, the road enters Uncompahgre National Forest at mile 5.1. Here you will see snowy peaks rising from the forest ahead. At mile 7.4 the road, 618, goes right, across a bridge. (Pass this turnoff to reach Woods Lake in about 1.5 miles.) Road 618 becomes single-lane dirt as it climbs among huge aspens and courses westward north of Lizard Head Wilderness, where Flat Top Peak rises to 11,596 feet Soon you're on a shelf, with terrific views across the valley of the San Miguel River to the lofty Sneffels Range. When you emerge from the trees, plateau country will spread out before you to the west. The road descends through beetle-killed Engelmann spruce. To the west rises 12,613-foot Lone Cone, the western end of the San Juans. Soon the road brings you to the marshes and willows on Beaver Creek, where the road improves. At the junction 0.7 mile beyond Lone Cone Guard Station, in Beaver Park, turn south (left) on more rudimentary Road 611. The views of the mountains are outstanding here. The road gradually ascends to more than 11,000 feet on a stretch of rocky roadbed. Here, in San Juan National Forest, begins a fabulously scenic, ear-popping descent via switchbacks to Black Mesa Road (611). When you reach it, go east (left) and descend for 11.3 miles to Dunton Guard Station and Dunton Road. Highway 145 is 10 easy miles to the left via a stretch of one-lane shelf, or 23 miles to the right along the West Dolores River.

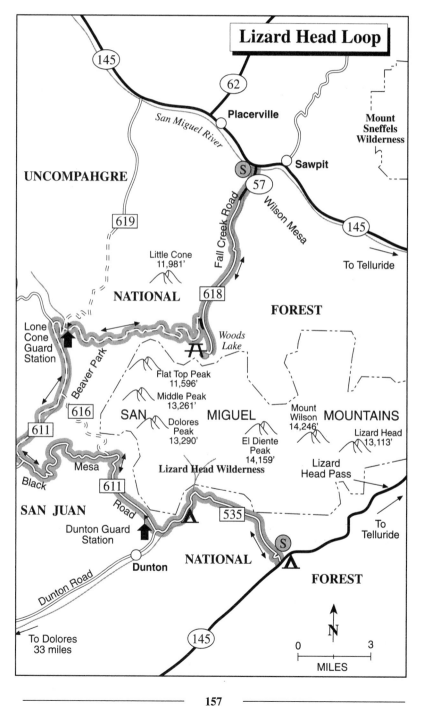

Black Bear Pass

LOCATION: Between Red Mountain Pass on U.S. 550 and Telluride. San Juan and Uncompahgre national forests. San Juan, San Miguel counties.

HIGHLIGHTS: This is one of Colorado's most spectacular 4WD roads, but it also is dangerous. The wildflowers are fantastic as you climb to 12,840 feet, and the view of the box canyon occupied by Telluride is awesome. You will cross Ingram Falls on the descent, then pass Bridal Veil Falls, Colorado's longest (350 feet).

DIFFICULTY: This one's for experienced four-wheelers. I'd leave the kids behind. It's moderately difficult for the first 6.4 miles from U.S. 550 through Mineral and Ingram basins, but difficult (due to fear as much as anything) and dangerous for the next 1.1 miles on a narrow shelf road. There are many tight switchbacks with killer drop-offs. A short wheelbase vehicle is best. A snowbank can block the road on the east side, so inquire locally before setting out. The road usually opens by mid-July. It's one-way (westbound) for 7.5 miles from Red Mountain Pass to the top of Bridal Veil Falls. The section from Bridal Veil Falls to Telluride is easy (and two-way), making that leg a fun drive up from Telluride.

TIME & DISTANCE: 2.5 hours; 11.8 miles.

MAPS: Uncompahgre National Forest. Trails Illustrated No. 141 (Silverton, Ouray, Telluride, Lake City). DeLorme p. 76.

INFORMATION: San Juan National Forest, Columbine West Ranger District; GMUG, Ouray Ranger District; Silverton Visitor Information Center. San Juan Public Lands Center.

GETTING THERE: Take U.S. 550 (the San Juan Skyway/Million Dollar Highway) south from Ouray or north from Silverton to the top of Red Mountain Pass. Turn west at the sign.

REST STOPS: Anyplace except switchbacks and other tight spots.

THE DRIVE: A series of easy switchbacks climbs toward Mineral Basin, providing breathtaking vistas of a meringue of 13,000–14,000-foot peaks. In Mineral Basin, the road climbs gradually past some small lakes toward a crest. There, look out over Ingram Basin, presided over by Ingram, Ajax and Telluride peaks and honeycombed by mines. From here the road angles left and then right as it drops into Ingram Basin. There, it makes a series of switchbacks and crosses a talus field as it skirts the alpine tundra and goes around Ingram Lake. If you find these switchbacks difficult, turn back even though the road is one-way. The road is very rocky in places now. By mile 6 it parallels Ingram Creek, where you'll crawl over rock outcrops. Note the steel cables suspended along the basin, remnants of the aerial tram that served the mines. At mile 6.4, where the creek is rushing through the rocks, is a good place to take a break. From here the road is narrow with long drop-offs and tight switchbacks, some of which will require multiple attempts. Roadbed rocks will cause your vehicle to pitch side to side, so watch the rock wall and the drop-off. Use low-range gears, and have someone guide you through the difficult places. At mile 6.5 drive through Ingram

Falls (your tires will be wet and slippery). At 7.5 is the old hydroelectric plant atop Bridal Veil Falls. The hard part ends here. At 8.3 gaze up at Bridal Veil Falls from the parking area, then continue your descent to Telluride.

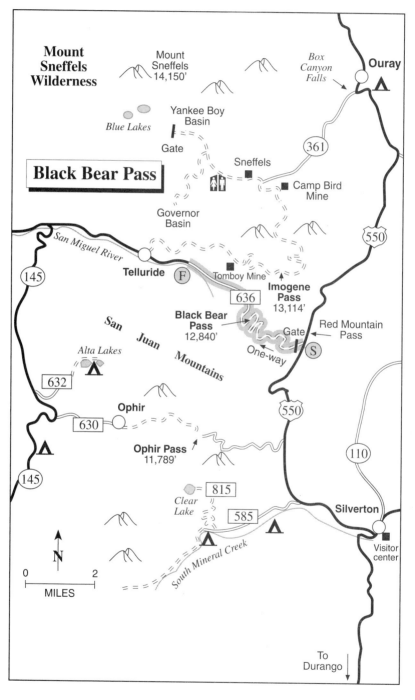

Mount Sneffels Wilderness

Mount Sneffels 14,150'

Blue Lakes

Yankee Boy Basin

Gate

Black Bear Pass

Sneffels

Camp Bird Mine

Governor Basin

San Miguel River

Telluride F

Tomboy Mine

636

Black Bear Pass 12,840'

One-way

Imogene Pass 13,114'

Gate

S

Red Mountain Pass

San Juan Mountains

Alta Lakes

632

Ophir

630

Ophir Pass 11,789'

550

Clear Lake

815

585

South Mineral Creek

145

110

550

Silverton

Visitor center

Box Canyon Falls

Ouray

361

550

N

0   2
MILES

To Durango

Black Bear Pass *(Tour 55)*

Ophir Pass *(Tour 56)*

Ophir Pass

LOCATION: San Juan Mountains. Links U.S. 550 north of Silverton and state Highway 145 south of Telluride. San Juan and Uncompahgre national forests. San Miguel and San Juan counties.

HIGHLIGHTS: Terrific vistas of glaciated mountains, basins and valleys, especially on the west side, where you can gaze at the San Miguel Mountains; the crossing at 11,789-foot Ophir Pass; wildflowers; a fun drive between two popular destinations, Telluride and Silverton. 1.9 miles north of the Ophir turnoff on Highway 145 is the 4.5-mile (one-way) drive to Alta Lakes, via the ghost town of Alta.

DIFFICULTY: The east side is an easy unpaved road. The west side, which I rate moderate, is a rocky, fairly steep shelf road along talus slopes with precipitous drop-offs. Note: Some maps depict this as one-way (east to west). Others don't. People go both ways. The road is usually open by mid-June.

TIME & DISTANCE: 1 hour; 10 miles.

MAPS: San Juan National Forest. Trails Illustrated No. 141 (Silverton, Ouray, etc.). Get the Silverton Chamber of Commerce's *Jeep Roads and Ghost Towns of the San Juans*. DeLorme p. 76.

INFORMATION: San Juan National Forest, Columbine West Ranger District; GMUG, Norwood Ranger District. Silverton Chamber of Commerce Visitor Information Center, at U.S. Highway 550 and Colorado 110. San Juan Public Lands Center.

GETTING THERE: From Telluride: Take Highway 145 south for 7.1 miles from the junction west of Telluride. Where the highway bends west, turn east (left) onto forest Road 630. **From Silverton:** Take U.S. 550 about 4.8 miles north from the junction with Highway 110 (Silverton's main street). Go west (left) on county Road 8/forest Road 679.

REST STOPS: There is primitive camping in the canyon bottom on the west side. The easy east-side road has many pullouts. There is camping along South Fork Mineral Creek (see Clear Lake, Tour 59).

THE DRIVE: East of Highway 145, a good road takes you 2 miles to a cluster of old and not-so-old buildings that comprise Ophir, or Old Ophir. Actually, two Ophirs sprouted near each other here in the 1870s. (The site of New Ophir was back by the highway.) The word Ophir (OH-fer) is thought to derive from a Biblical source of gold referred to in 1 Kings 9:28. Follow the signs for the pass. Soon you will enter pine and aspen forest, then pass tailings piles and ponds. The road will narrow and begin climbing along the northern wall of the long, dramatic canyon of the Howard Fork of the San Miguel River. Silver Mountain rises steeply to the north. Yellow Mountain, furrowed by spectacular gulches, dominates the skyline to the south. Between lies a lush valley. As you follow the road along the shelf you'll see the pass ahead, flanked by high peaks. The road is very narrow, with one tight switchback at the head of the canyon. From U.S. 550 the road is an easy cruise among forested mountains and canyons. Almost 3 miles from the highway the road climbs toward the gap between talus slopes that frame a stunning view of the San Miguel Mountains to the west.

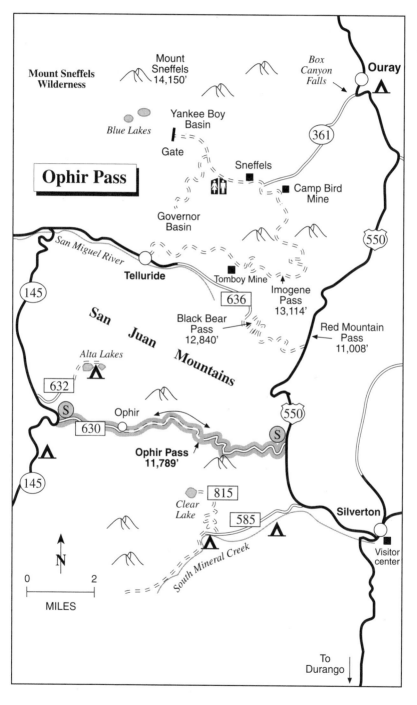

Engineer Mountain Road

LOCATION: San Juan County. San Juan Mountains southeast of Ouray. East of U.S. 550.

HIGHLIGHTS: Part of the 65-mile Alpine Loop National Back Country Byway, this outstanding route (often called Engineer Pass Road) includes old mine sites, the famous ghost town of Animas Forks (Tour 61) and meadows splashed with wildflowers. The drive along the narrow shelf above the gorge of the Uncompahgre River is absolutely spectacular, as are the views of glacial gulches and the craggy peaks of the Lizard Head and Mt. Sneffels wilderness areas.

DIFFICULTY: Moderate, but only because it is a long, rocky climb on the Alpine Loop's roughest leg. Some might prefer to go in the opposite direction, downhill from Animas Forks.

TIME & DISTANCE: 2 hours; 9.2 miles.

MAPS: Silverton Chamber's *Jeep Roads and Ghost Towns of the San Juans*. Uncompahgre National Forest. Trails Illustrated No. 141 (Silverton, Ouray, Telluride, Lake City). DeLorme p. 77.

INFORMATION: Silverton Visitor Information Center, at U.S. 550 and state Highway 110. BLM's Gunnison Field Office. San Juan Public Lands Center. Get a copy of the BLM's excellent *Alpine Explorer Recreation Guide to the Alpine Triangle*.

GETTING THERE: From U.S. 550 about 3.5 miles south of Ouray, turn east at the Alpine Loop sign onto Road 878. **From Animas Forks**, follow the signs for Engineer and Cinnamon passes. At a Y about 2.5 miles north of Animas Forks, go left at the sign for Ouray. (Engineer Pass and Lake City are to the right.)

REST STOPS: The ghost town of Animas Forks is one of Colorado's most famous. Enjoy (but don't pick) the wildflowers in the lush, fragile meadows high above timberline. There are toilets near the site of Mineral Point and at Animas Forks.

THE DRIVE: From U.S. 550, at about 9,200 feet, the narrow road ascends on a shelf hewn into the walls of the Uncompahgre River gorge. The roadbed is rough, but you'll want to take it slow anyway just to savor the stunning canyon scenery, which is such a contrast to the vast mountaintop panoramas you'll get after the long climb to more than 12,000 feet on the way to Animas Forks. 2.4 miles from the highway, or about 6.8 miles before Animas Forks, the occasionally difficult, rough and sometimes boggy 4x4 trail up Poughkeepsie Gulch branches south along the Uncompahgre River. (It climbs 4.5 miles to Lake Como, a pretty lake in a glacial cirque that is the headwaters of the river, and to Hurricane and California passes. It is closed when conditions are too wet.) As you follow Mineral Creek on what remains a primitive forest road, you will eventually reach a sharp bend in the road at treeline. Just to the south is the site of Mineral Point, a mining camp established in 1873. (The nearby ruins are the old San Juan Chief Mill.) From here to Animas Forks you will pass lovely alpine meadows. Please leave the wildflowers for others to enjoy.

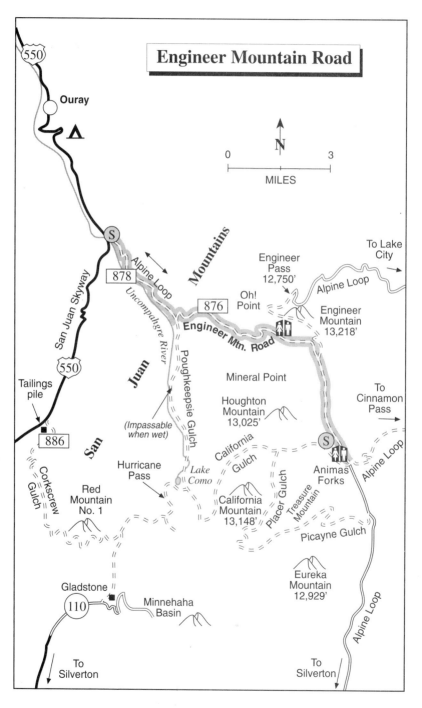

Engineer Mountain Road

Corkscrew Gulch

LOCATION: North of Red Mountain Pass, east of U.S. 550 between Ouray and Silverton. Ouray County. Uncompahgre National Forest.

HIGHLIGHTS: You'll find this an exhilarating white-knuckler with fabulous mountain scenery. This convenient tour off U.S. 550 links up with a network of spectacular roads to Silverton, Animas Forks, Picayne and Placer gulches and other scenic areas.

DIFFICULTY: Moderate. Steep with tight switchbacks.

TIME & DISTANCE: 45 minutes; 3.7 miles from top to bottom. From the top of the gulch, the time and distance to your final destination is additional.

MAPS: Trails Illustrated No. 141 (Silverton, Ouray, Telluride and Lake City). Silverton Chamber's *Jeep Roads and Ghost Towns of the San Juans.* Uncompahgre National Forest. DeLorme pp. 76–77.

INFORMATION: Silverton Chamber of Commerce Visitor Information Center, at the intersection of U.S. 550 and Colorado 110. GMUG, Ouray Ranger District. San Juan Public Lands Center.

GETTING THERE: From U.S. 550, turn east at a huge tailings pile 7.6 miles south of Ouray. Cross the bridge and drive into the trees ahead. Go right at the Y and follow Road 886 up Corkscrew Gulch. From the east end of Silverton, take Highway 110, a graded road, for 6.6 miles to the mine at Gladstone. Angle left there onto Road 10. Go 1.5 miles, then make a hairpin left at the fork, onto Road 11.

REST STOPS: Stop at the top of the gulch, at about 12,150 feet. If you descend to Silverton, first detour left at Gladstone and take the road through the trees south of the mine. It follows the South Fork of Cement Creek 1.6 miles to a glacial basin with a pretty lake.

THE DRIVE: Use your low-range gears going up or down this steep gulch. At the bottom, just north of the town site of Ironton, the road goes along the perimeter of a mammoth tailings pile. It's part of Idarado Mining Company's Superfund environmental remediation project. Ironton, founded in 1882, housed miners who extracted silver and lead from nearby Yankee Girl and Guston mines. When famed road and railroad builder Otto Mears laid tracks over Red Mountain to Ironton Park, Ironton town became a transportation center between Ouray and the Red Mountain mining district. The scenery even attracted tourists, and at Ironton's peak two trains arrived from Silverton daily. In the gulch was a railroad turntable that made it unnecessary to back trains downhill. Corkscrew Gulch itself is a spectacular, and aptly named, gash where the narrow and steep road coils skyward. At the top, the views of sharp ridges, red peaks and glacial cirques, especially in early evening's golden light, are among the premier sights in the volcanic San Juans. From the top, one option is to continue over Hurricane and California passes and down California Gulch to Animas Forks, and then on to Silverton. Or you can go to Silverton via the old gold mining center of Gladstone, named for late-19th century British Prime Minister William E. Gladstone.

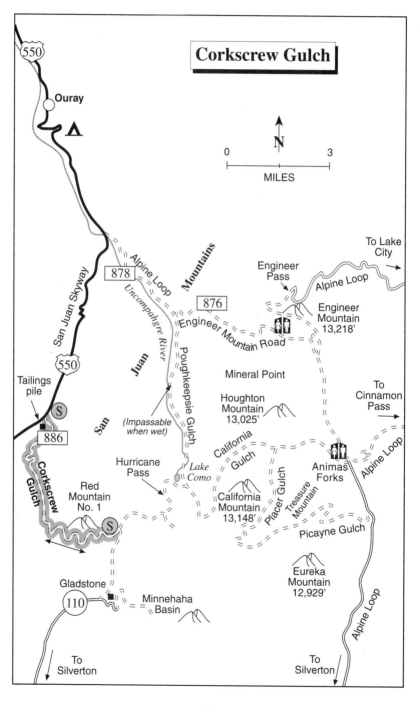

Corkscrew Gulch

550

Ouray

N

0   3

MILES

San Juan Skyway

550

Alpine Loop

878

Uncompahgre River

Mountains

To Lake City

Engineer Pass

Alpine Loop

876

Engineer Mountain Road

Engineer Mountain 13,218'

Tailings pile

886

Corkscrew Gulch

San Juan

Poughkeepsie Gulch

(Impassable when wet)

Mineral Point

Houghton Mountain 13,025'

To Cinnamon Pass

Hurricane Pass

Lake Como

California Gulch

Animas Forks

Alpine Loop

Red Mountain No. 1

S

California Mountain 13,148'

Placer Gulch

Treasure Mountain

Picayne Gulch

Gladstone

110

Minnehaha Basin

Eureka Mountain 12,929'

Alpine Loop

To Silverton

To Silverton

Clear Lake

LOCATION: West of Silverton. San Juan County. San Juan National Forest.

HIGHLIGHTS: Breathtaking high-elevation vistas along a 2,000-foot climb to a sparkling lake in a glacial cirque. This is a convenient drive from the Silverton area.

DIFFICULTY: Easy, although the final 4.4 miles are on a rocky shelf road. Almost a mile before the lake is a bend where a large snowbank can block the road well into July, but you can hike to the lake from there.

TIME & DISTANCE: 1 hour; 8.2 miles from U.S. 550.

MAPS: Trails Illustrated No. 141 (Silverton, Ouray, Telluride, Lake City). San Juan National Forest. Silverton Chamber of Commerce's *Jeep Roads and Ghost Towns of the San Juans*. DeLorme p. 76.

INFORMATION: Silverton Chamber of Commerce Visitor Information Center, at the intersection of U.S. 550 and Colorado 110. San Juan National Forest, Columbine West Ranger District. San Juan Public Lands Center.

GETTING THERE: 2 miles north of U.S. 550 and Highway 110 at Silverton, turn west onto forest Road 585 (San Juan County Road 7).

REST STOPS: There is primitive camping along South Mineral Creek, including designated areas. South Mineral Campground is 4.3 miles from the highway. Silverton has all services.

THE DRIVE: From U.S. 550, the well-maintained road along South Mineral Creek meanders up a long, beautiful gulch flanked by soaring walls. (Note the small waterfalls and avalanche chutes.) Beavers are busy in this area, evidenced by the ponds along the creek. Beyond South Mineral Campground the road narrows to a single lane and continues up the gulch for another 2.8 miles. After crossing the creek, it ends in a boggy area at the site of the old Bandora mine. But at mile 3.7 from the highway, before the campground, the narrow shelf road (815) to Clear Lake branches up the canyon's north wall, to the right. It's a rocky drive as it switchbacks through forest. But the views of the gulch and the 13,000-foot-plus peaks around it, salted with snowfields and sculpted by glaciers, are terrific. Eventually the road becomes a narrow ledge along the face of the canyon wall. Then you will see Clear Creek cascading down from the lake. Shortly after that an old mine site will appear up ahead. Here you should be able to see whether the snowbank has cleared. If it has, continue on up, passing a small lake. Soon you will see Clear Lake, a real jewel, and a parking area. If the snowbank is blocking the road, it's still worth the short hike to the lake, which lies at about 11,800 feet Remember that physical activity is more taxing at high elevations.

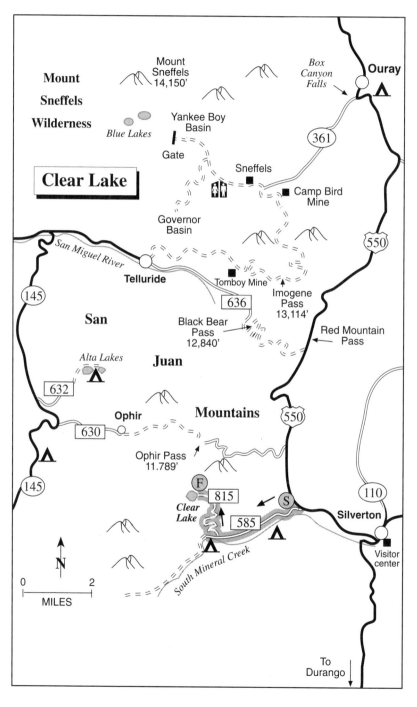

Mount Sneffels Wilderness

Mount Sneffels 14,150'

Box Canyon Falls

Ouray

Blue Lakes

Yankee Boy Basin

Gate

Clear Lake

Sneffels

Camp Bird Mine

361

Governor Basin

San Miguel River

Telluride

Tomboy Mine

636

Imogene Pass 13,114'

550

145

San

Black Bear Pass 12,840'

Red Mountain Pass

Juan

Alta Lakes

632

Mountains

Ophir

630

Ophir Pass 11.789'

550

145

F

815

Clear Lake

585

S

Silverton

110

Visitor center

South Mineral Creek

N

0   2
MILES

To Durango

Placer Gulch *(Tour 60)*

Animas Valley and Picayne Gulch *(Tour 60)*

Placer Gulch/Picayne Gulch

LOCATION: Near Silverton, between California Gulch and the ghost town of Animas Forks, on the Alpine Loop National Back Country Byway. San Juan County.

HIGHLIGHTS: This is a gorgeous, interesting and convenient loop along two dramatic gulches that take you high above timberline, to about 12,800 feet, and away from the busier roads of the Alpine Loop. A convenient and very scenic drive. Great wildflowers, too.

DIFFICULTY: Easy to moderate.

TIME & DISTANCE: 1 hour; 6.7 miles. Travel from Silverton to Animas Forks (Tour 61) adds almost 13 miles one way.

MAPS: Trails Illustrated No. 141 (Silverton, Ouray, Telluride and Lake City); Silverton Chamber's flyer *Jeep Roads and Ghost Towns of the San Juans*. Uncompahgre National Forest. DeLorme pp. 76–77.

INFORMATION: Silverton Chamber of Commerce Visitor Information Center, at the intersection of U.S. 550 and Colorado 110. San Juan Public Lands Center.

GETTING THERE: I recommend going up Placer Gulch and down Picayne (a.k.a. Picayune) Gulch to avoid a steep climb on a loose roadbed. From Animas Forks, drive 1.1 miles up California Gulch, then turn south at the entrance to Placer Gulch. If you're descending from California Pass, the Placer Gulch turn is 2.8 miles from there. To go up Picayne Gulch, turn west at the sign about 1.5 miles south of Animas Forks, along the road from/to Silverton.

REST STOPS: About mid-way is a knoll that provides an awesome alpine vista from about 12,700 feet.

THE DRIVE: You are likely to see countless wildflowers as you drive up Placer Gulch, along a rocky one-lane road below California Mountain, to your right. Watch for marmots scampering among the boulders as you follow a marshy stream ever higher. In about a mile you will see some mine ruins and tailings where an environmental remediation project is underway to improve the water quality of the Upper Animas River Basin. The mess left by the miners gets worse, unfortunately, as you reach the head of the gulch. There, go left across the brook and climb a narrow shelf. The road is rougher here as you switchback above the mines to head east below Hanson Peak. Soon you will see a knoll that provides a tremendous vista across a meringue of mountains and canyons. You're high above timberline now, headed around Treasure Mountain over a divide between treeless Placer Gulch and Picayne Gulch, which changes from grassy, treeless slopes at its higher reaches to wooded slopes farther along the steep descent toward Animas Forks.

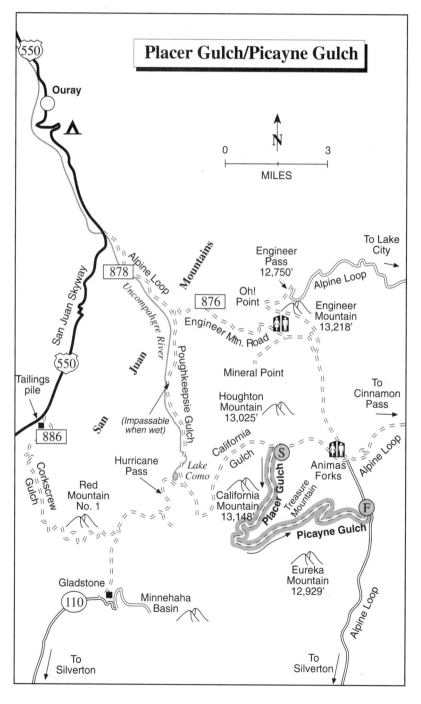

Placer Gulch/Picayne Gulch

550

Ouray

N

0   3
MILES

To Lake City

Engineer Pass 12,750'

Alpine Loop

878   Alpine Loop

Mountains

876

Oh! Point

Engineer Mountain 13,218'

Engineer Mtn. Road

San Juan Skyway

Uncompahgre River

Mineral Point

Poughkeepsie Gulch

To Cinnamon Pass

550

Juan

Houghton Mountain 13,025'

Tailings pile

886

San

(Impassable when wet)

California Gulch

S

Alpine Loop

Animas Forks

Corkscrew Gulch

Hurricane Pass

Lake Como

California Mountain 13,148'

Placer Gulch

Treasure Mountain

F

Red Mountain No. 1

Picayne Gulch

Gladstone

110

Minnehaha Basin

Eureka Mountain 12,929'

Alpine Loop

To Silverton

To Silverton

Animas Forks

LOCATION: San Juan County, in a high valley in the San Juan Mountains southeast of Ouray and northeast of Silverton along the famous Alpine Loop National Back Country Byway.

HIGHLIGHTS: Although Animas Forks is accessible in 2WD vehicles, this popular ghost town is a crossroads for a number of fabulously scenic 4WD routes. It's a convenient and rewarding side trip from U.S. 550—the famous San Juan Skyway—between Silverton and Ouray. It's usually accessible by Memorial Day.

DIFFICULTY: Easy. Side routes require 4WD and high clearance.

TIME & DISTANCE: 2–3 hours; 12.8 miles one-way.

MAPS: Silverton Chamber of Commerce's *Jeep Roads and Ghost Towns of the San Juans.* Uncompahgre National Forest. Trails Illustrated No. 141 (Silverton, Ouray, Telluride and Lake City). DeLorme pp. 76–77.

INFORMATION: Silverton Visitor Information Center, at U.S. 550 and Colorado 110. BLM, Gunnison Field Office. San Juan Public Lands Center. Get the BLM's booklet *Alpine Explorer Recreation Guide to the Alpine Triangle.*

GETTING THERE: From U.S. 550, the easiest access is to go east through Silverton on state Highway 110 (Greene Street, Silverton's main drag) from the intersection at the information center. Follow the signs for the Alpine Loop up the Animas River Valley.

REST STOPS: Silverton has food, fuel, lodging, a pleasant park at the east end, 4WD tours and rentals. There are toilets along the way.

THE DRIVE: Silverton, once a raucous mining and railroad town, dates back to 1871. Today, the seat of San Juan County is busy extracting the ore from tourists' wallets. It is the northern terminus of the popular steam-powered Durango and Silverton Narrow Gauge Railroad, whose locomotives fill the valley with the pungent smell of burning coal. Pavement ends less than 2 miles from town. Then you'll be on maintained dirt-and-gravel county Road 2 as you drive up a deep valley which, though scarred by more than a century of mining, remains beautiful. Two miles beyond the pavement is the site of Howardsville, the old county seat for the former La Plata Company of the 1870s. To the right is county Road 4 to Stony Pass (Tour 64). The road to Animas Forks continues past Maggie Gulch (Tour 62) and Minnie Gulch (Tour 63), and crosses the river. Then it narrows, and begins to climb up a high-walled valley. At mile 10.5 the road up Picayne (a.k.a. Picayune) Gulch (Tour 60) will be on the left. A bit beyond that is the rocky 4x4 road up Burns Gulch, on the right. It dead-ends after 2 scenic miles. Less than a mile farther roads fork to Cinnamon and Engineer passes (Tours 65 and 66), and to U.S. 550/Ouray via Engineer Mountain Road (Tour 57). From there you can see Animas Forks, at the 11,160-foot-high confluence of the river's three forks. The first prospectors wintered here in 1873, looking for gold and silver below the Continental Divide. By the summer of 1885 the population reached 450. Some estimates count more than 1,000 souls, though few braved the brutal winters. The town faded when metal prices fell in the 1920s. It was abandoned by the 1930s.

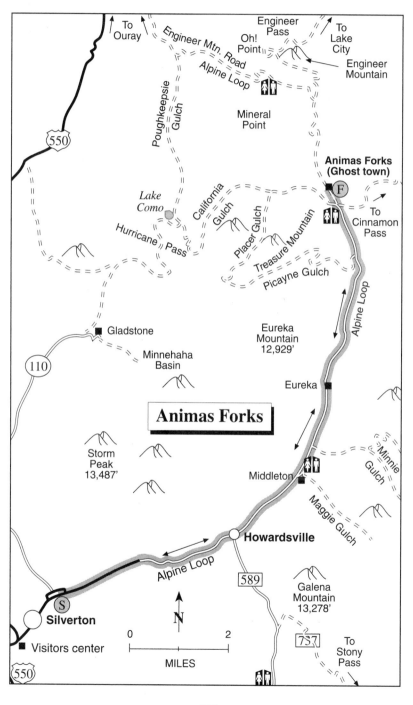

Animas Forks *(Tour 61)*

Maggie Gulch *(Tour 62)*

Maggie Gulch

LOCATION: This spur off the Alpine Loop is on the western slope of the Continental Divide in the San Juan Mountains of San Juan County, east of the historic mining town of Silverton, near Minnie Gulch (Tour 63).

HIGHLIGHTS: This is a great drive for folks who are visiting the historic mining town of Silverton and want to sample the area's outstanding backcountry routes without a major time commitment. The drive up this long, deep gulch includes stretches of shelf road, waterfalls, alpine scenery, wildflowers, an old mine site and fantastic mountain vistas.

DIFFICULTY: Easy to moderate. Driving on a shelf high above the gulch can be intimidating for inexperienced off-highway drivers.

TIME & DISTANCE: About 2 hours and 8 miles round-trip from the site of Middleton.

MAPS: Trails Illustrated No. 141 (Silverton, Ouray, Telluride, Lake City). Silverton Chamber of Commerce's *Jeep Roads and Ghost Towns of the San Juans.* Uncompahgre National Forest or San Juan National Forest. DeLorme pp. 76–77.

INFORMATION: Silverton Chamber of Commerce Visitor Information Center, at the intersection of U.S. 550 and Colorado 110. BLM's Gunnison Field Office. San Juan Public Lands Center.

GETTING THERE: Go east through Silverton, following the Alpine Loop toward Animas Forks. At the site of Middleton, about 1.8 miles past Howardsville and the road to Cunningham Gulch/Stony Pass, turn right at the public toilets. Immediately go left after the toilets, and just follow the road up.

REST STOPS: At the old mine, at the end of the drive.

THE DRIVE: In the 1890s Middleton was a small, short-lived mining camp on the main road to Animas Forks, midway between Howardsville and Eureka. The mountains here have given up not only silver and gold, but lead, zinc and copper as well. The single-lane shelf road up Maggie Gulch climbs steeply above the Animas River Valley. Soon you will see small waterfalls cascading down the walls of the gulch toward the rushing stream far below. As you continue, you will eventually see a large waterfall pouring out of a gap at the head of the canyon. The road passes close to the falls, and beyond them it climbs above timberline to a more open and verdant gulch just below the Divide. There are many old mining relics here. At the end of the road is a particularly interesting site that includes an old stamp mill and other artifacts. The ground there is strewn with rusty nails, so watch where you park and walk. The descent on the way back to the Animas River Valley provides inspiring views of the peaks and canyons to the north, so don't be put off by the fact that this is a dead-end drive. If you'd like to see more of this area, go up nearby Minnie Gulch.

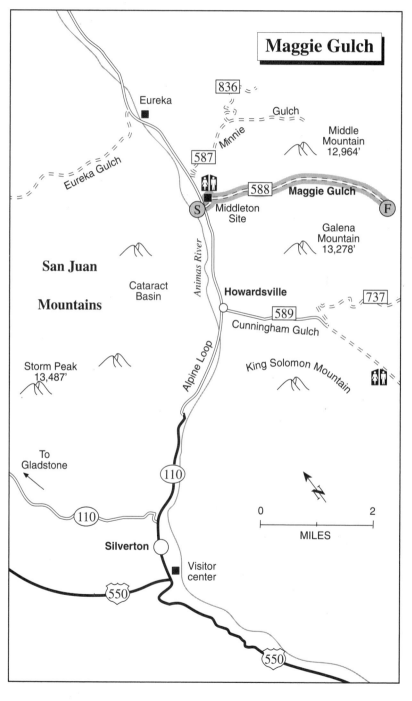

Maggie Gulch

836

Minnie Gulch

Eureka

Eureka Gulch

587

Middle
Mountain
12,964'

588

Maggie Gulch

S Middleton
Site

F

Animas River

Galena
Mountain
13,278'

San Juan

Mountains

Cataract
Basin

Howardsville

589

Cunningham Gulch

737

Storm Peak
13,487'

Alpine Loop

King Solomon Mountain

To
Gladstone

N

110

0   2

110

MILES

Silverton

Visitor
center

550

550

Minnie Gulch

LOCATION: This spur off the Alpine Loop is on the western slope of the Continental Divide, in the San Juan Mountains; San Juan County, east of the historic mining town of Silverton.

HIGHLIGHTS: Like nearby Maggie Gulch (Tour 62), this scenic drive is great for anyone who is visiting the Silverton area and wants to sample its outstanding backcountry routes without a major time commitment. The scenery is different from that in Maggie Gulch—more narrow, rocky and forested—but there also are open alpine areas and a number of impressive old buildings and other artifacts.

DIFFICULTY: Easy to moderate. There is one rough and loose wash crossing that can be a bit of a challenge.

TIME & DISTANCE: 2 hours and about 8.7 miles round-trip.

MAPS: Trails Illustrated No. 141 (Silverton, Ouray, Telluride, Lake City). Silverton Chamber of Commerce's *Jeep Roads and Ghost Towns of the San Juans.* Uncompahgre National Forest or San Juan National Forest. DeLorme pp. 76–77.

INFORMATION: Silverton Chamber of Commerce Visitor Information Center, at the intersection of U.S. 550 and Colorado 110. BLM's Gunnison Field Office. San Juan Public Lands Center.

GETTING THERE: Go east through Silverton, following the Alpine Loop (Highway 110) toward Animas Forks. Turn right about 2.4 miles beyond Howardsville and the turnoff to Cunningham Gulch/Stony Pass (or 0.6 mile beyond the turnoff at Middleton to Maggie Gulch).

REST STOPS: There are public toilets at Middleton.

THE DRIVE: The narrow old road climbs through forest of aspen and pine, providing glimpses of the long, history-rich valley of the Animas River, where mines produced gold, silver, lead, copper and zinc. Soon you will pass a rickety three-story frame building and a collapsed log cabin, which are privately owned. At mile 1.5 another road branches off to the left, or north. This narrow track goes about 1.6 miles to the remains of the Caledonia and Kitti Mack mines, providing more spectacular vistas and passing more structures, including the A-frames of an old aerial tram. (You might encounter a late-summer snowbank near the end, where the turnaround can be difficult. So it might be best to walk to the end.) From the Y, the main road continues past a pair of old roadside cabins (privately owned; don't take anything) that cling to the mountainsides above a rushing stream. Less than a mile from the Y a neat waterfall will be on the left. Runoff has created quite a gully to cross here. Don't take it too slow, or you might have difficulty getting to the opposite side. When you emerge from the trees the gulch widens, and soon you will be in a more open, more alpine setting. The road will take you along a talus slope, and ends about 1.6 miles beyond the Y, amid treeless tundra at about 11,200 feet, just below the Continental Divide.

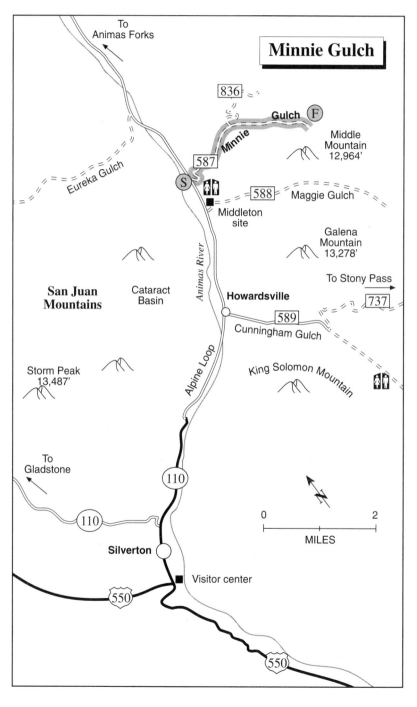

Minnie Gulch

To Animas Forks

836

Gulch (F)

Middle Mountain 12,964'

Minnie

587

(S)

588   Maggie Gulch

Middleton site

Galena Mountain 13,278'

Animas River

To Stony Pass

737

San Juan Mountains

Cataract Basin

Howardsville

589

Cunningham Gulch

Storm Peak 13,487'

Alpine Loop

King Solomon Mountain

To Gladstone

110

0   2

110

MILES

Silverton

Visitor center

550

550

Stony Pass Road

LOCATION: On the Continental Divide east of Silverton. San Juan and Hinsdale counties. Rio Grande National Forest.

HIGHLIGHTS: The scenery is nothing short of spectacular along this old wagon road over Stony Pass (12,588 feet), at the edge of Weminuche Wilderness. It fell into disuse after 1882, when the Denver and Rio Grande Railroad linked Durango and Silverton. On the east side, it traverses drainages that form the headwaters of the Rio Grande River, which you can ford on the Beartown Road. You'll see many old mining relics. Wildflowers abound early- to mid-summer.

DIFFICULTY: Stony Pass Road is moderate. The Forest Service rates rocky Beartown Road to Kite Lake moderate to more difficult. The pass is generally not free of snow until mid- to late-summer. Beartown Road is generally free of snow 1 to 3 weeks earlier. Pole Creek, about a half-mile above the Beartown Road turnoff, and the upper Rio Grande River can be deep or impassable early in the season. Snow can close the roads by late September to mid-October.

TIME & DISTANCE: Silverton to Highway 149 is 3.5 hours and 42 miles. Beartown Road (506) adds almost 12 miles and 2.5–3 hours.

MAPS: *Jeep Trails of the San Juans.* Trails Illustrated No. 140 (Weminuche Wilderness) and No. 141 (Silverton, Ouray, Telluride, Lake City). Rio Grande and San Juan national forests. DeLorme p. 77.

INFORMATION: Rio Grande National Forest, Divide Ranger District's Creede Office. Silverton Visitor Information Center. Get the USFS' flyers for Stony Pass Road and Beartown Road. San Juan Public Lands Center.

GETTING THERE: From Silverton, follow the Alpine Loop toward Animas Forks. In 4 miles, at Howardsville, turn right (south) onto county Road 4/forest Road 589. Drive about 1.7 miles up Cunningham Gulch. At a Y, veer left onto county Road 3, Stony Pass Road/forest Road 737. Or take state Highway 149 south from Lake City for about 29.6 miles, or southwest from Creede for 20.1 miles. Turn west onto Road 520 to Rio Grande Reservoir/Recreation Area.

REST STOPS: There are toilets in Cunningham Gulch, near the west end of the Stony Pass road. Primitive campsites and picnic sites are plentiful. There are developed campgrounds on the east side.

THE DRIVE: From Silverton, on the west side, the drive up Cunningham Gulch is scenic and easy. It's only 4 more miles to the pass via Road 737, but it's a steep climb on a single-lane shelf in a dramatic, narrow canyon. From Highway 149 on the east side, a very good road climbs up a picturesque valley past Rio Grande Reservoir. Then it becomes rocky and rough. It's about 32.5 miles to the pass; much of it through forest of aspen, spruce, fir, streamside willows, and gorgeous valleys and meadows, or "parks." There is a surprising amount of water (streams and pools) to ford as well. The road is rocky, with substantial potholes in places, but the high-elevation scenery is worth every bump. Rocky and slow Beartown Road, noted for wildflowers, branches south about 10 miles from the reservoir, or about 6.8 miles below the pass on the east side. It follows Bear Creek past the site of Beartown, an 1890s mining camp, then climbs steeply to end in 5.9 miles at sterile Kite Lake.

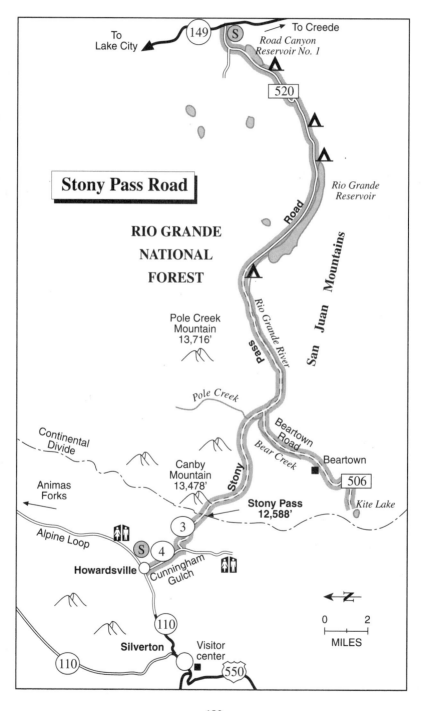

Stony Pass Road

Cinnamon Pass

LOCATION: San Juan and Hinsdale counties. San Juan Mountains southeast of Ouray, northeast of Silverton.

HIGHLIGHTS: Part of the Alpine Loop National Back Country Byway, this magnificent tour includes the ghost towns of Animas Forks, Argentum and Carson; 12,640-foot Cinnamon Pass; the glaciated western slope of the Continental Divide and lots of wildflowers.

DIFFICULTY: Easy; side trips are moderate. The leg between Animas Forks and the pass is rocky, but most of the descent from the pass to state Highway 149 is tamer. The forest road to Carson is slippery when wet. The drive up Cottonwood Creek is fairly rocky. The pass is usually open by June.

TIME & DISTANCE: 3 hours; 25 miles from Highway 149 south of Lake City to Animas Forks. Silverton adds 12 miles. Carson adds 7.3 miles round-trip. Cottonwood Creek adds 9.1 miles round-trip.

MAPS: Silverton Chamber of Commerce's *Jeep Roads and Ghost Towns of the San Juans.* Uncompahgre National Forest. Trails Illustrated No. 141 (Silverton, Ouray, Telluride, Lake City.). DeLorme p. 77.

INFORMATION: Silverton Information Center, at U.S. 550 and Highway 110. BLM's Gunnison Field Office. San Juan Public Lands Center. Get the BLM's *Alpine Explorer Recreation Guide to the Alpine Triangle.*

GETTING THERE: From the west: Start at the ghost town of Animas Forks (Tour 61). At the fork in the road just before Animas Forks, where there's a toilet, angle right, following the signs for Engineer and Cinnamon passes. After another fork, take a hard right at a small waterfall. **To start on Highway 149:** About 1.7 miles south of Lake City, turn toward Lake San Cristobal Recreation Area.

REST STOPS: There are toilets and campgrounds on the way. You also can stop at Lake San Cristobal and Red Mountain Gulch Picnic Area, at the east end. Lake City and Silverton have all services.

THE DRIVE: From Animas Forks, the road is a narrow, twisting, rocky shelf above timberline, in a landscape of fragile alpine tundra and glacial basins. About 3 miles from Animas Forks, you will see the pass. There, the sweeping view of snowy peaks and rocky basins takes in seven of the San Juans' thirteen 14,000-foot peaks. From there, the single-lane road is tame, though the scenery is not, as you follow the Lake Fork of the Gunnison River down a long gulch. About 2 miles from the pass, you're back in the piney forest. On the south side of the road is the short, beautiful spur to American Basin, noted for its wildflowers. Three miles farther, in Burrows Park, is the site of Argentum, where two 19th-century buildings recall bygone times along this road, which was completed in 1877. From here it's a meandering cruise. About 4 miles from Argentum, or 12 miles from Highway 149, near the old Sherman town site, take the small rocky road that angles west along Cottonwood Creek. It will take you past cliffs, a gorge, beaver ponds and wetlands. On the main road, between Mill Creek and Williams

Creek Campgrounds, watch on the south side of the road for the moderate spur up Wager Gulch to the late-1800s ghost town of Carson, just below the Continental Divide. Continuing to Lake City, the road descends through narrows and passes Lake San Cristobal, dammed by the massive Slumgullion Slide earth flow.

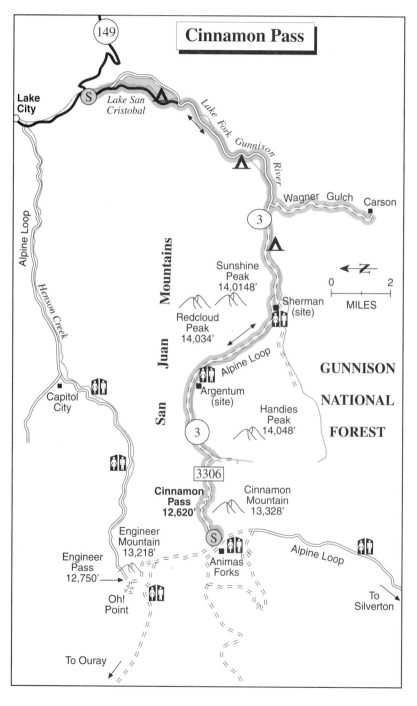

Cinnamon Pass

149

Lake City

Lake San Cristobal

Lake Fork Gunnison River

Wagner Gulch   Carson

3

Alpine Loop

Henson Creek

San   Juan   Mountains

Sunshine Peak
14,0148'

Redcloud Peak
14,034'

Sherman (site)

N
0   2
MILES

Capitol City

Argentum (site)

Alpine Loop

Handies Peak
14,048'

3

GUNNISON

NATIONAL

FOREST

3306

Cinnamon Pass
12,620'

Cinnamon Mountain
13,328'

Engineer Mountain
13,218'

Engineer Pass
12,750' →

Animas Forks

Alpine Loop

To Silverton

Oh! Point

To Ouray

Engineer Pass to Lake City

LOCATION: A leg of the famous Alpine Loop between Lake City and Ouray/Silverton. San Juan, Ouray and Hinsdale counties.

HIGHLIGHTS: Ghost town of Animas Forks; 12,800-foot Engineer Pass, from which you can see seven of the 13 San Juan peaks that reach 14,000 feet; wildflowers; fall colors; vast alpine landscape.

DIFFICULTY: Easy on the east side; moderate on the west side from Animas Forks to the pass. This is a busy route. Use the turnouts, and remember that uphill traffic has the right of way. The road is usually open by mid-June.

TIME & DISTANCE: 3 hours; 24 miles between Animas Forks and Lake City. To or from Silverton or Ouray is additional.

MAPS: Silverton Chamber of Commerce's *Jeep Roads and Ghost Towns of the San Juans*. Uncompahgre National Forest. Trails Illustrated No. 141 (Silverton, Ouray, etc.). DeLorme pp. 67, 76–77.

INFORMATION: Silverton Information Center at U.S. 550 and Highway 110. BLM's Gunnison Field Office. San Juan Public Lands Center. Get the BLM's *Alpine Explorer Recreation Guide to the Alpine Triangle*.

GETTING THERE: Take state Highway 149 to Lake City; turn west at the sign for Engineer Pass. **From Ouray,** take rough Engineer Mountain (a.k.a. Engineer Pass) Road (Tour 57) to Animas Forks. **From Silverton,** follow Tour 61 to Animas Forks.

REST STOPS: There are numerous places of interest, particularly spectacular Oh! Point. There are toilets at Animas Forks and elsewhere along the way. Roadside camping is allowed on public lands, except between Lake City and Capitol City with the exception of the meadow at Nellie Creek.

THE DRIVE: It seems unlikely that a rich vein of tourists was what toll-road and railway builder Otto Mears had in mind when he built this wagon road from Lake City along Henson Creek to Animas Forks in 1877. But rich it is. From Animas Forks, the narrow, rocky and steep road once used by miners and stagecoaches climbs the east wall of a basin. The road requires your full attention, so stop when you want to take in the dramatic views down the Animas Valley to the south and, to the west, the chiseled peaks of the Lizard Head and Mt. Sneffels wildernesses. In 4.6 miles detour to Oh! Point for a head-spinning view of the San Juans from about 12,900 feet. From there the road angles east around the north side of Engineer Mountain, reaching the pass less than a mile farther. The road improves, and makes a long descent. Visit the old cabin at Palmetto Gulch, then continue past Thoreau's Cabin, part of Colorado's Hut-to-Hut system. At mile 8.5 you will see the 4x4 track up Hurricane Gulch. Less than a mile farther is the site of Corydon Rose's cabin. Built in 1875, it was a stagecoach stop, bar, restaurant, post office and social hub. From here the improved road descends more gradually, passing the smokestack of Lee's Smelter, and then Whitmore Falls (hike down to see them). At the wooded bottom of the canyon the road passes through the site of Capitol City, founded in

1877 with the hope that it would become the state's political hub. (The side road up North Fork Henson Creek dead-ends in 4.3 miles, and isn't particularly scenic.) Soon the main road passes through dramatic narrows, and arrives at Lake City.

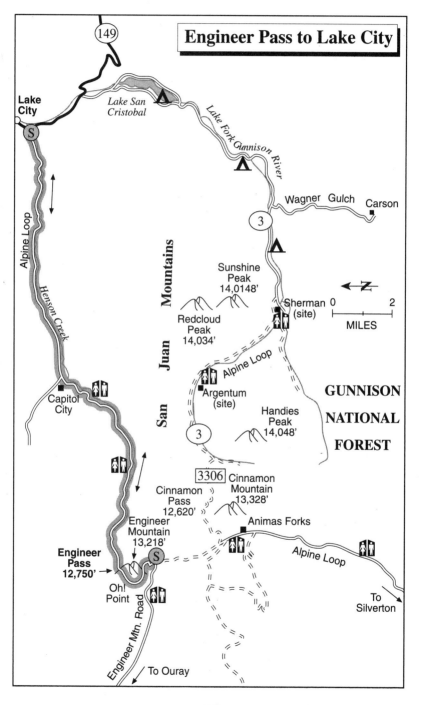

Engineer Pass to Lake City

Lake City

Lake San Cristobal

Lake Fork Gunnison River

Wagner Gulch — Carson

San Juan Mountains

Alpine Loop

Henson Creek

Sunshine Peak 14,0148'

Redcloud Peak 14,034'

Sherman (site)

0 — 2 MILES

Alpine Loop

Argentum (site)

Handies Peak 14,048'

GUNNISON

NATIONAL

FOREST

Capitol City

3306 Cinnamon Mountain 13,328'

Cinnamon Pass 12,620'

Engineer Mountain 13,218'

Animas Forks

Alpine Loop

Engineer Pass 12,750'

Oh! Point

Engineer Mtn. Road

To Silverton

To Ouray

Hermit Pass

LOCATION: Sangre de Cristo (Spanish for Blood of Christ) Range, west of Westcliffe. Custer County. San Isabel National Forest.

HIGHLIGHTS: You'll enjoy fantastic glaciated mountain scenery along a road that climbs to almost 12,800 feet, in mountains named for the way they seemed to reflect the blood-red light of the setting sun. The vistas extend east across the Wet Mountain Valley and the Wet Mountains to the Great Plains, and west across the San Luis Valley to the San Juan Mountains.

DIFFICULTY: Easy to moderate. Last 5.7 miles to the top are very rocky, but not difficult. There is one spot near the top that can be blocked by a snowbank well into July, but the road can be open by mid-June.

TIME & DISTANCE: 2 hours; 29.4 miles round-trip from state Highway 69.

MAPS: San Isabel National Forest. DeLorme p. 71.

INFORMATION: Pike and San Isabel national forests, San Carlos Ranger District.

GETTING THERE: From the south side of Westcliffe, turn west off Highway 69 onto Hermit Road (county Road 160) toward Hermit Lake. Drive west across the Wet Mountain Valley directly toward the Sangre de Cristo Range. In 2.8 miles, where the paved road bends south, continue straight, on the unpaved road. After 3.3 more miles keep left at the Y, continuing toward Hermit Lake.

REST STOPS: There is a campground at the base of the mountains, in the Middle Taylor Creek State Wildlife Area. You will also see many spots for primitive camping.

THE DRIVE: When one looks at the high ranges of Colorado, it's often hard to believe there are driveable roads in them. So it is as you drive across the pretty Wet Mountain Valley toward the vaulting ramparts of the Sangre de Cristo Range. This rocky road, No. 301, climbs through conifer forest along Middle Taylor Creek past its source at Hermit Lake (you will have to hike in), eventually exceeding timberline to reveal glacier-scoured canyons and peaks. About 10.7 miles from where the pavement ends, high among tundra basins and rocky cliffs, lies spangled and aptly named Horseshoe Lake. From there the road climbs along a narrow, eye-popping divide between two deep canyons toward a gap between Rito Alto Peak (13,794 feet) to the north and Hermit Peak (13,350 feet) to the south. Here you'll be greeted with more magnificent views of glaciers' handiwork. From there, the narrow road angles left (south), and climbs 0.6 mile up the flanks of Hermit Peak to a wide knoll at the boundary of San Juan and Rio Grande national forests. It is along this final leg that you might encounter a snowbank in the road. If you do, it's a short hike up. Just remember that the air is much thinner up here than down in the valley.

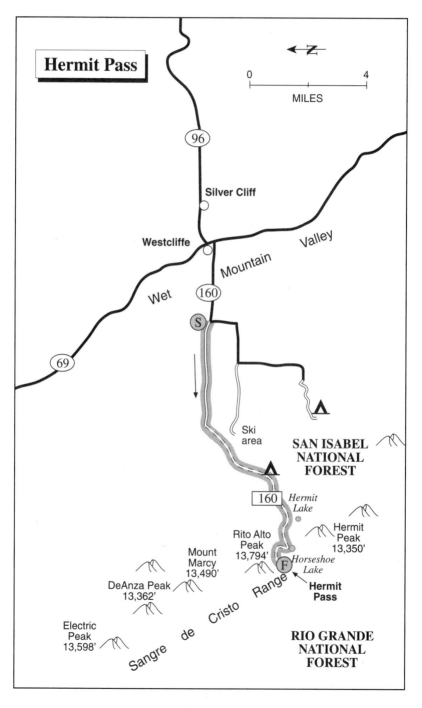

Hermit Pass

0 ———————————— 4
MILES

N ←

96

Silver Cliff ○

Westcliffe ○

Mountain   Valley

Wet

160

69

S

↓

Ski
area

▲

**SAN ISABEL
NATIONAL
FOREST**

160   *Hermit
Lake*

Hermit
Peak
13,350'

Rito Alto
Peak
13,794'

Mount
Marcy
13,490'

*Horseshoe
Lake*

F

**Hermit
Pass**

DeAnza Peak
13,362'

Sangre   de   Cristo   Range

Electric
Peak
13,598'

**RIO GRANDE
NATIONAL
FOREST**

Cinnamon Pass *(Tour 65)*

Great Sand Dunes National Monument and Preserve *(Tour 68)*

Medano Pass Road

LOCATION: Sangre de Cristo (Spanish for Blood of Christ) Range between Wet Mountain Valley and Great Sand Dunes National Monument and Preserve. San Isabel and Rio Grande national forests. Huerfano and Saguache counties.

HIGHLIGHTS: From grassy meadows and piñon-juniper woodlands to ponderosa pines, aspens, the highest sand dunes in North America and multiple stream crossings, few routes can beat this one for variety. Zebulon Pike crossed into Spanish Territory via the Indian trail over 10,040-foot Medano Pass in 1807, while exploring Louisiana Territory. The range's name derives from the way the mountains seemed to reflect the blood-red light of the setting sun.

DIFFICULTY: Easy on the east side, with a rocky spot or two. Moderate on the steeper west side, with numerous stream fordings that can be deep and hazardous early in the season. There are some substantial mudholes, rocky and narrow stretches, and soft wind-blown sand (it might be advisable to lower your tire pressure to 15–20 psi for better traction). You can air up again at the RV dump station at the end/beginning of the road in the monument. The road is usually open by mid-June.

TIME & DISTANCE: 2 hours; 20 miles.

MAPS: San Isabel National Forest. DeLorme p. 81.

INFORMATION: Pike and San Isabel national forests, San Carlos Ranger District; Great Sand Dunes National Monument and Preserve; Rio Grande National Forest, Conejos Peak Ranger District. Note: In the national monument, all vehicles must remain on designated roads (a good rule anywhere, actually). ATVs and trail motorcycles are not allowed in the monument.

GETTING THERE: From state Highway 69: Turn west onto County/forest Road 559 about 23.6 miles south of Westcliffe. Follow it to the pass. **From Great Sand Dunes:** Take the main road about 1.5 miles beyond the entrance station toward Pinyon Flats Campground. At the RV dump station before Pinyon Flats, turn left (west) at the sign for Medano Pass Primitive Road (forest Road 235).

REST STOPS: You'll see three primitive (no water or toilets) picnic areas along the road in the monument. There is year-round camping at the monument's Pinyon Flats Campground. There also are many primitive campsites in the national forests.

THE DRIVE: If you start on the east side, the graded road will take you through scenic grass and sagebrush rangeland, much of it privately owned, into hills forested with piñon pines and junipers. The road becomes single-lane dirt in 6.8 miles, but rock in the roadbed helps to keep it passable when wet. Then it climbs steadily to the pass, which isn't a dramatic crossing. The adventure is on the west side. There, the narrow road is fairly steep, and in places it gets chewed up by the spinning wheels of climbing vehicles. It crosses Medano Creek a number of times. You may encounter substantial holes, and it won't be long before you begin to notice sand in the road. Then you'll see the great dunes themselves, 39 square miles of them rising to nearly 700 feet. The Rio Grande River changed course over thousands of years, leaving deposits of sand that wind continues to carry across the San Luis Valley. As the wind rises over the Sangre de Cristo Range, heavier grains are left behind. Medano Creek carries them back to the valley, where wind picks them up again and carries them to the dunes.

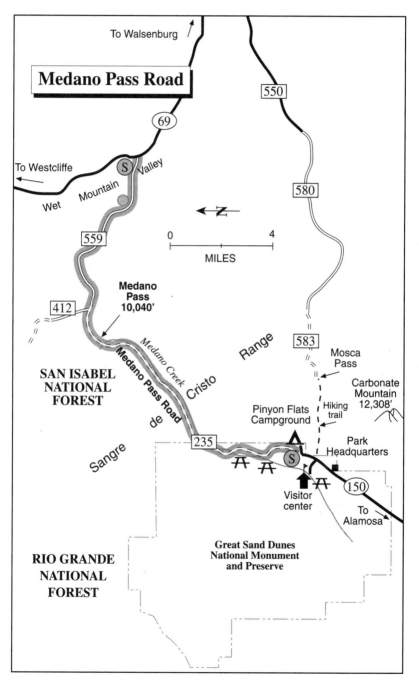

Bachelor Historic Loop

LOCATION: North of Creede, on Colorado Highway 149; Rio Grande National Forest. Mineral County.

HIGHLIGHTS: This scenic and history-filled loop climbs to more than 11,000 feet as it circles through a spectacular canyon in a once-raucous mining district. Bob Ford, the killer of outlaw Jesse James, is buried in the local cemetery. (He was murdered here in 1892.) Visit the Creede Underground Mining Museum, early on the drive. The Nelson Mountain spur leads to a gorgeous sub-alpine "park," or large mountain grassland. This is a great tour of Colorado mining history.

DIFFICULTY: Easy, on a well-maintained dirt and gravel road that is steep and narrow in places. Narrow East Willow Creek Road is easy, but it makes a 1,000-foot climb out of (or down into, depending on your direction) a deep, high-walled canyon. Nelson Mountain Road is generally not passable until late June. It is steep and rocky at first, and boggy higher up. I rate it moderate.

TIME & DISTANCE: 17 miles; 2 hours. Nelson Mountain adds an hour and 4–5 miles. East Willow Creek Road is 5.3 miles and 45 minutes.

MAPS: Get the *Bachelor Historic Tour* brochure. The Creede Forest Service office has flyers about this and other routes. DeLorme p. 78.

INFORMATION: Rio Grande National Forest's Creede Office, 3rd and Creede Avenue; Chamber of Commerce, north of the courthouse.

GETTING THERE: From downtown Creede, just drive north toward the obvious gash in the mountains.

REST STOPS: There are picnic tables in Willow Creek Canyon, and many points of interest along the way. Creede has all services.

THE DRIVE: In 1890 Nicholas C. Creede discovered silver along East Willow Creek, and launched his "Holy Moses" mine. Thus was born the wild boom town that bears his name. The original town site was at the confluence of West and East Willow Creeks, between the dramatic walls of Willow Creek Canyon. Follow the tour north up this magnificent cleft. At the confluence (tour stop #1), East Willow Creek Road branches right. I recommend that you return to it after completing the main tour. Continuing on the serpentine road, you will pass numerous mine and mill sites, some perched precariously on the cliffs above. Stop #8 is the turnoff to Nelson Mountain Road (787). (Deerhorn Park Road is closed). Road 787 climbs about 2 miles to a gorgeous "park," a large mountain meadow. Although the track crosses the delicate meadows, I suggest stopping when you reach the park. The scenery here, below 12,033-foot Nelson Mountain and the Continental Divide, takes in the magnificent La Garita Mountains to the east. Continuing the tour, be sure to drive up the scenic gulch to Equity Mine, and note the huge beaver ponds along the way. (Beyond the mine, late-summer four-wheelers make the potentially difficult and muddy trek up West Willow Creek to the Divide via roads 503 and 505). Here the tour bends south via Road 504. There are great views of the San Juans to the south as you approach the site of Bachelor, 10,500 feet high. The so-called "town in the clouds," named for the initial absence of women, boasted 1,200 residents in the 1890s. Near the end, visit the cemetery where Bob Ford's bones lie.

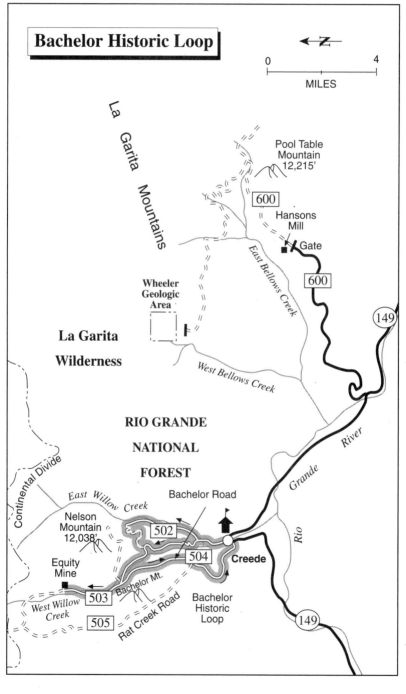

Bachelor Historic Loop

0   4

MILES

La Garita Mountains

Pool Table Mountain 12,215'

600

Hansons Mill

Gate

East Bellows Creek

600

149

Wheeler Geologic Area

La Garita Wilderness

West Bellows Creek

RIO GRANDE

NATIONAL

FOREST

Rio Grande River

Bachelor Road

East Willow Creek

Nelson Mountain 12,038'

502

504

Creede

Rio Grande

Equity Mine

503

Bachelor Mt.

West Willow Creek

505

Rat Creek Road

Bachelor Historic Loop

149

Continental Divide

Wheeler Geologic Area Road

LOCATION: East of Creede, north of Highway 149 at Wagon Wheel Gap. Rio Grande National Forest. Mineral County.

HIGHLIGHTS: This remote 640-acre area includes 60 acres of pinnacles, domes and spires of volcanic ash deposited 26.5 million to 29 million years ago, as well as sub-alpine scenery. It used to be a national monument, but visitors were deterred by the difficult access and it was turned over to the Forest Service in 1950.

DIFFICULTY: Easy for 10 miles on Pool Table Road. The Forest Service gives a "more difficult" rating to the next 13.7 miles of rough and slow 4WD Wheeler Geologic Area Road, which can be impassable when wet. It's closed during the muddy spring season, generally May through early June. It's usually open between mid-June or early July through October. Near the end it is narrow, muddy and rutted as it twists between trees. The going is particularly difficult for large vehicles. Mechanized travel is prohibited in the geologic area, so you must hike the last 0.6 mile to the formations.

TIME & DISTANCE: About 10 hours; 47.4 miles round-trip.

MAPS: Rio Grande National Forest. ACSC's *Indian Country*. Trails Illustrated Nos. 139 (La Garita, etc.) and 142 (South San Juan/Del Norte). DeLorme pp. 78–79.

INFORMATION: Rio Grande National Forest's Creede Office. Get the USFS' informative flyer about the drive and the area.

GETTING THERE: Take Highway 149 to Wagon Wheel Gap, about 7.5 miles south of Creede. Turn northeast on Pool Table Road, No. 600. Drive about 10 miles to the end of the 2WD road, at the site of Hanson's Mill (where there used to be a sawmill). Wheeler Geologic Area Road continues for almost 14 miles.

REST STOPS: The only camping facility at the geologic area is a shelter built about 1915. There is no water at the formations. The Forest Service recommends camping about a quarter-mile downhill from them, where there's a spring and deadfall for firewood. You'll find primitive camp sites and a pit toilet at the Hanson's Mill site.

THE DRIVE: Millions of years ago massive amounts of volcanic ash spewed from vents in the Earth's crust and settled on the land. Over time, wind and water sculpted the ash into the shapes we see today. They've given the area a number of nicknames: To the Ute Indians they were The Sand Stones, and tribal renegades are said to have hidden out there. Other monikers have included City of Gnomes, Dante's Lost Souls and Phantom Ships. From Hanson's Mill, Road 600 climbs northeast through spruce-fir forest to a signed junction in 0.4 mile. (The left fork is a dead-end.) Continue straight. The road climbs gently, angles east, then bends hard to the northwest and crosses East Bellows Creek. It traverses relatively level ground for 2.6 miles, except where it crosses Trujillo Creek and the Cañon Fernandez drainage. It becomes a legal corridor through the La Garita Wilderness (where mechanized travel is otherwise prohibited) as it descends to the Cañon Nieve drainage. It begins to wind and twist about 0.75 mile from the end, eventually forcing you to use existing muddy tracks to squeeze between the trees. The road then crosses a small park, and ends at a fence. Hike from there.

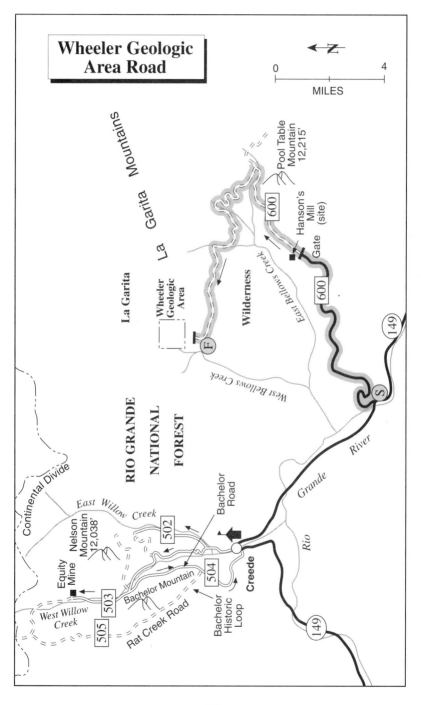

Wheeler Geologic Area Road

0   4

MILES

La Garita Mountains

Pool Table Mountain 12,215'

600

Hanson's Mill (site)

Gate

La Garita

600

149

Wheeler Geologic Area

Wilderness

East Bellows Creek

F

S

West Bellows Creek

Rio Grande River

RIO GRANDE NATIONAL FOREST

Continental Divide

East Willow Creek

Bachelor Road

502

Nelson Mountain 12,038'

Equity Mine

503

504

Creede

West Willow Creek

505

Bachelor Mountain

Bachelor Historic Loop

Rat Creek Road

Rio Grande

149

Vista Variety Tour

LOCATION: Northwest of Del Norte; Rio Grande and Saguache counties. Rio Grande National Forest.

HIGHLIGHTS: In this single drive, you can experience views that include high-desert grasslands, distant mesas, canyons, valleys, streams, mountain "parks," and dense aspen and spruce forests.

DIFFICULTY: Easy.

TIME & DISTANCE: 3 hours; 58.6 miles round-trip (this is a dead-end road).

MAPS: Rio Grande National Forest. ACSC's *Indian Country*. DeLorme p. 79.

INFORMATION: Rio Grande National Forest's Divide Ranger District, Del Norte Office.

GETTING THERE: 9 miles west of the traffic light in Del Norte, turn north off U.S. 160 onto Rio Grande County Road 18. Cross the Rio Grande River, then turn right (east) at the T intersection, onto county Road 15. At the Y go left (north) on Embargo Creek Road (forest Road 650). Stay on Road 650 all the way.

REST STOPS: Stop anywhere that appeals to you. Cathedral Campground is to the west, on Road 640.

THE DRIVE: The Forest Service map doesn't hint at the inspiring beauty and variety of ecosystems this drive offers. Heading north from the Rio Grande River, the road courses through a wide valley of rolling hills, meadows, piñon-juniper woodlands and cottonwoods. Almost 7 miles from the highway it enters Rio Grande National Forest. Soon the hills begin to close in around you, and tall pines begin to appear. As you gradually climb, outstanding views across rolling hills of grass and sagebrush spread out to the south. By mile 12 you're leaving high desert behind. Ahead, the road takes you into aspen and pine forest. By about mile 19.5 you will be at Groundhog Park, one of those large, open and grassy areas that are common high in the Rockies. You will also notice that this area has been logged. The road will take you around the periphery of the park, possibly becoming muddy and rougher. By this point you've climbed from about 8,150 feet elevation at the highway to about 11,000 feet. The road dead-ends about 6 miles beyond Groundhog Park, but the park could be the end of your tour because the scenery becomes primarily dense forest.

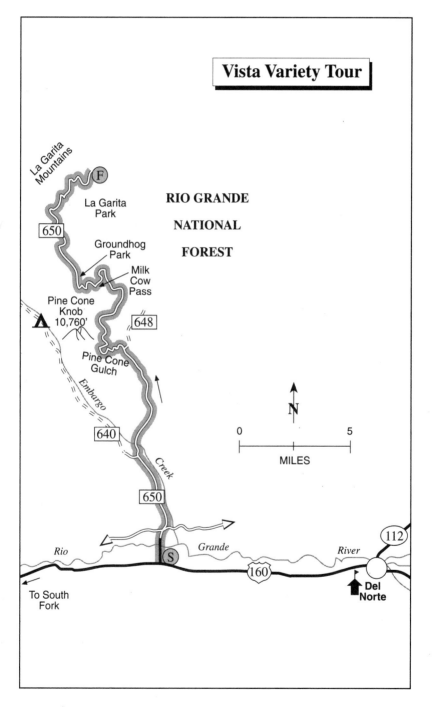

Vista Variety Tour

La Garita Mountains

F

La Garita Park

RIO GRANDE

NATIONAL

FOREST

650

Groundhog Park

Milk Cow Pass

648

Pine Cone Knob 10,760'

Pine Cone Gulch

Embargo

640

Creek

650

N

0   5

MILES

Rio   Grande   River   112

S

160

Del Norte

To South Fork

English Valley-Natural Arch

LOCATION: Rio Grande and Saguache counties, north of Del Norte; Rio Grande National Forest.

HIGHLIGHTS: This area is home to an array of wildlife that could include pronghorn (a.k.a. antelope), bighorn sheep, mule deer, golden eagles and prairie falcons. Bring your binoculars! A spur will take you to a large natural arch, and there are many spectacular cliffs and buttes, with contrasting views of the San Juans to the south. The eroded labyrinths of Elephant Rocks are worth a visit as well.

DIFFICULTY: Easy. Can be muddy after rains.

TIME & DISTANCE: 2–3 hours; about 25 miles.

MAPS: Rio Grande National Forest. ACSC's *Indian Country*. DeLorme p. 79.

INFORMATION: Rio Grande National Forest's Divide Ranger District, Del Norte Office.

GETTING THERE: In Del Norte, on U.S. 160, turn north at the only traffic light in town onto county Road 112. In a half-mile go left onto county Road 15, toward the airport. The road will bend left. At mile 0.6 past the auto salvage yard, turn right onto a small 4WD road, English Valley Road (661). There probably won't be a sign. Just don't go past that beguiling rock formation, Indian Head, north of the county road.

REST STOPS: The arch is neat, and jumbled Elephant Rocks, on the way back to Del Norte, are intriguing. The BLM has a 10-site campground at Penitente Canyon, west of La Garita. (The canyon is popular among rock climbers.) There is a pleasant park in Del Norte.

THE DRIVE: Early to mid-morning and evening are always best for wildlife viewing. But even if you can't time it just right, this is a beautiful, sculpted high-desert landscape that presents stark contrast to the soaring Rocky Mountain peaks in the distance. English Valley Road is a fun little track that will bounce you toward impressive reddish-brown volcanic cliffs and buttes. At mile 2, go straight at the Y. Keep left at the Y at mile 3.2, at the base of a tilted butte. At mile 6.4 you'll reach Road 660, a good hard-packed dirt road. Ahead, Eagle Mountain rises to 10,462 ft. Go right (east) through volcanic hills dotted by piñon pines and junipers. At mile 7.7 is a view of spectacular red-rock cliffs and hills, and beyond them, across the broad San Luis Valley, the distant crest of the Sangre de Cristo Range. To the south rise the San Juans. On the left at mile 8.7 is Road 659. Take it 1.6 scenic miles to a high volcanic "dike," a wall of more erosion-resistant rock left behind after softer rock eroded away. You will see a large cavity that has eroded through the rock. Along the way are massive Eagle Rock and high cliffs. Continue east on Road 660 from the arch turnoff until you reach Road 38A, in four miles. Go right (south). You will eventually see Elephant Rocks off to the right (west). About 30 million years ago volcanic activity deposited a layer of ash about 50 feet thick, and over time erosion created this labyrinth of grottos and canyons. Continue south on Road 33 to Road 112 and Del Norte.

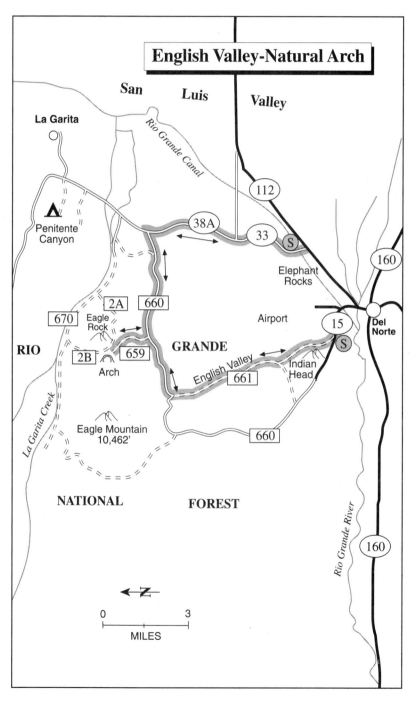

English Valley-Natural Arch

San Luis Valley

La Garita

Rio Grande Canal

112

38A

33

S

Penitente Canyon

Elephant Rocks

160

2A 660

670

Eagle Rock

Airport

15

S

Del Norte

2B 659

GRANDE

Arch

English Valley 661

Indian Head

Eagle Mountain 10,462'

660

RIO

La Garita Creek

NATIONAL FOREST

Rio Grande River

160

N

0 3

MILES

Bolam Pass

LOCATION: Between the Purgatory Ski Area on U.S. 550 (San Juan County) and Cayton Campground on Colorado Highway 145 (Dolores County). San Juan National Forest.

HIGHLIGHTS: You'll have fantastic views of Lizard Head and the San Miguel Mountains from Bolam Pass, 11,180 feet high along an historic toll road. The long, grassy valley of Hermosa Park, with its abundant wildflowers, is very pretty. The old Graysill vanadium and uranium mine is interesting.

DIFFICULTY: Moderate. There are some rocky stretches. You might encounter snow in the road well into summer, but it may be clear by mid-July.

TIME & DISTANCE: 3 hours; 23 miles.

MAPS: San Juan National Forest. DeLorme p. 76.

INFORMATION: San Juan National Forest, Mancos-Dolores and Columbine West ranger districts. Dolores Public Lands Office. You can get information, maps, etc. at the old Forest Service guard station on Highway 145 north of Rico.

GETTING THERE: From the west, 6 miles north of Rico at Cayton Campground on Highway 145, take forest Road 578 south. **From the east,** just north of Purgatory Ski Area, turn west at the sign for Hermosa Park Road (578). Following the paved road, go right at about mile 0.4. Then take the dirt road straight ahead where the paved road bends left. Soon you will see signs for Hermosa Park Road, Sig Creek Campground and Bolam Pass. Follow Road 578.

REST STOPS: Cayton and Sig Creek campgrounds, as well as many primitive campsites.

THE DRIVE: On the eastern slope, the easy two-lane dirt road climbs rapidly, eventually paralleling the East Fork of Hermosa Creek through lovely Hermosa Park. This was once a leg of the old Scotch Creek Toll Road, a difficult passage that served the Rico mining area in the 1880s. But now it's a recreational journey through the picturesque meadows, draws, narrows and aspen stands of Hermosa Park. About 10.5 miles from the highway you'll cross a rocky streambed, and the road will become rockier. When you reach Road 550, you could go up Hotel Draw and connect with the Scotch Creek-Roaring Forks drive (Tour 74). But then you'd miss Bolam Pass. About 4 miles farther the road becomes a rocky shelf of red earth as it climbs to Graysill Mine. From 1945 until 1963 miners dug for vanadium, used to harden steel, and uranium. At its peak 3,000 tons of ore a year were shipped to a mill in Durango. Some of the Durango "yellow cake" (uranium) was used in the first atomic bomb. In addition to the usual harsh living conditions that went with mining in the San Juans, the men were exposed to radon gas. Only 20 endured the winters and the gas year-round. Next on the tour comes the pass, a rocky place with a great view of neighboring mountains. From there it's 7 miles down a draw to Highway 145.

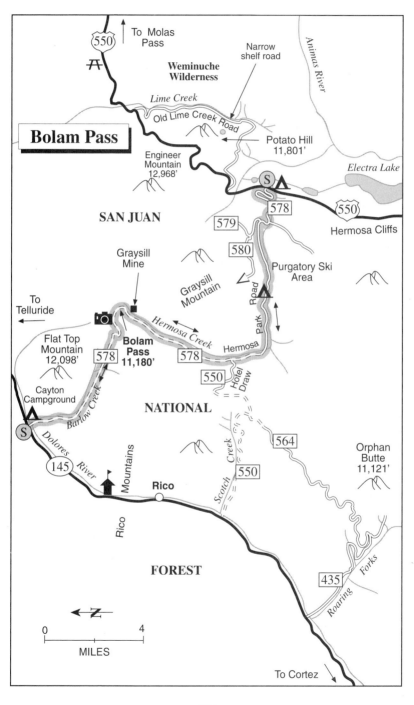

Bolam Pass

To Molas Pass

Weminuche Wilderness

Narrow shelf road

Animas River

Lime Creek

Old Lime Creek Road

Potato Hill 11,801'

Electra Lake

Engineer Mountain 12,968'

SAN JUAN

578

579

580

550

Hermosa Cliffs

Graysill Mine

Graysill Mountain

Purgatory Ski Area

To Telluride

Hermosa Creek

Park Road

Flat Top Mountain 12,098'

578

Bolam Pass 11,180'

578

Hermosa

Cayton Campground

550

Hotel Draw

Barlow Creek

NATIONAL

Scotch Creek

564

Orphan Butte 11,121'

550

Dolores River

145

Rico Mountains

Rico

FOREST

435

Roaring Forks

N

0   4

MILES

To Cortez

203

Scotch Creek-Roaring Forks

LOCATION: San Juan National Forest. South of Rico, northwest of Durango; Montezuma and Dolores counties.

HIGHLIGHTS: This beautiful loop will take you along the historic Scotch Creek Toll Road, an important link in the 1870s and 1880s between the mines at Rico and the Animas Valley. It also will take you along the crest of a divide with outstanding mountain vistas, then through the canyon of Roaring Forks Creek to state Highway 145.

DIFFICULTY: The Scotch Creek leg is moderate (lower your antenna so brush doesn't break it off, and be prepared to remove possible dead-fall from the roadway). Roaring Forks Road (435) and Road 564 atop the divide are easy.

TIME & DISTANCE: 2 hours; 25.4 miles.

MAPS: San Juan National Forest. DeLorme p. 76.

INFORMATION: San Juan National Forest, Mancos-Dolores Ranger District. Dolores Public Lands Office. You also can get information, maps, etc. at the old Forest Service guard station on Highway 145 north of Rico.

GETTING THERE: The loop begins and ends at Highway 145 south of Rico. The Scotch Creek leg (Road 550) is 2.6 miles south of Rico. The Roaring Forks Creek leg (Road 435) is 8.3 miles south of Rico.

REST STOPS: There are many places to stop, especially along Scotch Creek, including primitive campsites and scenic points.

THE DRIVE: The minerals and metals buried around Rico held great promise in the late 1800s, but development was hindered by lack of a reliable transportation link to the Animas Valley. The Pinkerton Trail along Scotch Creek served for a time. In 1882 that was replaced with the Scotch Creek Toll Road, which was still a difficult route for freight wagons. (One freighter took 35 days and 22 yoke of oxen to haul two steam boilers the 35 miles from Rockwood to Rico.) In 1891, the road lost its importance when the Rio Grande Southern Railroad reached Rico. Today, the rough and narrow but very pretty 6.4 miles from the highway up to Road 564 follows Scotch Creek along a narrow canyon of mixed forest, cliffs and talus slopes. When you reach Road 564, turn south. (north, or left, will take you 4.8 miles down Hotel Draw to Hermosa Park Road and the Bolam Pass drive, Tour 73, for a great alternate loop.) Serpentine and undulating Road 564 basically runs north-south on the crest of a high divide, paralleling the Colorado Trail. Much of this rutted road passes through logged conifer forest. But as it rises to almost 11,000 feet, you eventually will see outstanding mountain vistas. The descent (or ascent, depending on your direction) through aspen stands and along Roaring Forks Road (435) is on a much better dirt and gravel road.

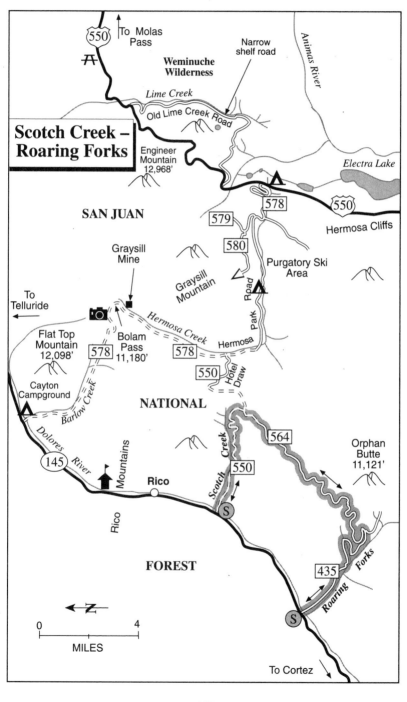

Scotch Creek – Roaring Forks

To Molas Pass

US 550

Weminuche Wilderness

Narrow shelf road

Animas River

Lime Creek

Old Lime Creek Road

Engineer Mountain
12,968'

Electra Lake

SAN JUAN

578

US 550

579

Hermosa Cliffs

580

Purgatory Ski Area

Graysill Mine

Graysill Mountain

Road

To Telluride

Hermosa Creek

Flat Top Mountain
12,098'

578

Bolam Pass
11,180'

578

Hermosa

Park

Cayton Campground

Barlow Creek

550

Hotel Draw

NATIONAL

Dolores River

Scotch Creek

564

Orphan Butte
11,121'

145

Rico Mountains

Rico

550

S

435

Roaring Forks

Rico

FOREST

N

0   4

MILES

To Cortez

Graysill Mine *(Tour 73)*

Old Lime Creek Road *(Tour 75)*

Old Lime Creek Road

LOCATION: East of U.S. 550 between Purgatory Ski Area and Molas Pass. It skirts the western edge of the Weminuche Wilderness. San Juan National Forest. San Juan County.

HIGHLIGHTS: This historic little road is a spectacular, if short, alternative to U.S. 550, its modern-day replacement. It was carved into the western wall of the canyon of Lime Creek. Along the way you can take the one-mile (one way) hike to pretty Potato Lake.

DIFFICULTY: Easy, but rocky in places and very narrow.

TIME & DISTANCE: 1.5 hours; 10.9 miles.

MAPS: San Juan National Forest. Trails Illustrated No. 140 (Weminuche Wilderness). DeLorme p. 76.

INFORMATION: San Juan National Forest, Columbine West Ranger District. San Juan Public Lands Center.

GETTING THERE: Take U.S. 550 south from Silverton over Molas Pass, or north from Durango toward Purgatory. The north portal is 4.3 miles south of Molas Pass. The south portal is just under 2 miles north of Cascade, at a sharp bend in the highway.

REST STOPS: There is a shady picnic or primitive camping area with a toilet along Lime Creek at mile 5.6.

THE DRIVE: Long before whites arrived in the San Juan Mountains searching for gold and silver, Ute Indians were using this route as a hunting trail. Captain Charles Baker became one of the earliest prospectors to use the trail, passing this way in 1860. It became an actual road during the mining days of the late 1800s. Then this transportation link between Silverton and Durango was used for hauling gold, silver and supplies. During the 1930s the Depression-era Civilian Conservation Corps made improvements, including the stonework you will see along the narrowest and highest canyonside segments. Most traffic now uses U.S. 550. But Old Lime Creek Road (591) still offers an adventurous, if short, alternative to the paved highway. It wends around 11,871-foot Potato Hill, first through forest, then along a dramatic shelf high above the gorge occupied by Lime Creek. Across the way rise the 12,000–13,000-foot peaks of Weminuche Wilderness. Along the drive the road descends to the bottom of the canyon, providing easy access to the pretty stream. The trailhead to Potato Lake, a popular hike, is 2.9 miles from the south end of the road.

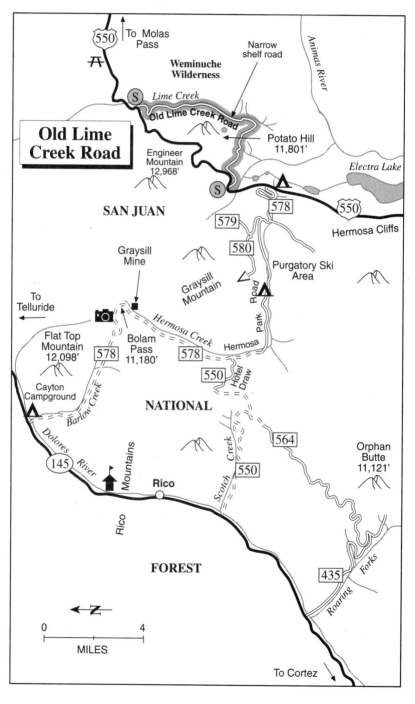

Old Lime
Creek Road

To Molas
Pass

Weminuche
Wilderness

Narrow
shelf road

Animas River

550

S Lime Creek
Old Lime Creek Road

Potato Hill
11,801'

Electra Lake

Engineer
Mountain
12,968'

S

578

579

580

SAN JUAN

Hermosa Cliffs

550

Graysill
Mine

Graysill
Mountain

Purgatory Ski
Area

To
Telluride

Flat Top
Mountain
12,098'

578

Hermosa Creek

Hermosa Park Road

Bolam
Pass
11,180'

578

Hermosa

Cayton
Campground

550

Hotel Draw

NATIONAL

Barlow Creek

Scotch Creek

564

Orphan
Butte
11,121'

Dolores River

145

Rico Mountains

Rico

550

Roaring Forks

435

FOREST

0   4

MILES

N

To Cortez

La Plata Canyon

LOCATION: Northwest of Durango, in the La Plata Mountains. San Juan National Forest. La Plata County.

HIGHLIGHTS: A beautiful and convenient drive along the La Plata River, up a canyon with many waterfalls, through the old mining camp of La Plata City to a spectacular glacial basin. Kennebec Pass, a 11,500-foot-high gap cut through the ridge at the head of the canyon, is quite a sight. The vista across the La Plata Mountains from Indian Trail Ridge, just below the pass, are terrific as well. This drive provides hiking access to the Colorado Trail. Lots of wildflowers, too.

DIFFICULTY: Easy for the first 10 miles or so, then moderate to the top. The last mile is a single-lane shelf road. There are a number of places where snowbanks can block the road into summer, so check ahead on whether the road is open.

TIME & DISTANCE: 3 hours; about 30 miles round-trip. The spur to Columbus Basin adds almost 3 miles round-trip.

MAPS: San Juan National Forest. DeLorme p. 86.

INFORMATION: The Durango Visitor Center, south of the U.S. 550/U.S. 160 junction. San Juan National Forest, Columbine West Ranger District. San Juan Public Lands Center.

GETTING THERE: Take U.S. 160 to Hesperus, west of Durango. Turn north onto La Plata Canyon Road, county Road 124.

REST STOPS: Snowslide Campground at mile 5.7; Kroeger Campground at mile 6.2; Lewis Creek Recreation Site, a walk-in tent campground at mile 9.3. You'll see many places to stop, including primitive campsites, along the river. There is a toilet at the trailhead on Indian Trail Ridge, just below the pass.

THE DRIVE: The road, paved for 4.6 miles, heads toward a yawning forested canyon where an expedition led by Spanish explorer Juan Maria de Rivera in 1775 is thought to have discovered gold. By the 1870s gold and silver miners were seeking their fortunes along the La Plata River. The boom sprouted La Plata City, where some original buildings remain at mile 7.7, and short-lived Parrot City, once the county seat, near Mayday. Mining faded early in the 20th century, although some gold mining did go on into the 1950s. The roadbed becomes quite rocky by mile 6, and begins to climb by the time it passes through the site of La Plata City. At mile 12 is a Y. A sign warns that the left branch, Road 571 to Kennebec Pass, requires 4WD. To the right is the side trip to beautiful Columbus Basin, via Road 498. In a couple of miles the road enters verdant Cumberland Basin, a glacial valley high above timberline below Snowstorm Peak and Cumberland Mountain. Soon you'll reach a parking area for hikers. If there are vehicles at the pass, consider parking here and walking the remaining 0.9 mile of narrow shelf road, which ends at a windy gap cut into the head of the basin (there's little room to turn around). Beyond the gap is a sheer drop-off.

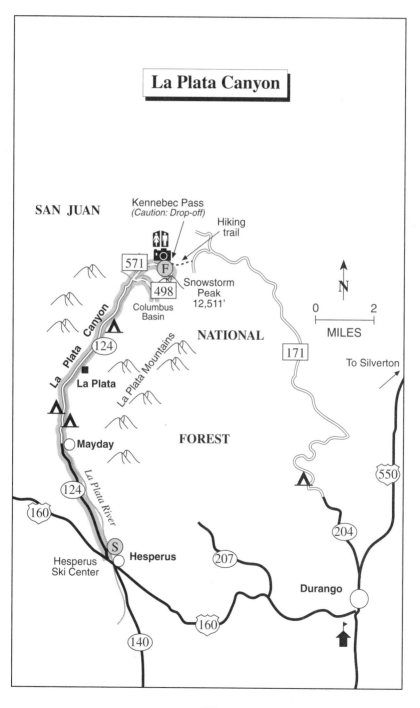

La Plata Canyon

SAN JUAN

Kennebec Pass
(Caution: Drop-off)

Hiking trail

571

498

Snowstorm
Peak
12,511'

Columbus
Basin

La Plata Canyon

La Plata Mountains

124

La Plata

NATIONAL

171

To Silverton

0   2
MILES

N

124

Mayday

La Plata River

FOREST

550

160

204

207

S

Hesperus

Durango

Hesperus
Ski Center

160

140

Middle Mountain Road

LOCATION: On Middle Mountain northeast of Durango, between Vallecito Reservoir and Weminuche Wilderness. San Juan National Forest. La Plata County.

HIGHLIGHTS: You'll see fine views of lofty peaks, glacial basins, forested mountains and canyons as well as the site of Tuckerville, a 1929 mining camp, at the end of the drive. While you will have to back-track on this drive, the return trip provides its own outstanding mountain vistas. This a convenient and worthwhile drive out of Durango.

DIFFICULTY: Easy.

TIME & DISTANCE: 1.5 hours; 24.4 miles round-trip.

MAPS: Trails Illustrated No. 140 (Weminuche Wilderness). San Juan National Forest. DeLorme pp. 86–87.

INFORMATION: San Juan National Forest, Columbine West and Columbine East ranger districts.

GETTING THERE: From either Durango, on U.S. 550, or Bayfield, on U.S. 160, make your way to the northeastern end of Vallecito Reservoir. There you will see the turnoff for Middle Mountain Road, No. 724.

REST STOPS: There are many primitive campsites, and a parking area at mile 10.6 with good views.

THE DRIVE: The graded single-lane dirt and gravel backway climbs the eastern wall of the valley of Vallecito Creek, through aspen and conifer forest. After 4 miles you will be able to look west across the deep vale to the craggy, snowy peaks and basins of the southern Weminuche Wilderness. Eventually you will emerge from the forest to be greeted by expansive vistas to the east and south as well. The road, much smaller now, will cross a meadow, Runlett Park, and traverse a south-facing mountain slope, where you will have a stunning view down the deep, dark canyon of Indian Creek and the drainage of the Los Pinos River. At mile 12.3 the road delivers you to a forest clearing, the site of Tuckerville. On Feb. 10, 1928, the Mt. Runlett Metals Company of Cortez ran an advertisement in the Durango Evening Herald to promote its new mining venture in Cave Basin, to the north. "This investment absolutely guaranteed against loss," the ad promised. But Tuckerville never grew beyond a handful of log cabins and a dining hall. In 1929, the few mines in the area closed, and the camp was literally abandoned overnight.

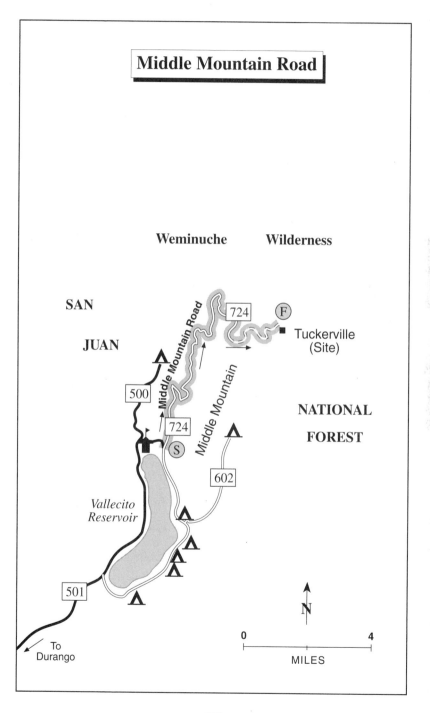

Middle Mountain Road

Weminuche   Wilderness

SAN

JUAN

724

F

Tuckerville
(Site)

Middle Mountain Road

500

724

S

Middle Mountain

NATIONAL

FOREST

602

Vallecito
Reservoir

501

To
Durango

N

0   4

MILES

Elwood Pass-Beaver Creek

LOCATION: On the Continental Divide in the San Juan Mountains west of Alamosa, between Pagosa Springs and Del Norte. San Juan and Rio Grande national forests. Mineral and Rio Grande counties.

HIGHLIGHTS: A scenic and historic loop from U.S. 160 that includes a stop at Silver Falls; four-wheeling on the old military and wagon road over Elwood Pass (11,875 feet); scenic Schinzel Flats; the ghost town and Superfund mine site at Summitville; the 12,616-foot summit of Grayback Mountain; and a pretty cruise along Beaver Creek.

DIFFICULTY: U.S. 160 to Quartz Creek via Road 667 is easy; Quartz Creek to Elwood Pass is moderate to difficult; Elwood Pass to South Fork is easy; Grayback Mountain is moderate. Elwood Pass usually opens by mid-July.

TIME & DISTANCE: 6 hours; 60 miles.

MAPS: San Juan and Rio Grande national forests. Trails Illustrated No. 142 (South San Juan/Del Norte). DeLorme pp. 79, 88–89.

INFORMATION: San Juan National Forest, Pagosa Ranger District; Rio Grande National Forest, Conejos Peak Ranger District.

GETTING THERE: If you prefer to do the rough segment first, start on U.S. 160 about 9.7 miles north of Pagosa Springs and 9 miles south of Wolf Creek Summit. Turn west on forest Road 667 toward East Fork Campground (this is how I describe the drive). To start at the north end, take U.S. 160 southwest 1.4 miles from the junction with Highway 149 at South Fork. Turn south onto Beaver Creek Road.

REST STOPS: There are campgrounds, primitive campsites, and historic ruins. Restored Elwood Cabin, at Schinzel Flats, can be rented by contacting the USFS' Conejos Peak Ranger District. The old cabin at Silver Falls can be rented by contacting the Pagosa Ranger District.

THE DRIVE: In 1874, the San Juan Prospector newspaper recounted a trip over Elwood Pass beneath the headline, "A Perilous Journey." Four years later the Army Corps of Engineers recommended against linking Ft. Garland, in San Luis Valley, with Ft. Lewis, in Pagosa Springs, with a road over Elwood Pass. Yet it was built. Today the drive from U.S. 160 along the East Fork of the San Juan River on East Fork Road (667) begins as an easy cruise past pretty Silver Falls, through a mix of cliffs, forest and meadows. At mile 9.1, at the junction with Quartz Meadow Road (684), East Fork Road becomes a rough 4x4 trail. Cross Elwood Creek about 1.4 miles farther, then go left in 0.4 mile (there's a left-pointing arrow carved on a tree). A rougher stream crossing follows. The road beyond is rocky and steep as you climb to a shelf above the gorge of Elwood Creek, skirt the South San Juan Wilderness and pass McCormick Cabin, an old mine cabin. Eventually you will cross the pass and come out on a graded road (380) at Schinzel Flats. Go left to the Summitville gold mine, a huge Superfund reclamation project. (Acid drainage from the mine, along with naturally occurring heavy metals, have left the Alamosa River lifeless.) Take Road 330 for 4.5 miles to the rocky, eroded road up Grayback Mountain Then descend on Road 330 to the junction with Road 332.

The roads are good from here. Del Norte is 20 uninteresting (to me) miles to the right. I prefer the scenic 24-mile descent along Beaver Creek to U.S. 160 via roads 332, 360, and 20.

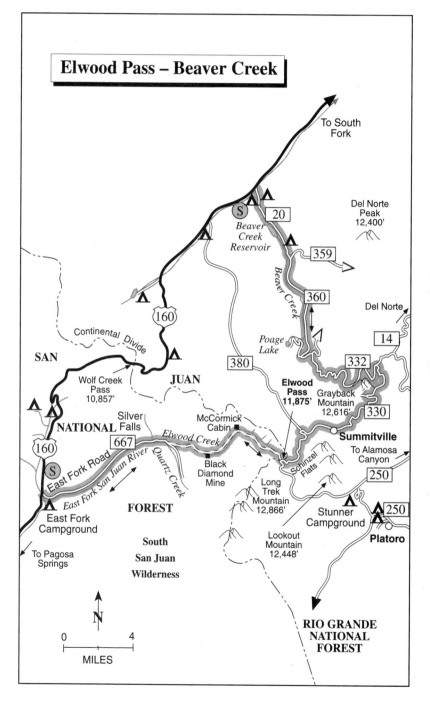

Elwood Pass – Beaver Creek

To South Fork

Del Norte Peak 12,400'

Beaver Creek Reservoir

20

359

Beaver Creek

360

Del Norte

14

Continental Divide

160

Poage Lake

380

332

SAN

Wolf Creek Pass 10,857'

JUAN

Elwood Pass 11,875'

Grayback Mountain 12,616'

330

Silver Falls

McCormick Cabin

Summitville

NATIONAL Falls

667

Elwood Creek

To Alamosa Canyon

East Fork Road

Quartz Creek

Black Diamond Mine

Schinzel Flats

250

East Fork San Juan River

FOREST

Long Trek Mountain 12,866'

Stunner Campground

250

East Fork Campground

Platoro

To Pagosa Springs

South San Juan Wilderness

Lookout Mountain 12,448'

N

0   4

MILES

RIO GRANDE NATIONAL FOREST

215

Alamosa River to Platoro

LOCATION: San Juan Mountains southwest of Alamosa. Rio Grande National Forest. Rio Grande and Conejos counties.

HIGHLIGHTS: This is a scenic loop from the San Luis Valley on the eastern slope of the Continental Divide. It will take you through the old town sites of Stunner and Jasper, and over Stunner Pass.

DIFFICULTY: Easy.

TIME & DISTANCE: 3 hours; 57 miles.

MAPS: Rio Grande National Forest. Trails Illustrated No. 142 (South San Juan/Del Norte). ACSC's *Indian Country*. DeLorme pp. 89–90.

INFORMATION: Rio Grande National Forest, Conejos Peak Ranger District.

GETTING THERE: You can begin or end at either Highway 17 about 22 miles west of Antonito, or southwest of Alamosa near the junction of Highways 15 and 370. Either way, just follow the loop made by Road 250. **To go via the Alamosa River Canyon first** (as described in The Drive) take Gunbarrel Road (north-south Highway 15) to a junction about 2 miles south of the junction with Highway 370, then turn west onto Road 250. **To go via Platoro first,** take Highway 17 west from Antonito to Road 250, and drive north through Platoro.

REST STOPS: There are developed campgrounds along the way. You will find food, lodging, fishing and other amenities at Platoro.

THE DRIVE: From Highway 15, Road 250 follows Cat Creek into the mountains, along a narrow and scenic canyon called The Canyon. At mile 5.7 it passes a large log barn. By mile 9.7 you've reached a Y. Keep right, and drive along Terrace Reservoir. Soon the road runs along the Alamosa River. (Acid runoff from the Summitville gold mine and Superfund site, higher in the mountains, along with naturally occurring heavy metals, have left the river lifeless. In 1990, mine runoff killed off the stocked fish in the reservoir.) The road follows the creek up the beautiful canyon, wooded with pines and cottonwoods. After about 20 miles it passes through what remains of the short-lived 1880s mining town of Jasper, where many of the old, privately owned cabins are still occupied. At mile 27.7 is the junction with Road 380. The old roadside cabin is the Stunner telephone cabin, built in 1911 as shelter for crews working on a telephone line across the Continental Divide. Here you can angle right and drive higher into the mountains to Summitville and Elwood Pass (Tour 78), to come out at U.S. 160. But this tour continues ahead to Stunner Campground, where you can see the site of the Stunner mining camp. Gold fever attracted some 400 miners, gamblers and camp followers to this spot in 1892, but it wasn't long before news of more promising strikes elsewhere lured them away. From there, descend to the creek crossing, a nice but buggy place for primitive camping (don't drink the tainted water), and make the highly scenic 5-mile cruise through Stunner Pass down to Platoro. Platoro combines the Spanish words for the two precious metals that spawned the town in the 1880s: "plata" (silver) and "oro" (gold). Today, businesses are mining tourism and outdoor recreation. From

Platoro you have a long, easy and scenic cruise down the valley of the Conejos River to Highway 17.

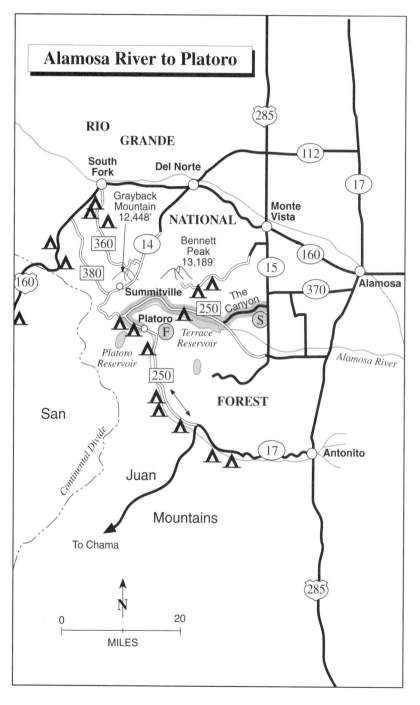

Alamosa River to Platoro

RIO
GRANDE

South Fork

Del Norte

Grayback Mountain 12,448'

NATIONAL

Bennett Peak 13,189'

Monte Vista

360

14

380

15

160

Summitville

The Canyon

250

Alamosa

370

S

Platoro

F

Terrace Reservoir

Platoro Reservoir

250

FOREST

Alamosa River

San

Continental Divide

Juan

17

Antonito

Mountains

To Chama

N

0   20
MILES

285

285

112

17

160

Pagosa Junction *(Tour 80)*

Juanita *(Tour 80)*

Pagosa Junction

LOCATION: The Southern Ute Indian Reservation north of the New Mexico border. Archuleta County, between U.S. 160 and U.S. 84.

HIGHLIGHTS: You will love this gentle meander through the bucolic hills, vales and mesas of southern Colorado, much of it along the San Juan and Navajo rivers. It's especially pretty on early summer evenings and autumn afternoons. Interesting sights include the old Catholic mission church at Juanita, and the Denver and Rio Grande Railroad stop at Pagosa Junction. There also are great views of the craggy, soaring San Juan Mountains, which contrast with the picturesque hills.

DIFFICULTY: Easy, on maintained county roads.

TIME & DISTANCE: 2.5 hours; about 45 miles.

MAPS: ACSC's *Indian Country*. Or refer to *Recreational Map of Colorado*. DeLorme pp. 87–88.

INFORMATION: Pagosa Springs Area Chamber of Commerce.

GETTING THERE: From Pagosa Springs, take U.S. 160 west for 13.1 miles. Turn south onto Cat Creek Road (700) and drive to Carracas Road (500) and Pagosa Junction. Then take Carracas Road east along the river, and make a short detour south to Juanita on Juanita Road (551). Follow Road 500 (Trujillo Road) to Montezuma Mesa Road (524). Take Montezuma Mesa Road east to Coyote Park Road (359) and turn south. At Edith Road (391), turn east toward Chromo. **From U.S. 84 at Chromo,** north of the New Mexico line: Turn west onto Edith Road and reverse the directions above.

REST STOPS: The roads pass through reservation and private property, so you won't be able to wander from the roadside.

THE DRIVE: Sometimes a cruise through bucolic countryside is as rewarding as a white-knuckle crossing of the Continental Divide. Instead of four-wheeling, what you get on this tour are riverside meadows, pastures and cottonwood groves, hills dotted with piñon pines and junipers, high mesas skirted with yellow cliffs, lonely canyons and views across pastoral valleys. These easy roads vary from two-lane gravel to a single lane of dirt. In places they provide outstanding views across rolling Pagosa Country to the high San Juans. Silent and seemingly forgotten Pagosa Junction (also called Gato), once a wye where the main railroad line between Chama, New Mexico, and Pagosa Springs split, seems frozen in time. The line was abandoned in 1935. Today, the old water tower still stands near a cluster of buildings beside the narrow-gauge tracks occupied by old rail cars. On a hill overlooking the valley of the San Juan River sits a picture-postcard church, and across the river stretches a vintage steel-truss bridge. A few miles southwest of the junction, at Carracas, the pioneering Dominguez-Escalante expedition of 1776 camped while searching for a route from Santa Fe, New Mexico, to Monterey, California. They called the site "Nuestra Señora de las Nievas" (Our Lady of the Snows). East of Pagosa Junction, on Juanita Road (551) just beyond the bridge over the San Juan River, an old Catholic church recalls the former town of Juanita.

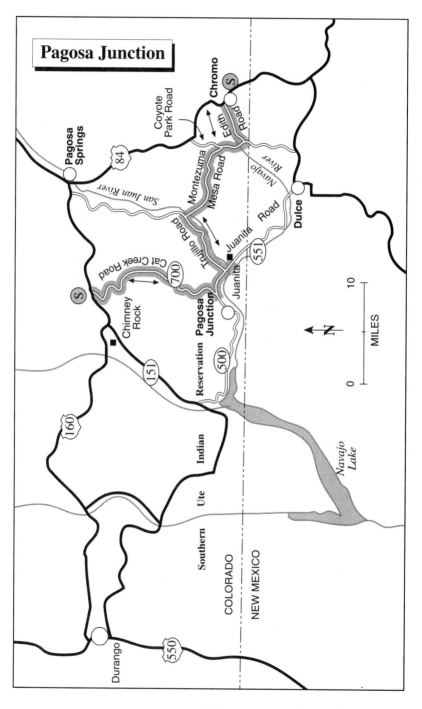

Pagosa Junction

Durango & Silverton Narrow Gauge Railroad, Silverton *(Tour 61)*

APPENDIX

Collisions can happen anywhere.

Information Sources

AAA Colorado Headquarters
4100 East Arkansas Avenue
Denver, CO 80222
(303) 753-8800
fax (303) 758-8515
www.aaacolo.com

**Arapaho and Roosevelt
National Forests**
www.fs.fed.us/r2/arnf/

Boulder Ranger District
2140 Yarmouth Avenue
Boulder, Colorado 80301l
(303) 541-2500
(970) 498-2727 (TTY)
(303) 541-2515 (Fax)

Canyon Lakes Ranger District
1311 South College Avenue
Fort Collins, CO 80524
(970) 498-2770

Clear Creek Ranger District
101 Chicago Creek Road
P.O. Box 3307
Idaho Springs, CO 80452
(303) 567-2901

**Forest to Grassland
Information Center**
1311 South College Avenue
Fort Collins, CO 80524
(970) 498-2770
(970) 498-2707 (TTY)

Pawnee National Grassland
660 O Street
Greeley, CO 80631
(970) 353-5004
www.fs.fed.us/arnf/districts/png

Sulphur Ranger District
9 Ten Mile Drive
P.O. Box 10
Granby, CO 80446-0010
(970) 887-4100

Supervisor's Office
240 W. Prospect Road
Fort Collins, CO 80526
(970) 498-1100

Aspen Chamber Resort Assoc.
425 Rio Grande Pl.
Aspen, CO 81611
(970) 925-1940

(800) 262-7736
www.aspenchamber.com

**Automobile Club
of Southern California**
3333 Fairview Road
Costa Mesa, CA 92626
(714) 427-5950
www.aaa-calif.com

**Breckenridge Resort
Chamber Assoc.**
311 South Ridge
Breckenridge, CO 80424
(970) 453-6018
www.gobreck.com

**Colorado Association
of Four-Wheel Drive Clubs**
P.O. Box 1413
Wheat Ridge, CO 80034
(303) 857-7992
www.cohvco.org/ca4wdci

**Colorado Geological Survey
Department of Natural Resources**
715 State Centennial Building
1313 Sherman Street
Denver, CO 80203
General info.: (303) 866-2611
http://geo.fortlewis.edu/ARC

Colorado State Parks
1313 Sherman Street No. 618
Denver, CO 80203
(303) 866-3437
www.parks.state.co.us/home

Colorado Tourism Board
(800) 265-6723
www.colorado.com

DeBeque (town)
(970) 283-5531

DeLorme Publishing Company
P.O. Box 298
Yarmouth, ME 04096
(207) 846-7000
www.delorme.com

Dolores Public Lands Office
100 N. 6th Street
P.O. Box 210
Dolores, CO 81323
(970) 882-7296

**Durango Area
Chamber Resort Assoc.**
111 S. Camino del Rio
P.O. Box 2587
Durango, CO 81302
(970) 247-0312
(800) 525-8855
www.durango.org
Visitor center is located along the river
just south of the U.S. 550/U.S. 160
junction

Grand Mesa Byway Association
P.O. Box 122
Cedaredge, CO 81413
(800) 436-3041

**Grand Mesa/Uncompahgre/
Gunnison (GMUG) National Forests**
www.fs.fed.us/r2/gmug/

**Grand Valley Ranger District—
Collbran**
P.O. Box 330
218 High Street
Collbran, CO 81624
(970) 487-3534

**Grand Valley Ranger District—
Grand Junction**
2777 Crossroads Blvd., Ste. A
Grand Junction, CO 81506
(970) 242-8211

Gunnison Ranger District
216 North Colorado
Gunnison, CO 81230
(970) 641-0471

**Gunnison Ranger District—
Lake City**
P.O. Box 89
Lake City, CO 81235
(970) 641-0471 or 944-2500

Norwood Ranger District
P.O. Box 388
1150 Forest Avenue
Norwood, CO 81423
(970) 327-4261

Ouray Ranger District
2505 South Townsend
Montrose, CO 81401
(970) 240-5300

Paonia Ranger District
P.O. Box 1030
North Rio Grande Avenue
Paonia, CO 81428
(970) 527-4131

Supervisor's Office
2250 Highway 50
Delta, CO 81416
(970) 874-6600

GTR Mapping
(Recreational Map of Colorado)
P.O. Box 1984
Cañon City, CO 81215-1984
(800) 268-8920
www.gtrmapping.com

**Gunnison County
Department of Public Works**
(970) 641-0044

**Lake City Chamber of Commerce
Visitor Information Center**
(on Silver Street in the center of town)
P.O. Box 430
Lake City, CO 81235
(800) 569-1874
www.lakecityco.com

**Medicine Bow-Routt
National Forests**
www.fs.fed.us/r2/mbr/

**Hahns Peak/Bears Ears
Ranger District**
925 Weiss Drive
Steamboat Springs, CO 80487-9315
(970) 879-1870

**Montrose Public Lands Center
(USFS and BLM)**
2505 S. Townsend
Montrose, CO 81401
(970) 240-5300

Parks Ranger District
P.O. Box 158
100 Main Street
Walden, CO 80480
(970) 723-8204

Parks Ranger District
P.O. Box 1210
2103 E. Park Avenue (Highway 40)
Kremmling, CO 80459
(970) 724-9004

Supervisor's Office
2468 Jackson Street
Laramie, WY 82070-6535
(307) 745-2300

Yampa Ranger District
300 Roselawn Avenue
P.O. Box 7

Yampa, CO 80483
(970) 638-4516

**National Recreation
Reservation Service**
(campground reservations)
(877) 444-6777
www.reserveusa.com

**National Geographic Maps/
Trails Illustrated**
P.O. Box 4357
Evergreen, CO 80437-4357
(303) 670-3457 or (800) 962-1643
www.nationalgeographic.com/trails/maps

National Park Service
U.S. National Parks By Name
www.nps.gov/parklists/byname.htm

**Bent's Old Fort
National Historic Site**
35110 Highway 194 East
La Junta, CO 81050-9523
(719) 383-5010
www.nps.gov/beol

**Black Canyon of the Gunnison
National Park**
102 Elk Creek
Gunnison, CO 81230
(970) 641-2337 x 205
www.nps.gov/blca/

Colorado National Monument
Fruita, CO 81521-0001
(970) 858-3617
www.nps.gov/colm/

**Curecanti National
Recreation Area**
102 Elk Creek
Gunnison, CO 81230
(970) 641-2337 x 205
www.nps.gov/cure/

Dinosaur National Monument
4545 E. Highway 40
Dinosaur, CO 81610-9724
(435) 789-2115
www.nps.gov/dino/

Dinosaur Nature Association
1291 East Highway 40
Vernal, UT 84078-2830
To order books, etc.
(800) 845-3466
www.dinosaurnature.com/

**Florissant Fossil Beds
National Monument**

P.O. Box 185
Florissant, CO 80816-0185
(719) 748-3253
www.nps.gov/flfo/

**Great Sand Dunes
National Monument and Preserve**
11500 Highway 150
Mosca, CO 81146-9798
(719) 378-2312
www.nps.gov/grsa/

Hovenweep National Monument
McElmo Route
Cortez, CO 81321
(970) 562-4282
www.nps.gov/hove/

Mesa Verde National Park
P.O. Box 8
Mesa Verde National Park, CO
81330-0008
(970) 529-4465
www.nps.gov/meve/

National Park Reservation Service
(800) 365-2267
http://reservations.nps.gov

Rocky Mountain National Park
1000 Highway 36
Estes Park, CO 80517
(970) 586-1206 gen'l info.
(970) 586-1333 recorded info.
www.nps.gov/romo/

Rocky Mountain Nature Assoc.
Rocky Mountain National Park
Estes Park, CO 80517
(800) 816-7662
www.rmna.org/bookstore/

North Star Mapping
(Jeep Trails of the San Juans)
P.O. Box 22238
Flagstaff, AZ 86002

**Ouray Chamber Resort Assoc.
Visitor Information Center**
1222 Main Street
P.O. Box 145
Ouray, CO 81427
(970) 325-4746
(800) 228-1876
www.ouraycolorado.com

**Pagosa Springs Area
Chamber of Commerce**
402 San Juan
P.O. Box 787
Pagosa Springs, CO 81147

(970) 264-2360
(800) 252-2204
www.pagosaspringschamber.com

Pike and San Isabel National Forests
www.fs.fed.us/r2/psicc

Leadville Ranger District
2015 North Poplar
Leadville, CO 80461
(719) 486-0749

Pike's Peak Ranger District
601 S. Weber Street
Colorado Springs, CO 80903
(719) 636-1602

Salida Ranger District
325 West Rainbow Blvd.
Salida, CO 81201
(719) 539-3591

San Carlos Ranger District
3170 E. Main Street
Cañon City, CO 81212
(719) 269-8500

South Park Ranger District
P.O. Box 219
320 Highway 285
Fairplay, CO 80440
(719) 836-2031

South Platte Ranger District
19316 Goddard Ranch Court
Morrison, CO 80465
(303) 275-5610

Supervisor's Office
1920 Valley Drive
Pueblo, CO 81008
(719) 545-8737

**Rangely Area
Chamber of Commerce**
209 East Main Street
Rangely, CO 81648
(970) 675-5290

Rio Grande National Forest
www.fs.fed.us/r2/riogrande/

Conejos Peak Ranger District
15571 Colorado Rt. T5
La Jara, CO 81140
(719) 274-8971

**Divide Ranger District
Del Norte Office**
13308 West Highway 160

Del Norte, CO 81132
(719) 657-3321

**Divide Ranger District
Creede Office**
3rd and Creede Avenue
Creede, CO 81130
(719) 658-2556
Note: Open May–November

Saguache Ranger District
46525 state Highway 114
Saguache, CO 81149
(719) 655-2547

Supervisor's Office
1803 West U.S. Highway 160
Monte Vista, CO 81144
(719) 852-5941

Roosevelt National Forest
See Arapaho and Roosevelt National
Forest

Routt National Forest
See Medicine Bow-Routt National
Forest

San Isabel National Forest
See Pike and San Isabel national forests

San Juan National Forest
www.fs.fed.us/r2/sanjuan/

Columbine Ranger District East
367 S. Pearl Street
P.O. Box 439
Bayfield, CO 81122
(970) 884-2512

Mancos-Dolores Ranger District
100 N. Sixth
P.O. Box 210
Dolores, CO 81323
(970) 882-7296

Pagosa Ranger District
180 Second Street
P.O. Box 310
Pagosa Springs, CO 81147
(970) 264-2268

Supervisor's Office
15 Burnett Ct.
Durango, CO 81301
(970) 247-4874
(970) 385-1243 fax

San Juan Mountains Association
P.O. Box 2261
15 Burnett Ct.

Durango, CO 81302
(970) 385-1210
www.sanjuanmountainsassociation.org

**San Juan Public Lands Center
(USFS and BLM)**
15 Burnett Ct.
Durango, CO 81301
(970) 247-4874

San Miguel County
Road and Bridge Dept.
(970) 327-4835

Shrine Mountain Inn
(970) 476-6548 for summer restaurant
schedule and reservations;
(970) 925-5775 for lodging reservations

Sidekick Off Road
(4WD guidebooks, maps, videos, etc.)
12188 Central Avenue #352
P.O. Box 727
Chino, CA 91708
(909) 628-7227
(909) 628-5392 fax
www.sidekickoffroad.com

**Silverton Chamber of Commerce
Visitor Information Center**
(south end of Greene Street at U.S. 550)
P.O. Box 565
Silverton, CO 81433
(970) 387-5654
(800) 752-4494
www.silverton.org

Telluride Chamber Resort Assoc.
700 West Colorado
P.O. Box 653
Telluride, CO 81435
(970) 728-3041
(800) 525-3455

U.S. Bureau of Land Management
www.co.blm.gov

   Anasazi Heritage Center
27501 Highway 184
Dolores, CO 81323
(970) 882-4811
(970) 882-7035 fax
www.co.blm.gov/ahc/hmepge.htm

   **Arkansas Headwaters
Recreation Area**
(State Park and BLM office)
307 West Sackett
P.O. Box 126
Salida, CO 81201

(719) 539-7289
(719) 539-3771 fax

Colorado State Office
2850 Youngfield Street
Lakewood, CO 80215-7076
(303) 239-3600

Front Range Center
3170 East Main Street
Cañon City, CO 81212
(719) 269-8500
(719) 269-8599 fax

Glenwood Springs Field Office
50629 Highways 6 and 24
(Zip 81601)
P.O. Box 1009
Glenwood Springs, CO 81602
(970) 947-2800
(970) 947-2829 fax

Grand Junction Field Office
2815 H Road
Grand Junction, CO 81506
(970) 244-3000
(970) 244-3083 fax

Gunnison Field Office
216 North Colorado Street
Gunnison, CO 81230
(970) 641-0471
(970) 641-1928 fax

Kremmling Field Office
2103 E. Park Avenue
P.O. Box 68
Kremmling, CO 80459
(970) 724-3000
(970) 724-9390 fax
www.co.blm.gov/kra/kraindex.htm

La Jara Field Office
15571 county Road T5
La Jara, CO 81140
(719) 274-5193
(719) 274-6301 fax

Little Snake Field Office
455 Emerson Street
Craig, CO 81625
(970) 826-5000
(970) 826-5002 fax
www.co.blm.gov/lsra/lsraindex.htm

Western Slope Center
2815 H Road
Grand Junction, CO 81506
(970) 244-3000
(970) 244-3083 fax

Royal Gorge Field Office
3170 East Main Street
Cañon City, CO 81212
(719) 269-8500
(719) 269-8599 fax

San Juan Field Office
15 Burnett Ct.
Durango, CO 81301
(970) 247-4874
(970) 385-1375 fax
www.co.blm.gov/sjra/sjra.html

Saguache Field Office
46525 Highway 114
Saguache, CO 81149
(719) 655-2547
(719) 655-2502 fax

Uncompahgre Field Office
2505 South Townsend Avenue
Montrose, CO 81401
(970) 240-5300
(970) 240-5367 fax

White River Field Office
73544 Highway 64
Meeker, CO 81641
(970) 878-3601
(970) 878-5717

**USDA Forest Service
Rocky Mountain
Region Headquarters**
Mailing address:
P.O. Box 25127
Lakewood, CO 80225
Location:
740 Simms Street
Golden, CO 80401
(303) 275-5350

**Vail Valley Tourism
and Convention Bureau**
100 East Meadow Drive
Vail, CO 81657
Visitor Center:
(800) 525-3875
(970) 476-1000

White River National Forest
www.fs.fed.us/r2/whiteriver/

Aspen Ranger District
806 West Hallam
Aspen, CO 81611
(970) 925-3445

Blanco Ranger District
317 East Market Street

Meeker, CO 81641
(970) 878-4039

Dillon Ranger District
680 River Pkwy.
P.O. Box 620
Silverthorne, CO 80498
(970) 468-5400

Eagle Ranger District
125 West 5th Street
P.O. Box 720
Eagle, CO 81631
(970) 328-6388

Holy Cross Ranger District
24747 U.S. Highway 24
P.O. Box 190
Minturn, CO 81645
(970) 827-5715

Rifle Ranger District
0094 county Road 244
Rifle, CO 81650
(970) 625-2371

Sopris Ranger District
620 Main Street
P.O. Box 309
Carbondale, CO 81623
(970) 963-2266

Supervisor's Office
900 Grand Avenue
P.O. Box 948
Glenwood Springs, CO 81602
(970) 945-2521

**Winter Park/Fraser Valley
Chamber of Commerce
and Visitor Center**
78841 U.S. Highway 40
P.O. Box 3236
Winter Park, CO 80482
(970) 726-4118
(800) 903-7275
www.winterpark-info.com

Miscellaneous Internet sites:

4X4NOW.com
Articles, books, maps, videos, etc.

**Alpine Loop National
Back Country Byway**
www.co.blm.gov/gra/gra-al.htm
www.gorp.com/gorp/activity/byway/co.
alpin.htm

BLM/Colorado Scenic Byways
www.co.blm.gov/rectouring.htm

Colorado Railroad Museum
www.crrm.org

Durango Visitor Guide
www.godurango.com

Flat Tops Scenic and Historic Byway
www.fs.fed.us/r2/mbr/rd-
yampa/scenicbyway.shtml

Mesa Verde Museum Association
www.mesaverde.org

Moffat County Scenic Drives
www.colorado-go-west.com/scenic2.html

ParkNet Park Bookstore
National Park Cooperating
Associations
http://165.83.219.72/hafe/bookshop/ind
ex.cfm

Public Lands Information Center
www.publiclands.org

**Rocky Mountain Region
Map Order Form**
Maps of the national forests and grasslands of the Rocky Mountain Region
www.fs.fed.us/r2/maps.htm

Telluride Gateway
www.telluridegateway.com/

The Denver Post Online
www.denverpost.com/

**USDA Forest Service
Rocky Mountain Region**
www.fs.fed.us/r2/

Wilderness Press
1200 5th Street
Berkeley, CA 94710
www.wildernesspress.com

References

Benson, Maxine. 1994. *1001 Colorado Place Names*. University Press of Kansas.

Brown, Robert L. 1995. *Jeep Trails to Colorado Ghost Towns*. The Caxton Printers, Ltd.

Chronic, Halka. 1980. *Roadside Geology of Colorado*. Mountain Press Publishing Company.

DeLong, Brad. 1996. *4-Wheel Freedom: The Art of Off-Road Driving*. Paladin Press.

Eberhart, Perry. 1969. *Guide to the Colorado Ghost Towns and Mining Camps*. Swallow Press.

Gregory, Lee. 1996. *Colorado Scenic Guide: Northern Region*. Third edition. Johnson Books.

Griffin, Wayne W. 1994. *Central Colorado 4-Wheeling*. Who Press.

Heck, Larry E. 1995. *4-Wheel Drive Trails and Ghost Towns of Colorado*. Pass Patrol, Inc.

Huber, Thomas P. 1997. *Colorado Byways: A Guide Through Scenic and Historic Landscapes*. University Press of Colorado.

Koch, Don. 1987. *The Colorado Pass Book: A Guide to Colorado's Backroad Mountain Passes*. Pruett Publishing Company.

Litvak, Dianna. 1996. *Colorado Travel Smart Trip Planner*. John Muir Publications.

McTighe, James. 1984. *Roadside History of Colorado*. Johnson Books.

Metzger, Stephen. 1996. *Colorado Handbook*. Moon Publications.

Mutel, Cornelia Fleischer, and Emerick, John C. 1992. *From Grassland to Glacier: The Natural History of Colorado and the Surrounding Region*. Johnson Books.

Norton, Boyd and Barbara. 1995. *Backroads of Colorado*. Voyageur Press, Inc.

Alpine Explorer: Recreation Guide to the Alpine Triangle. U.S. Department of Interior, Bureau of Land Management.

Colorado Atlas and Gazetteer. 1995. DeLorme Mapping.

Microsoft Encarta Encyclopedia 99. 1999. Microsoft Corporation.

National Geographic Maps/Trails Illustrated. Maps Nos. 1001-220.

Recreational Map of Colorado. 1994. GTR Mapping.

Index

About the author

Tony Huegel is the author of six family-oriented guides for owners of sport-utility vehicles: *California Desert Byways, Sierra Nevada Byways, California Coastal Byways, Utah Byways, Colorado Byways* and *Idaho Byways*. He grew up in the San Francisco Bay Area, and is now an Idaho-based journalist.

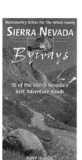

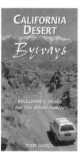
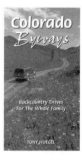